SEAS and ISLANDS

THE LIVING COUNTRYSIDE

A Reader's Digest selection

SEAS AND ISLANDS

First Edition Copyright © 1986
The Reader's Digest Association Limited, Berkeley Square House,
Berkeley Square, London W1X 6AB

Copyright © 1986
Reader's Digest Association Far East Limited
Philippines Copyright 1986
Reader's Digest Association Far East Ltd

Reprinted with amendments 1995

Originally published as a partwork,
The Living Countryside
Copyright © 1981, 1982, 1983, 1984
Eaglemoss Publications Ltd and Orbis Publishing Ltd

PRINTED IN SPAIN

ISBN 0 276 39660 X

Front cover picture: A nesting colony of gannets on a remote and
precipitous sea cliff. This handsome species is the largest of
Britain's many sea-going birds.

SEAS *and* ISLANDS

THE LIVING COUNTRYSIDE

PUBLISHED BY THE READER'S DIGEST ASSOCIATION LIMITED
LONDON   NEW YORK   MONTREAL   SYDNEY   CAPE TOWN

Originally published in partwork form
by Eaglemoss Publications Limited and Orbis Publishing Limited

Consultant

Keith Hiscock

Contributors

Penny Anderson	**William Condry**	**Ray Ingle**
Sheila Anderson	**Frances Dipper**	**Fred Naggs**
Roger Bailey	**Eric Edwards**	**Imants Priede**
Alan Bowers	**Peter Evans**	**Bryan Sage**
Keith Brander	**Michael Everett**	**Annabel Seddon**
Nigel E Buxton	**Jim Flegg**	**Hilary Soper**
Tom Cairns	**Peter Hawkey**	**Sue Wells**
Andrew Campbell	**Keith Hiscock**	**Alwyne Wheeler**

Contents

SEAS *and* ISLANDS

Introduction

To the underwater explorer the sea-bed presents an amazing variety of scenes. As the sea-bed progresses from mud to sand to gravel, to pebbles and on to rock, the communities associated with each type of surface change dramatically. And in the ascent from deep to shallow water, so the plants begin to take over from the animals.

The richness of the life associated with the sediments can only be viewed by taking samples since the vast majority of species living there are buried below the surface. They are animals – mainly worms, shrimp-like crustaceans and cockle-like molluscs. In contrast, many of the organisms living on rocks appear more like plants, with feathery feeding structures, leaf-like fronds or brightly coloured flower-like polyps. All these animals rely ultimately on the abundance of organic food in the water.

Animals dominate the sea-bed in deep waters where the light is too dim for plants to grow. In water shallow enough the rocks are clothed by seaweeds – plants which have no flowers and absorb their nutrients from the waters around them, not from any roots. The kelps, the largest of these plants, form forests with a dense canopy of fronds. Kelp forests provide a specialised habitat colonized by a community of plants, fishes and other organisms.

Even life on land is influenced by the sea, as it continues to influence terrestrial life. Islands, in particular, owe many of their characteristics to the salt spray and the battering of uninterrupted gales. They present special difficulties for colonization but are also havens for many species persecuted on the mainland by predators or by over-efficient agriculture. Many of them have some of the best coastal scenery in the British Isles and are especially important for their birds and flowers.

Left: A view of the sea from Lundy Island. Thrift grows in profusion among the short grass on the clifftop.

THE WORLD OF OPEN SEAS AND ISLANDS

The seas around Britain, largely unpolluted by man, remain our only natural wilderness, while our islands are havens for wildlife – sanctuaries for both man and a multitude of plants and animals. How we resolve the conflicts of development, fishing and conservation will determine whether our seas and islands remain the very special places they are today.

Above: Pilot whales in the open sea. These large mammals can be seen fairly frequently in British waters. Although they spend most of their lives well out to sea, they do sometimes come close inshore, particularly in the autumn when they can be seen off the south-west coast of Britain, and off the Shetlands.

Life on earth started in the sea and at one time almost all life existed solely there. Marine creatures therefore had a head start in an amenable environment, with the result that the greatest variety of life is now found in the sea. The teeming marine communities of our oceans and coastal waters are powered by sunlight, by the nutrients dissolved in their waters, and by the forces which keep that water in motion – wind, the rotation of the earth and tidally induced currents.

Part of that motion is in oceanic currents which carry water masses round the world. One of these current systems – the Gulf Stream – is the major force that determines much of the marine ecology of the coastal waters around the British Isles. This great 'river' of the sea, which starts its journey in the warm waters off Mexico, ensures that the climate of Britain is much milder than that of other places in the world on a similar latitude – countries bordering the Gulf of Alaska and the Bering Sea, for instance. The Gulf Stream cuts into the cold waters which approach the British Isles from the north. The northern waters are colonized by plants and animals different from the ones which inhabit the warmer waters to the south. The marine life surrounding the British Isles is therefore particularly rich, including a mixture of both northern and southern species.

Open water communities The communities of the sea can be classified and described in many different ways. An obvious division is between those living in the open waters and those which are attached to, or crawl over, the sea-bed. In open waters minute planktonic algae and animals drift with the water currents, some actively migrating from shallow to deep water by day and night. Their numbers are greatly affected by the concentrations of nutrients in the water. Some of the richest plankton communities, and therefore the fish and larger vertebrate animals that feed on them, are found where nutrient-rich waters from the depths of the ocean upwell into the well-lit surface waters where planktonic algae can photosynthesise. These algae are eaten by very small animals which provide a diet for larger animals, which themselves are eaten by even larger animals until they in turn are consumed by plankton-feeding fish such as the herring. This is the basis of the extremely complex food web which exists in the sea.

The obvious next stage is for the larger fish to feed on the smaller fish. But not all large fish rely on smaller ones for food. In fact the largest fish, the basking shark, feeds directly on plankton, filtering 1500 tons of water an hour by opening its cavernous mouth and trapping tens of thousands of small crustaceans and other animals on its gill rakers. The same goes for some of the large sea mammals. Some whales feed on plankton, while others take fish.

Sea-bed communities On the sea-bed, the survival of plants and animals depends on a different, much more variable, range of conditions. Most areas of the sea-bed are covered by sediments and the animals which live on and in them are greatly influenced by their different types. The communities that occur in coarse, well-oxygenated sediments are very different from those living in the fine sediments which are de-oxygenated just below their surface. Creatures living here need special adaptations to survive in such deadly conditions – many animals, for instance, extend siphons or some other structure to the sediment surface to draw in a stream of water for breathing or feeding, or they extend the respiratory/food-gathering parts of their bodies above the surface. Nevertheless, bur-

Above: There are large numbers of animals in the sea which spend the greater part of their lives settled in one place – on the rocks of the sea-bed, clamped firmly to the leg of an oil-rig, even on each other. Here a colony of hydroids has settled on a mussel shell.

Below: A colony of jewel anemones. These beautiful animals normally live below the low tide mark, usually on rock faces.

rowing into sediments provides all-important protection from many predators, particularly the fish.

Rock surfaces are colonized by seaweeds in shallow depths where light penetrates sufficiently for their growth. The seaweeds draw their nutrients directly from the surrounding waters and attach themselves to the sea-bed by holdfasts, not roots. Animals living attached to rocks are mainly dependent on food suspended in the water, which they capture by either active or passive suspension feeding. The passive feeders thrive best in areas where water movement is strong and food is brought to them, while the active feeders can create their own feeding currents in sheltered areas, thus colonizing habitats such as sea lochs.

Yet other factors are important to species living in shelter – they need, for instance, to have some mechanism for maintaining themselves free from silt or they will be smothered. Local topographical features and the type of substrate are important for rock-living species. Characteristic communities occur in such habitats as caves, cliffs or on pebble bottoms.

Man-made structures are another type of sea-bed and, although the species living on them are the same as those that live on rock, some thrive particularly well on these artificial substrates. This leads to the development of unusual communities, often dominated by spectacular growths of mussels, plumose anemones and sea squirts.

There are many predators living on both sediments and rocks. In sediments some of the most vicious are worms armed with several arrays of chitinous teeth. The crustaceans, worms and echinoderms (starfishes, sea

Above: A male pea crab (*Pinnotheres pisum*). These small crabs spend nearly all their lives inside the shells of bivalve molluscs – chiefly mussels, fan mussels and cockles. They take up residence in the host during the first stage of their lives after the active larval stage which is spent swimming freely in the sea.

Below: The goldsinny, a member of the colourful group of fishes known as wrasses, lives in rocky subtidal areas around Britain's coasts. It is most often seen by divers, though it is also found in rock pools.

urchins and so on) living in and on the sediments provide food for some of our most important commercial fish species. On rock, plants and animals also have to face predators and many mobile species only emerge at night when the creatures which feed on them, such as the wrasses, are asleep.

Where sea meets land The energy of the sea both destroys and builds. Coastal erosion on the North Sea coast of England, in particular, is a scene of constant battle between man and the sea. But the sediments created by the erosion of our coasts and by the outflows of our great rivers (mainly from the past) provide a source of sand which, when thrown up on to the shore and blown inland by the wind, creates sand dunes – havens of rich plant and animal life often left untouched by man because of their unsuitability for his crops.

In the Outer Hebrides the sand dunes are of quite a different type. The sand deposited by the waves and blown by the Atlantic gales includes much calcium carbonate derived from shelled marine animals. The resulting soil, together with the traditional agricultural practices of cattle grazing and cutting the sward after the flowers have seeded, creates a unique habitat – Hebridean machair – that is very fertile and extremely rich in plants.

Marine communities round islands Island waters are particularly rich in their variety of marine life because they offer so many different habitats to the drifting larvae that colonize the sea-bed. But islands are isolated, and sometimes the larvae of coastal species fail to reach them, so that some of the habitats there may be impoverished, compared to their mainland counterparts. On the other hand, they may provide havens from the stressful conditions, including pollution, which often exist near the coast. Islands are often places where species which were once widespread along our shores have their last strongholds, from where they will either sink into extinction or spring forth again when conditions become more favourable.

Marine communities are not static and depend on the balance between death and the recruitment of new individuals for their continued survival. For some species there may be cycles of high and low abundance. Such cycles have been most studied in fish, which have for long been a natural resource of our island waters and which have seen both natural and man-induced changes. The catching of fish is a job which becomes more sophisticated with every passing year, but the resource is potentially finite and fisheries have collapsed because of over-fishing as well as because of natural fluctuations in populations. Developments in fisheries move fast, and in recent years fish farming, particularly in the sea lochs of the west coast of Scotland, has grown into an enormous and successful industry.

Island communities – land and air For the terrestrial animals, including man, islands are places for escape and solitude, but they also present special problems and opportunities to the plants and animals they support. They may offer the first landfall to migrating birds or birds blown off course by strong winds – even from the other side of the Atlantic. And they provide escape and sanctuary, not just from man but from the other animals which pose a threat, such as foxes and weasels which failed to colonize the islands before they were created by rising seas following the last great ice age 7000 years ago. Conversely, many plants and animals suffering isolation on islands during those 7000 years have evolved distinct island races. But man has introduced mammals, particularly those he uses for food, to islands, and the consequences have often been severe for the native wildlife which relied so much on isolation.

Islands are frequently rich fishing grounds because they are near areas of nutrient-rich upwelling water, with a consequent abundance of plankton and fish. This richness provides food for the variety of birds and their young that find sanctuary on our islands. Many of these birds spend their lives at sea except for the few weeks when they come to land to breed and raise their young. Birds have seen many man-made and natural events which have affected their numbers. The large oil spills that occur when a tanker strikes a reef and disgorges its toxic cargo kill countless numbers of birds.

Another animal which relies on the availability of fish for its survival is the seal. Britain is the 'world headquarters' for the Atlantic grey seal, with over 50% of the world population. Numbers of both grey and common seal have increased substantially over the past few years, to the dismay of the salmon fishermen who believe that the stocks available to them are substantially reduced by the activities of the seals. Here, as with every natural community, the ideal is a balance in which all the elements interact without destroying one another.

Right: A herring gull wheels in flight over the Gower Peninsula. The remote coasts and islands of northern Britain — because of their very isolation — are thronged with seabirds of many species.

Below: A view of Village Bay on Hirta, one of the islands in the remote St Kilda group, with some of the gulls that haunt all four of St Kilda's main islands. St Kilda has several island specialities, including the St Kilda wren and the Soay sheep.

ROCKY SEA-BED COMMUNITIES

On the rocky sea-bed the plants and animals growing at any one location are determined by a complex framework of environmental conditions in which the penetration of light, strength of wave action and velocity of tidal streams are all-important.

Below: *Tubularia* hydroids growing in a 'turf' of hydrozoans. They can survive at depths where there is not enough sunlight for algae to live.

Until about 20 years ago, the rocky sea-bed around the British Isles was largely a mystery, but in the past 15 years or so scientists and naturalists have used improved diving techniques to observe, sample and photograph this colourful and fascinating world.

The amount of light penetrating to the sea-bed is one of the most vital factors determining the type and variety of life found there, but other factors, too, are important in influencing the distribution of species. One such factor is depth, and another is the strength of wave action (which decreases with increasing depth) and its effects on food supply, destruction of attached (sessile) species, dislodgement of mobile predators and the settlement of silt.

Food and feeding Animals fixed to the rock of the sea-bed have one major source of food: the organic material and plankton suspended in the water column. Such animals as hydroids, sea fans and bryozoans utilise this food supply in a passive manner by waiting for food to pass by in the water currents. The food is caught by minute anemone-like polyps or similar structures crowded along the branches. This might seem rather hit-or-miss,

but many species are highly adapted, having a flattened, fan-like structure which faces into the prevailing water currents to 'filter' the food. Other bottom-living species actively pump water through their filtration system; they include the fan worms and sea squirts.

Many species feed on the suspended material once it has settled to the bottom; they are the deposit feeders and include some worms, crustaceans, snails and bivalve molluscs. The most conspicuous of these is the black sea cucumber *Holothuria forskali*, which is over 20cm (8in) long and roams the sea-bed like an underwater vacuum cleaner, collecting silt and the organic material associated with it. A few species graze algae and animals from the rock, these including sea urchins and some molluscs. Others, such as the crabs, sea slugs, starfishes and fishes are active predators, often highly selective of their prey. Many species of crabs, lobsters and starfishes are also carrion eaters.

Waves and tidal streams Widely different animal communities develop on different areas of sea-bed under the influence of varying degrees of exposure to wave action and tidal streams.

Wave action can be extremely violent. A Force 8 gale can set up strong wave turbulence to a depth of 20m (66ft) near the coast, which results in waves moving along the sea bed at speeds of up to 3m (10ft) per second. However, the reduction of wave action with increasing depth means that, under the same Force 8 gale, water movement at a depth of 80m (270ft) is barely perceptible. This back and forth water motion can be highly destructive to erect sessile species since the constant movement causes tissue fatigue and tearing near the base, or else tears the whole plant or animal away from the rock. Secondary effects may also include the abrasion of rocks and organisms by the movement of boulders, stones, gravel and sand during storms.

The strength of tidal streams near the coast ranges from almost nothing to up to 10 knots

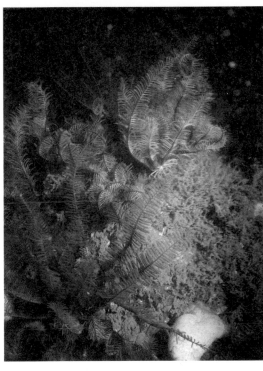

Above: One of the larger vertebrates found on the rocky sea-bed—the lumpsucker fish. Here the fish is guarding its nest and eggs.

Right: *Antedon bifida* feather stars—these crinoids often dominate large areas of the sea-bed. They are suspension feeders, the food being caught along the arms and transferred to the mouth at the central disc. The distribution of plants and animals on the rocky sea-bed is determined by the conditions of wave exposure, tidal flow, topography, scouring and other factors, but on any one patch of sea-bed, different communities develop according to chance historical events.

Sub-tidal communities

Sea water, together with particles of sediment suspended in the water, absorbs, scatters and reflects light so that the amount reaching the sea-bed is reduced rapidly with increasing depth. In shallow well-lit areas seaweeds (algae) dominate the sea-bed, particularly the brown and red algae. Kelp forms forests in shallow waters, the depths at which it lives ranging from less than 1m (3ft) below water level, where turbid waters predominate, to 25m (80ft) where the water is very clear. Kelps can only grow where more than 1% of surface illumination is usually present, but smaller foliose algae thrive where light intensity is less than this. In the depths where light is too dim for algae, such animals as sea firs (hydroids), sponges, sea anemones, sea mats (bryozoans) and sea squirts dominate the rock, together with crabs, lobsters, sea urchins, starfishes and fishes.

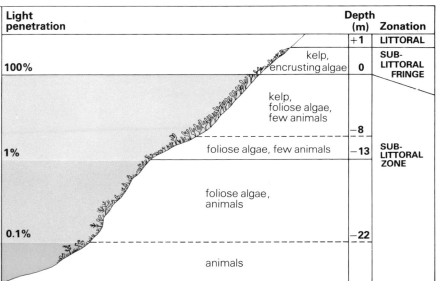

Light penetration		Depth (m)	Zonation
		+1	LITTORAL
100%	kelp, encrusting algae	0	SUB-LITTORAL FRINGE
	kelp, foliose algae, few animals	−8	
1%	foliose algae, few animals	−13	SUB-LITTORAL ZONE
	foliose algae, animals		
0.1%		−22	
	animals		

Above: A community of the orange sea squirt *Dendrodoa grossularia,* with the white sponge *Clathrina coriacea.* They are characteristic of shallow wave surge gullies. A yellow sponge and a purse sponge can also be seen. Both wave action and tidal streams bring food for suspension feeders and prevent smothering by silt and deoxygenation. These same forces, however, can also be highly destructive.

(11½ miles per hour) at the surface (about 1.5m/5ft per second near the sea-bed), depending on geographical location and coastal topography. Again, such forces can be highly destructive. However, both wave action and tidal streams bring food for suspension feeders and prevent smothering by silt and deoxygenation.

Distribution of communities The different susceptibilities and needs of the plant and animal species colonizing the rocky sea-bed, in relation to the strength of water movement and its effects, lead to the presence of widely different communities in different regimes of wave and tidal stream exposure.

In shallow areas exposed to violent wave action, for instance, a particularly distinctive community develops. Here, the sea squirt *Dendrodoa grossularia* and the sponge *Clathrina coriacea* thrive together, accompanied by a small variety of other sponge, hydroid and sea anemone species that are consistently found in this type of habitat. On coasts facing the most severe exposure to the Atlantic the forest of large kelp plants normally present in shallow water is reduced to a few scattered small plants, while the main species which settle and dominate the rock are fast-growing, short-lived algae and animals, such as some of the foliose algae and sponges, hydroids and barnacles. In the deeper, animal-dominated areas, rocks are often characterised by a low turf of hydroids and bryozoans, with erect species such as the branching sponges and sea fans restricted to gullies and potholes sheltered from the full force of wave oscillation.

Strong tidal flow encourages a different type of community from that able to survive strong wave action. Such areas as the narrowest parts of the Menai Straits, Ramsey Sound and Strangford Lough Narrows are populated by communities dominated by the sponge *Halichondria panicea* and the hydroid *Tubularia indivisa.* Again, there are other species usually associated with this distinctive community, forming a restricted range of organisms able to withstand such severe en-

Continental Shelf

The edge of the Continental Shelf is located to the west of Britain, where the water depth is in excess of 200m (656ft). Most of the seas immediately surrounding the coast of Britain, including the entire North Sea, are relatively shallow (less than 200m/656ft deep).

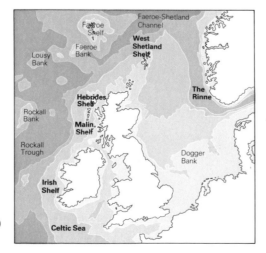

Depth (m)
0–50	100–200
50–100	200–1000
	1000+

vironmental conditions. But distinctive communities are also found at the other end of the spectrum, in the extreme shelter of sea lochs. These communities are characterised by large sea squirts such as *Ciona intestinalis*, species of *Ascidiella* and *Ascidia mentula* and by delicate fan worms including *Sabella pavonina* and *Bispira volutacornis*. In such extreme shelter there is often no kelp forest, the shallow water rocks instead being dominated by a green, cottonwool-like cover of filamentous algae and by the cord weed *Chorda filum*. Where kelp plants do occur, they are of the species *Laminaria saccharina*, which has short stipes and long crinkled fronds.

Geographical distribution There is a distinctive geographical element to the composition of sea-bed communities. The British Isles lie at the meeting point of three major biogeographical provinces: the Arctic-Boreal with its centre well to the north of the British Isles; the Mediterranean-Boreal which extends near the north of Scotland; and the Mediterranean-Atlantic which extends northwards to the English Channel and the western approaches.

In the south-west of Britain, communities dominated or characterised by a wide range of sponges, hydroids, anemones and their relatives, and erect bryozoans are present. Many of these species are found in abundance only in the south-west and, by chance, are some of the most colourful and spectacular forms of marine life. They include such species as the red sea fingers (*Alcyonium glomeratum*) and the sea fan (*Eunicella verrucosa*), yellow zoanthid anemones (*Parazoanthus axinellae*), the hydroid *Gymnangium montagui* and such cup corals as the yellow *Leptopsammia pruvoti*. Many seaweeds are also restricted to the south-west and some, such as the kelp *Laminaria ochroleuca*, can dominate the sea-bed. The distribution of some of these species appears to be closely associated with the proximity of oceanic water and they extend all round the western coasts of the British Isles.

To the far north the picture is different.

There are not as many species; many of the southern ones are lost and only a few northern species appear to replace them. These few northern species, which are not found or are only rarely encountered in the south, sometimes dominate the sea-bed. An outstandingly successful example is the horse mussel (*Modiolus modiolus*). This large mussel colonizes both rock and sediment, providing a habitat for a wide range of other marine species. *Modiolus* communities sampled from widely different areas are remarkably similar. Some of the most exciting discoveries in recent years have been made in the sea lochs of Scotland, where communities very similar to those of Norwegian fjords have been found. These

Above: Polyps of the yellow sea anemone (*Parazoanthus axinellae*) – a species rarely recorded and, until recently, thought to be restricted in distribution to south-west England and Wales. In 1982 it was recorded from the Hebrides.

Below: Waving fronds of a kelp forest. The species is *Laminaria hyperborea*; it is characteristic of temperate waters and forms forests in shallow water.

Below: A close-up of a rich rock community off the island of Lundy. The animals visible here include erect bryozoans, the sponge *Leucosolenia botryoides*, the Devonshire cup coral *Caryophyllia smithii*, and the sea slug *Greilada elegans*.

communities are characterised by such species as the sea anemone *Protanthea simplex* and by the brachiopods (lamp shells) *Crania anomala* and *Terebratulina retusa*. Northern species of seaweeds also take over as dominant or characteristic species on the coasts of Scotland; one abundant species is *Odonthalia dentata*.

There are other features of particular areas which give them a strong regional characteristic. One such is the abundant growth of brown dead men's fingers (*Alcyonium digitatum*) and plumose anemones (*Metridium senile*) in rocky areas of the north-east coast. Others are the communities associated with limestone where piddocks bore into the rock, thus providing holes that shelter a characteristic fauna, and certain areas of the upper Bristol Channel where the effects of a stressful water quality and suspended sand lead to the development of communities dominated by worms of the genus *Sabellaria*, which construct their dwelling tubes from sand.

Stability and change Man has influenced hardly at all the plants and animals that colonize the rocky sea-bed and the communities present there are some of the last natural ones existing in our islands. These communities appear reasonably similar when viewed from year to year, although considerable seasonal changes occur in a few species.

Above: The sea urchin *Echinus esculentus* exerts a major influence on the ecology of underwater rocky areas. It is present in large numbers in areas of south-west England, the Isle of Man, Scotland including the Shetland Isles, western and northern Ireland and the north-east coast of England. In places its density exceeds one per square metre. In such numbers the sea urchin can effectively keep the rocks clear of erect growth, with the exception of a small range of fast-growing resistant species or species with defensive equipment. However, it does not graze to bare rock in shallow areas where pink encrusting calcareous algae cover the rocks—the algae appear to be unaffected by the grazing urchins.

Opposite page: During the day the common lobster hides deep in crevices wherever the sea-bed is rocky. At night it emerges to feed.

Above right: The velvet swimming crab (*Liocarcinus puber*) is a predator and carrion eater on sub-tidal rocky sea-beds.

Right: Dense foliose algae dominating sandy rock in well-lit waters.

Some species are extremely long-lived; the sea fan, for instance, grows at a rate of only about 1cm ($\frac{3}{8}$in) a year, but reaches a height of 40cm (16in). Other species have a very short life but colonize, grow and die in a year, so providing a similar appearance on the sea-bed in a particular area at the same time each year. Some species, on the other hand, show variable recruitment and may dominate an area for a few years, then almost disappear.

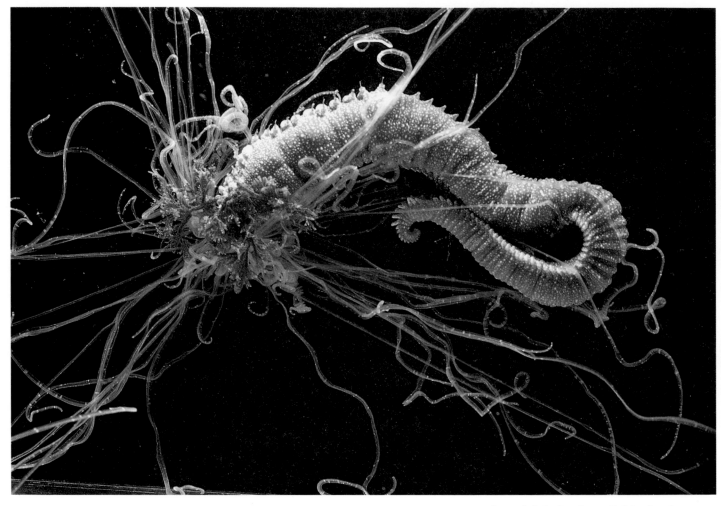

COMMUNITIES OF SEA-BED SEDIMENT

Off the shores of the British Isles are vast areas of underwater mud, sand and gravel. The surface of these sediments appears bare when compared with the rocky sea-bed, but within are huge numbers of worms, molluscs, crustaceans, brittle stars and sea urchins.

quantity of fish food available for bottom-living fishes. As he worked on the thousands of bottom samples collected it became clear to Petersen that animals were not distributed in a random fashion; distinct assemblages of organisms existed which could be characterised by a few large or abundant species. This definition, though adapted, altered and criticised, is a basis for most present descriptions of sea-bed communities. It was clear to Petersen and to later researchers that the collection of animals present was dependent mainly on sediment type, so it is little wonder that the naming of the communities has taken two main lines, one naming the communities by their dominant or character-

Since most of the animals dwelling in the sediment of the sea-bed are burrowers, it is difficult to gain a true idea of the numbers that actually exist. The only way to observe these animal communities is to sample the sediment, then wash away the mud and sand over a sieve, so exposing the animals to view. Research shows that the macrofauna (animals larger than 1mm) alone can number 80 species and 2500 individuals below just one square metre of sea-bed.

The discovery of 'communities' In the early part of this century CGJ Petersen (an eminent Danish fisheries scientist) began a series of investigations in the Danish seas that were intended to provide a basis for calculating the

Above: This type of polychaete worm is abundant in the bivalve mollusc *Macoma* community found in shallow water muddy areas extending on to the shore.

Right: The heart-urchin or sea potato (*Echinocardium cordatum*) belongs to the sand-dwelling community, and is found in depths of 10-20m (33-66ft) below the sea surface. Shown here are the urchin's upper surface (left) and the under surface (right).

istic species, the other by the sediment type they occupy.

North-east Atlantic communities Four sediment communities are particularly widespread in this area. In the shallow water muddy areas extending on to the shore, a community characterised by the bivalve mollusc *Macoma baltica* is usually found. Often the most conspicuous species, to the casual observer, are the lugworm *Arenicola marina*, visible only by its casts of excreted material, and the edible cockle, which lives very near the surface. The netted whelk (*Hinia incrassatus*) ploughs through the surface here, searching for bivalve molluscs such as *Macoma* to bore into and feed on. The deeper into the sediment an animal can burrow, the more protected it will be. All the species living below the shallow surface layers, often in deoxygenated sediment, need a connection to the surface, either in the form of an open burrow or by a long siphon such as that possessed by another bivalve inhabitant of this community, *Mya arenaria*. There are many small amphipod crustaceans and polychaete worms in a community such as this, and the worm *Pygospio* is often abundant, with the small mud tubes in which it lives packed closely together at the surface.

The *Chamelea* (or *Venus*) community is found in depths of about 10-20m (33-66ft) below the sea surface in sand. Here, the bivalves *Chamelea gallina* and *C. ovata* are present in large numbers, together with several other bivalve species, many of them important sources of food for fishes. The polychaete *Pectinaria* also lives in this community and constructs a tapered tube of sand grains in which it sits head down into the sediment, drawing water and food into its burrow. The heart-urchin, too, lives buried in the sediment. Apart from the fishes and other surface dwellers, there are predators within the sediment, including the starfish *Astropecten irregularis* and species of the snail *Lunatia*.

A third community can be found in muddy sand in depths of about 5-15m (16-50ft); this habitat is populated by vast numbers of bivalves of the species *Abra* (or *Syndosmya*). These molluscs, together with many of the other species in the *Abra* community, are fast-growing and provide a source of rapidly renewed food for flatfishes such as plaice and flounder. Large brittle stars (*Ophiura texturata*) are often common here.

In deeper water from about 15-100m (50-330ft) the muddy sea-bed is colonized by a rich community characterised by species of burrowing brittle stars (*Amphiura*), together with the urchin *Brissopsis lyrifera* and a wide range of polychaetes and crustaceans. To the observer swimming over the sea-bed, the arms of *Amphiura filiformis* appear as a meadow of rather sparse long grasses which rapidly withdraw if touched. A fascinating and unusual species often present in this com-

Four sediment communities

The *Macoma* community

1 Lugworm *Arenicola marina*.
2 Edible cockle (*Cerastium edule*).
3 Common shrimp (*Crangon crangon*).
4 Netted dog whelk (*Hinia reticulatus*).
5 Bristleworm *Pygospio*.
6 Bivalve *Macoma baltica*.
7 Bivalve *Mya arenaria*.
8 Mud snail *Hydrobia*.

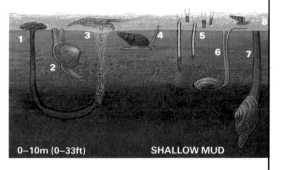

0–10m (0–33ft)   SHALLOW MUD

The *Chamelea* community

1 Heart-urchin or sea potato (*Echinocardium cordatum*).
2 Starfish *Astropecten irregularis*.
3 Snail *Lunatia*.
4 Common prawn (*Palaemon serratus*).
5 Striped Venus shell (*Chamelea gallina*).
6 Bivalve *Spisula elliptica*.
7 Bivalve *Tellina fabula*.
8 Bristleworm *Pectinaria* species.

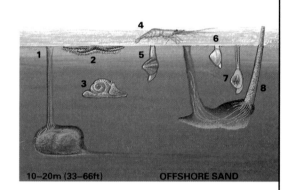

10–20m (33–66ft)   OFFSHORE SAND

The *Abra* community

1 Blunt gaper shell (*Mya truncata*).
2 Common whelk (*Buccinum undatum*).
3 Bivalve *Abra* species.
4 Bristleworm *Pectinaria* species.
5 Brittle star *Ophiura texturata*.
6 Bivalve *Cultellus pellucidus*.
7 Bivalve *Nucula* species.
8 Common basket shell (*Corbula gibba*).

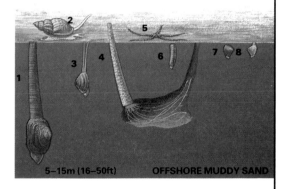

5–15m (16–50ft)   OFFSHORE MUDDY SAND

The *Amphiura* community

1 Sea urchin *Brissopsis lyrifera*.
2 Tower shell (*Turritella communis*).
3 Brittle star *Amphiura chiajei*.
4 Pelican's-foot shell (*Aporrhais pes-pelecani*).
5 Brittle star *Amphiura filiformis*.
6 Sea pen *Virgularia mirabilis*.
7 Bristleworm *Nephthys ciliata*.

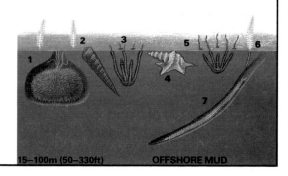

15–100m (50–330ft)   OFFSHORE MUD

munity is the sea pen *Virgularia mirabilis*. It grows to a height of up to 30cm (12in) above the sea-bed and, as a close relative of the sea anemones, the stalks are covered in anemone-like polyps. The sea pen extends for a similar length down into the sediment and is firmly anchored by a bulbous foot. The tower shell (*Turritella communis*) and the pelican's-foot shell (*Aporrhais pes-pelecani*) have unusual shells and are often found in this habitat.

Two plant communities Most communities are described according to the conspicuous burrowing animal present, but some marine algae can use relatively small pieces of gravel as a substratum for growth and, provided the gravel is stable for at least a few weeks, form

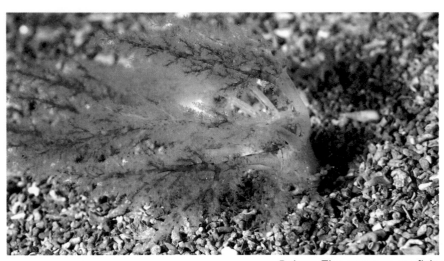

characteristic assemblages in the shallow well-lit zones during the summer. However, multicellular plants are not generally found on sediments because there is no firm base for attachment on the sediment particles.

There are, nevertheless, two remarkable exceptions to this rule: the beds of eel-grass (*Zostera marina*) which occur in shallow, sheltered waters (usually no deeper than 5m/ 16ft), and the beds of maerl (detached calcareous algae) which make up large areas of the sea-bed and also occur in sheltered conditions, particularly those off the west coasts of Ireland and Scotland. *Zostera marina* is the only flowering plant which inhabits sub-littoral areas of the British Isles. Rhizomes of the plant provide a firm anchorage into the sediment, and the leaves, which can grow to over a metre in length, form large meadows which are habitats for a variety of fishes and attached algae and invertebrates.

Maerl (*Phymatolithon calcareum* and another red algae, *Lithothamnion corallioides*) often occurs with *Zostera*, but also forms extensive beds deeper than the *Zostera*. The pink calcareous nodules are usually 1-3cm ($\frac{2}{5}$-1in) across but grow up to 10cm (4in), forming a substratum like coarse gravel. Only a proportion of the maerl is alive but the dead material remains to form deep beds which are exploited as a source of limestone fertiliser in some areas. Many rare or unusual species occur in this habitat, which has a very

Below: A characteristic inhabitant of coarse gravel is the burrowing sea cucumber *Neopentadactyla mixta*. It often occupies substrates which are highly mobile. The body of this creature, which is about 10cm (4in) long, is buried but the sticky tentacles appear above the sediment to catch suspended particles of organic matter. Each tentacle is withdrawn into the mouth one after the other to suck off the attached material.

Below: The common starfish (*Asterias rubens*) is another inhabitant of the muddy gravel habitat. Along with a few crabs and fishes, it is one of the few species to be seen on the surface of the sediment.

restricted distribution.

Food and feeding Most of the animals living in the sediment rely on plankton and suspended organic matter for food, taking that food by suspension or deposit feeding. Suspension feeders, such as some of the bivalve molluscs, draw in water through a siphon, filter off the organic material and pass the water out through another siphon. Other suspension feeders, such as fan worms, the sea pen, and those brittle stars with arms protruding from the sea-bed, catch their food as it floats past in water currents. Deposit feeders include bivalve molluscs, which use their inhalant siphon like a vacuum cleaner to draw in organic material from the surface of the sediment, and such species as the lugworm *Arenicola*, which eats large quantities of sand to extract organic material.

The animal species living in the sediment include many voracious predators. Among the larger species is the starfish *Astropecten*, which takes whole bivalves into its stomach and digests the tissue. The snail *Lunatia* has rasping teeth and probably also uses a chemical to bore a small conical hole into clam shells, into which its proboscis is inserted to feed on the animal within. Many worms are predators and such species as *Nereis* have vicious jaws, used to attack other worms. The several species of anemone which burrow into sediments are opportunistic carnivores and carrion eaters, waiting for prey to stumble into their tentacles or for carrion to come into contact. The fishes which live on or near the bottom are large consumers of sediment-living species, especially bivalve molluscs, and some duck species also dive for bottom-dwelling animals. With such a variety of predators it is hardly surprising that the long-lived species are generally those which dig deep and are equipped with thick shells. Thin-shelled animals living near the surface, such as *Abra*, reproduce in enormous numbers and have a short life-cycle.

Reproduction, settlement and survival The majority of north-east Atlantic species living on the sea-bed have planktonic larvae which spend up to a month drifting in the surface waters, feeding on phytoplankton and on each other. Vast numbers of larvae are produced and mortality is high before the survivors are ready to settle to the bottom.

Settlement appears to be far from random. In the open sea small differences in temperature and salinity, together with other aspects of water quality, may induce or discourage

growth, feeding and settlement. Thus, the survival of the larvae is different in different water bodies, and choice of settlement sites may be affected. Larvae of bottom-living species are often photopositive (attracted to light) or photonegative (repelled by light) and, at the end of their larval life, will go either near the surface and therefore settle in shallow water or to the bottom and settle in deeper water. Sensitivity to gravity or water pressure has a similar effect. The larvae of several species have been shown to select the type of substratum on which to settle. Once the larvae are on the bottom, it is a fight for survival of the fittest, including competition for living space and food and the interaction between predators and prey.

Many of the species present in the sea-bed sediment live for several years and include some of the large bivalve molluscs, large crustaceans such as the Norway lobster, and some of the echinoderms. Their survival often depends on the presence of a stable environment where sediments are not disturbed by storms or other forms of perturbation. In shallow wave-exposed areas, communities are frequently disturbed and generally consist of large numbers of a small variety of fast-growing species, particularly some polychaete worms and small bivalve molluscs. Apart from the changes resulting from storms, many sea-bed communities are very changeable, particularly because of

Above: Eel-grass (*Zostera marina*) is the only flowering plant to inhabit sub-tidal areas of the British Isles. It usually occurs in waters no deeper than 5m (16ft). Before the 1930s it was much more abundant than it is today, but at that time a bacterial or fungal infection decimated the populations, which have still not fully recovered in many areas.

Left: The tower shell (*Turritella communis*) is often found as a member of the burrowing brittle star *Amphiura* community in mud in deep water.

Below: The burrowing sea anemone *Cerianthus lloydii* living in a bed of maerl (*Phymatolithon calcareum*).

variable recruitment of their component species or heavy predation in some years. Such changes occur in the species characteristic of more stable communities but are usually reflected in low or high numbers in particular year classes rather than in generally low or high densities. In environments where physical conditions, including such factors as wave action, temperature and salinity, are stable, the communities are usually much more diverse than those that form in unstable environments.

Any environmental change beyond the usual is likely to cause stress and result in reduced numbers of species being present (although those organisms that are stress-tolerant thrive). This is the case for both natural disturbance and man-induced disturbance, including pollution. Much work has been done to study the effects of organic pollution on marine sediment communities (in particular that caused by sewage discharge and pulp mill effluents) and on the effects of activity from the North Sea oil industry.

LIFE ON WRECKS BENEATH THE SEA

A shipwreck is a disaster at the time it happens, but the wreckage may well last longer than the memory of the loss. Today, the life that springs from the death of a ship – or an aircraft – attracts an increasing number of naturalists and divers.

To man, a shipwreck is a disaster representing tragic loss of life and property, and often pollution of our seas and shores. Historic wrecks such as the *Titanic*, the *Torrey Canyon* and the *Mary Rose* are created by bad luck, human error and war. Time, however, is a great healer and soon many of these lost ships become places of interest and excitement to fishermen, divers and archaeologists.

Many wrecks have long ago been stripped of their valuables by salvagers and others who recover what the sea has taken. The naturalist, however, sees a different value in these wrecks–as sites for an incredible variety of marine life. Living space in the sea is at a premium, and new wrecks provide attach-

Right: Few, if any, species live exclusively on wrecks, but some are typical of them. The plumose anemone *Metridium senile* prefers an elevated position and its white, orange or green heads festoon many sunken gangways and railings. This picture of *Metridium* was taken on the wreck of the *Hispanica* in the Sound of Mull.

Below: Soft corals, sponges and a diver on the wreck of the *Glanmire* off St Abb's Head, Scotland.

ment places and homes for a myriad of animals and plants. In fact, any hard object left in the sea is soon colonized by so-called 'fouling' organisms.

Dangerous coasts Nobody knows exactly how many wrecks there are around the coasts of Britain and Ireland. Many are never found, and others are broken up beyond recognition. At a conservative estimate there are at least 250,000 recorded wreck incidents since about the year 1300 AD.

The beautiful rocky coasts of Devon and Cornwall and the west of Ireland and Scotland, exposed to the full fury of Atlantic storms, are notoriously dangerous to shipping. Wrecks of all sorts abound in the Scilly Isles, off the Manacle Rocks in Cornwall, and around Mull in the Hebrides.

Diversity of habitats Sessile (attached) marine plants and animals reproduce and spread by means of floating (or sometimes crawling) larvae and spores, and so what settles on a new wreck partly depends on its position and depth. Wrecks settling on soft sediments provide a sudden and unexpected hard substrate, and quickly become oases of life in otherwise superficially barren areas. The wreck of the *Fort Napier* in the shelter of Loch na Beiste in Skye lies on muddy sand and shell. Its many hanging spars provide a foothold for dead man's fingers (*Alcyonium digitatum*) and the beautiful sea anemones *Sargartia elegans* and *Metridium senile*, other-

wise scarce in this area.

Wrecks settling in rocky areas eventually become almost indistinguishable from their surroundings, although close examination reveals subtle differences. Iron surfaces are sometimes poorly colonized because of the mechanical instability of flaking rust, and so may have less cover than nearby rocks and a predominance of short-lived, rapidly growing species.

A large wreck presents a variety of micro-habitats, and on many wrecks different communities are found at the bow and stern, or from side to side where conditions of current and wave action differ. Seaweeds are restricted to shallow wrecks, and often cover the horizontal top sides, where the light can reach them (although the 'top' may be the side of the ship). Deeper sheltered horizontal surfaces and recesses are often covered in species tolerant of settling silt, such as the sponge *Suberites* and the sea squirt *Ascidiella*.

Surfaces of the wreck Colonial animals are well suited to an attached existence, and many wrecks are covered in 'turfs' of sponges, hydroids, bryozoans and colonial sea-squirts. All these are filter feeders, relying on the current to bring them food particles; they are particularly abundant where such currents are strong. They gain considerable benefit from their elevated position above the sea-bed.

Particular wrecks may be rich in a particular group or species of animal or plant,

Above: The sea slug *Facelina bostoniensis*, on the wreck of the *Alistair* in Strangford Lough.

Below: A goldsinny in a wreck off Plymouth. A piece of seaweed floats past.

depending on local conditions. The Dutch cargo ship *Breda* was sunk by German bombers in 1940 and lies in the shelter of Ardmucknish Bay near Oban in Scotland. All 122m (380ft) of her length are still there, and the vertical sides are covered by sea squirts, mainly *Ascidia mentula* and *Ciona intestinalis*, which are typical of sheltered Scottish waters.

The beautiful sea anemone *Protanthea simplex*-only recently discovered by SCUBA divers in British waters-also prefers still waters and adorns the sides of this wreck. The oaten pipes hydroid *Tubularia indivisa* is characteristic of areas of high water movement, and many wrecks in the Sound of Mull and the Menai Straits are dominated by this species.

Hard-shelled borers A few species of specialised animals are not content to live merely on or within a wreck, but burrow into the very fabric itself. The wooden parts of shipwrecks are quickly attacked by the shipworm (*Teredo*) and by piddocks, all bivalve molluscs; and by a small isopod crustacean, the gribble (*Limnoria lignorum*). Henry VIII's now famous wooden warship, the *Mary Rose*, only survived to the present day because when it sank it was rapidly buried by fine silt, thus avoiding the ravages of these creatures.

Abundant fish life Fish seem to be irresistably attracted to wrecks, and anglers have long taken advantage of this. However, only the diver is able to see the beautiful shoals of banded bib (*Trisopterus luscus*) which seem to abound around most wrecks. Solitary larger individuals often prefer the shelter of the dark recesses within the wreck, and many of these lack the banding of the younger fishes. Here too the small poor cod (*Trisopterus minutus*) can be found sheltering. Silvery pollack and saithe, and the ubiquitous ballan wrasse, are

Life on a wreck

This is an artist's impression of life colonizing a wreck. It would exceed the wildest hopes of any diver, whose view would be clouded by floating particles and poorly lit at the best of times. The picture shows the wreckage of a Catalina sea-plane near Millport on the island of Great Cumbrae in the Firth of Clyde. This aircraft was part of a squadron defending the Scottish sea lanes in World War II. It sank in 1941, not as a result of fighting but because of accidental opening of the seacocks, causing the fuselage to flood. It is therefore not a 'grave', and today it is one of the most frequently visited wrecks. To the naturalist, it is an example of a habitat that has not developed a

fully stable community, perhaps chiefly because it is subject to winter storms. It is colonized and recolonized by successive different species—such as mussels and barnacles—from year to year, and even at different times of year.

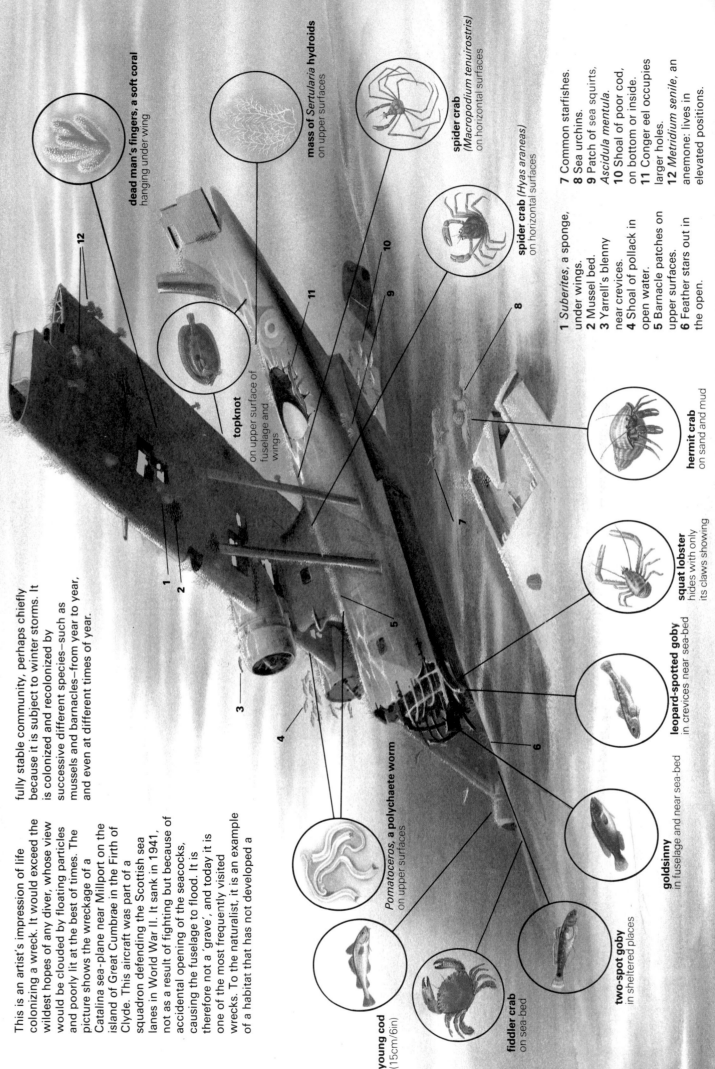

dead man's fingers, a soft coral
hanging under wing

mass of *Sertularia* hydroids
on upper surfaces

spider crab
(*Macropodium tenuirostris*)
on horizontal surfaces

spider crab (*Hyas araneas*)
on horizontal surfaces

topknot
on upper surface of
fuselage and wings

hermit crab
on sand and mud

squat lobster
hides with only
its claws showing

leopard-spotted goby
in crevices near sea-bed

goldsinny
in fuselage and near sea-bed

Pomatoceros, a polychaete worm
on upper surfaces

two-spot goby
in sheltered places

fiddler crab
on sea-bed

young cod
(15cm/6in)

1 *Suberites*, a sponge,
under wings.
2 Mussel bed.
3 Yarrell's blenny
near crevices.
4 Shoal of pollack in
open water.
5 Barnacle patches on
upper surfaces.
6 Feather stars out in
the open.
7 Common starfishes.
8 Sea urchins.
9 Patch of sea squirts,
Ascidula mentula.
10 Shoal of poor cod,
on bottom or inside.
11 Conger eel occupies
larger holes.
12 *Metridium senile*, an
anemone: lives in
elevated positions.

vicinity of a wreck. The rich turfs of sponges and hydroids provide abundant food for the colourful predatory sea slugs.

Changing occupants Wrecks, like rocky areas, can support fairly stable communities of plants and animals. However, such communities may take many years to develop fully. Divers are studying this development by looking at plant and animal communities on wrecks of known age, and making comparisons with the life on the surrounding rocks. The first colonizers of a new wreck are the short-lived, fast-growing species. These are then gradually replaced by longer-lived but slow-growing organisms, which can compete more strongly for space and light.

The kelp *Sacchoriza polyschides* is a very fast-growing annual, and this, along with the sea lettuce *Ulva lactuca*, which reproduces throughout the year, are often among the first colonizers of shallow wrecks. The perennial forest kelp *Laminaria hyperborea*, and encrusting animal species, take longer to become established, but eventually take over.

Conservation of wrecks Many wrecks are protected by law because of their historical, archaeological or salvage interests. Some are classified as war graves, and access to these is restricted. In these cases, the marine life gains incidental protection. Some people feel that other wrecks deserve equal protection simply for the rich and varied marine life that they support.

also common residents.

The many holes and crevices in a typical wreck provide ideal homes for conger eels, which lurk in portholes with apparently sinister intent. In spite of their ferocious reputation, congers do not attack divers or swimmers unless provoked by an incautious hand or stick. Smaller holes are inhabited by the tompot blenny (*Parablennius gattorugine*), which peers cheekily out from the safety of its refuge. The tompot is restricted to the south and west coasts, but the equally entertaining Yarrell's blenny (*Chirolophis ascani*) takes its place on the other coasts.

Rich turfs of encrusting species provide shelter and a meal of small worms and crustaceans for the scorpion fish *Taurulus bubalis*. This species is a master of camouflage, and alters its colour to suit the background. The topknot is one of the few species of flatfish living in rocky areas, and small specimens can often be found on wrecks. They, too, merge well into the background. When patches of the pink encrusting seaweed *Lithothamnion* are present, the topknot may well display beautiful pink spots for camouflage.

The so-called wreck fish (*Polyprion americanus*) gets its name from the habit of the young fishes of accompanying drifting wreckage, but it is not generally associated with sunken wrecks.

Other predators With their profusion of marine life, wrecks are good hunting grounds for many predators other than fishes. On the wreck of the *James Egon Layne* near Plymouth, cuttlefish can be seen stealthily hunting crabs and small fishes. They catch their prey by a lightning grab with their longest pair of tentacles. Lobsters and edible crabs also find refuges in holes and under timbers, and fishermen often lay pots in the

Above: Ship's timbers riddled with shipworms and encrusted with other molluscs.

Below: Yarrell's blenny on the sea-plane wreck near Millport, Great Cumbrae.

NOCTURNAL LIFE IN THE SEA

Night diving is richly rewarding for the marine naturalist, for night is a time of great activity among the animals living in the sea.

The sea is a place of perpetual activity, and night is no exception. Filter feeding animals such as anemones, dead man's fingers, barnacles and tube worms are as active by night as they are by day. Their food is brought to them by water currents, and they have no need for stealth or concealment. Their times of activity and inactivity are not necessarily related to the cycle of day and night.

However, there are many nocturnal sea creatures for which night offers better chances of finding food and evading predators, just as it does for nocturnal land animals such as owls and hedgehogs. Many, such as the brightly coloured squat lobster *Galathea strigosa*, hide in crevices during the day where fishes and

Above: The squat lobster *Galathea strigosa* emerges from its daytime crevice to wander in the safety of darkness. It feeds on algae and floating particles of detritus, as well as hunting small marine animals. Squat lobsters sometimes take up a night-time position clinging upside down to an overhanging rock.

Left: A terebellid worm, a member of the large group known as the polychaetes. This animal hides under boulders and in crevices by day, emerging at night to crawl on the sea-bed. Why it emerges at all is something of a mystery: its long whitish feeding tentacles function just as effectively while it is still in its hiding place.

octopuses cannot reach them. Some animals live in an eternal night because below a certain depth there is no light; such deep sea animals are specially adapted to a life of perpetual darkness.

Night fishes At night, many fishes and other normally timid and wary creatures lose their fear, and for the diver this is the best time to photograph them. Dazzled by a torch beam, the strangely shaped John dory (*Zeus faber*) poses with its fins outstretched. Normally aggressive conger eels sometimes allow a diver to stroke them, and the timid leopard-spotted goby (*Thorogobius ephippiatus*) emerges from its daytime crevice to feed on amphipods (small crustaceans) and worms. This beautiful, shy fish was once thought to be rare, but recently divers have found that it is widespread, living in steep, rocky areas of the sea-bed.

The venomous weever fish lies hidden in the sand for most of the day, and although it does feed during the day, it is more successful at night. It is also more active by day in areas where the water is dark and murky. This is also true of other animals, such as the long-clawed squat lobster (*Munida bamffica*), which normally hides under rocks in the day with just the claws showing. In deep, dark water they can be found in the open at all times.

In contrast to the night-active fishes, wrasse sleep soundly at night, wedged into crevices or deep among seaweeds. Often they can be picked up before they awake sufficiently to swim off. Shoals of pollack can be found resting quietly among kelp plants, their hunting over for a while. Some of these fishes, including wrasse, undergo subtle colour changes at night. Bars, stripes and spots appear and disappear, and many fishes become darker all over. (This can most easily be seen in an aquarium.)

Night senses Many animals in the sea rely on their senses of smell and touch, and are not perturbed by their lack of vision at night. Fishes have a lateral line sensory system that detects low frequency vibrations caused by other fishes moving through the water or their own 'bow wave' hitting other objects. They are thus well able to swim freely around at night. Some deep sea fishes have especially well developed lateral lines. Other nocturnal and deep sea fishes have very large eyes which are sensitive to low light intensities.

Skates possess another sense useful at night –electricity. Most can produce their own weak electrical fields that other skates can detect and recognise. In this way they can more easily locate others of their own species. If any object disturbs this electrical field, the fish can detect the change and thus 'see' in the dark. Dolphins and whales can hunt and move freely at night, using their sophisticated echolocation system much as bats do on land.

Bioluminescence This effect, also called phosphorescence, is one of the wonders of the sea at night. In calm summer weather, vast

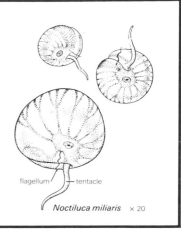

How 'cold light' is made
Bioluminescence is more widespread among marine organisms than it is among land animals. Light is formed in an interesting chemical reaction: substances known as luciferins combine with oxygen, aided by an enzyme, with light as a by-product. When a candle burns, the reaction is also an oxidation, but heat is made as well as light. Luminescence is a totally cold light–giving no heat, the reaction is a more efficient way of making light. The small dinoflagellate *Noctiluca miliaris* (right) has exceptional luminescent powers for its size: its body contains thousands of light-producing granules.

flagellum tentacle

Noctiluca miliaris × 20

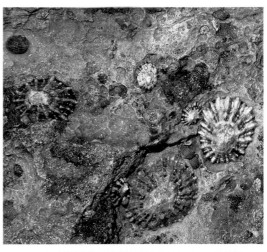

Above: The hermit crab's survival strategy is an alternative to nocturnality– with a shell to retreat into, it has adequate safety without the cover of night. It is therefore active by day and night.

Right: Limpets remain motionless by day, but forage at night.

Below: A leopard-spotted goby in night coloration: white on the upper fins, and a darker body colour with a pinkish tinge.

oxidation of a substance called luciferin.

Many other animals have the power of bioluminescence, especially fishes of the open ocean and deep sea. The little lantern fishes (myctophids) have special organs called photophores that emit light. The photophores contain gland cells which secrete a chemical that produces the light. In some species, the photophores contain luminous bacteria.

At night, lantern fishes rise towards the surface of the sea, where they can sometimes be seen from ships. The functions of the luminous organs are not well understood. In the eternal night of the deep sea they may serve the same function as the markings of shore fishes—allowing the fishes to recognise their own species. In the lantern fish, the number and pattern of the photophores provide the means for distinguishing the different species. The luminous organs may also light up the water in front of and beneath the fish, helping it to find prey, and they may also confuse predators.

Some deep sea shrimps and squids produce clouds of a luminous substance when attacked —rather like the ink clouds of shallow water squids.

Night migrations An amazing mass migration occurs every night in the sea. When darkness falls, the tiny planktonic animals migrate upwards, often for many hundreds of metres, to feed on the plant plankton in the upper levels. Considering their size, this is no

numbers of planktonic animals and plants accumulate at the sea surface and some of these, particularly dinoflagellates such as *Noctiluca miliaris*, produce light. When waves break, or a boat or a swimmer passes, the movement of the water disturbs the plankton and causes it to emit light. For the diver, it is like swimming through star dust as his fins and bubbles disturb the water. The cold light of phosphorescence is a product of the

Above: A velvet swimming crab, *Liocarcinus puber*, photographed in Lough Hyne in south-west Ireland. The mouthparts, eyes and claws are particularly clearly shown. Though small numbers of this species are seen in daytime, many more emerge at night to prowl on the sea-bed.

The sea at night

1 Anemones: active day and night.
2 Barnacles: active day and night.
3 *Noctiluca*: bioluminescent plant plankton, activated by water movement.
4 Leopard-spotted gobies: emerge at night to rest on rocky ledges outside their crevice homes, waiting to pounce on small animals passing by.
5 Ballan wrasse: sleep at night, wedged into crevices or in other resting places.
6 Squat lobster: active at night, either eating detritus or catching live prey.
7 Long-clawed squat lobster: active at night; this is a deep-water species, occurring less frequently on the shore.
8 Shoal of pollack: resting in a kelp bed.
9 Conger eel: emerges from its lair—either a gully or a hole in the rocks—to hunt stealthily by night. Sometimes congers go on extended night forays, far out to sea.
10 Greater weever fish: active at night in deep water.
11 John dory: an easy fish to study at night, for it becomes less timid.
12 Shoal of mackerel: feeding on plankton at night.
13 Lantern fishes: bioluminescent, rising towards the sea surface at night.
14 Skate: produces an electric field which it uses as a night sense.
Note: this illustration is a 'composite'—no diver would ever be so lucky as to see all these species in the same place at one time.

mean feat–equivalent perhaps to running a marathon before breakfast every morning. In the Atlantic, for every square metre of sea surface about six tonnes of plankton migrate up into the top 200 metres (100 fathoms). In turn, about four tonnes of shrimps and other small animals follow them up to prey on them, and some deep sea fishes follow the shrimps from as deep as 1500 metres (800 fathoms). This is often known as the ladder of migrations: each animal moves up by a certain number of rungs.

Seashore at night Activity on the seashore is controlled mostly by the tidal cycle. However, many more animals move about during a low tide at night than during one in the day. At night it is cool and damp, and there is much less danger of desiccation. Limpets normally cling tightly to the rock surface when the tide is out, and keep water beneath their shells. At night, they can move freely over the rocks feeding: they graze small algae from the surface of the rock. Logically enough, each limpet returns to its own exact place on the rock, for that is where it fits perfectly.

Darkness also provides protection from predatory seabirds. On sandy beaches in spring, the masked crab (*Corystes cassivelaunus*) gathers in mating groups during low tides at night. The large and beautiful worm *Phyllodoce paretti* hides in crevices in the day, but large numbers crawl over the shore at night.

Above: A corkwing wrasse. It was only by observing wrasses in an aquarium that scientists learnt that these fishes sleep at night, finding a suitable ledge or crevice in which to rest.

Right: The butterfish lurks in crevices during the day; here it is seen emerging at night to catch small animals such as shrimps and worms. Unlike the wrasse, most fishes sleep in short naps, which they take from time to time either by day or by night.

THE SECRET WORLD OF A SEA CAVE

Few creatures can survive in the dark, dank interior of a sea cave, but to those that can–particularly the seabirds and seals–there are considerable advantages, for a sea cave provides a degree of shelter and security hard to match elsewhere.

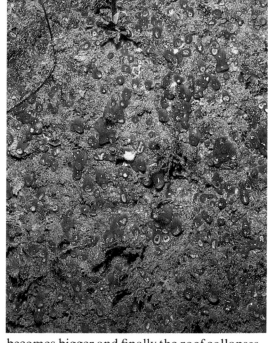

The life of a sea cave begins when the erosive power of waves breaking at the bottom of a cliff face exploits a weakness there and excavates a small hole. An obvious target for this process is a band of weak rock flanked by stronger material. Joints and cracks in a rock also allow a first exploring finger of erosion to begin its work. Sometimes the process is initiated by a rock-boring animal. In south-west England, for example, the common piddock slowly bores holes in the rock in which to live. If enough of these holes are bored the rock becomes considerably weakened and much more susceptible to erosion than the surrounding rock.

Once a weak point has been established, the pounding of the waves, and the erosive effects of sand grains, pebbles and even boulders being hurled against it, begin to gouge out a hole. Slowly the hole increases, and the bigger it becomes the greater is the effect of oncoming waves to trap air in it. The waves compress the air to such an extent that the release of pressure when the waves recede creates a vacuum that has almost an explosive power, further shattering the surrounding rock.

As the cave enlarges, blocks of rock periodically fall from its roof and eventually the roof is breached by a small hole leading up to the cliff top. If the hole is small enough the waves may force water through it in a dramatic spray. Slowly but surely the hole

Right: A colony of jewel anemones exposed at low tide on the wall of a sea cave. Jewel anemones occur all up the west coast of the British Isles and are found as far north as the Shetland Islands.

Opposite page: Fingal's Cave on the south-west coast of Staffa, Inner Hebrides. The dramatic appearance of this cave is due to the basalt columns from which it has been carved.

Below right: The chough is the rarest of our sea cave breeding birds and is now confined to remote coasts of Wales, Ireland, the Inner Hebrides and the Isle of Man. Its decline is probably due to its highly specialised feeding requirements–it eats ants and larvae in cliff-top turf, a habitat that is rapidly being put under the plough.

Below: Carragheen, a species of red seaweed able to survive in the gloomy interior of a sea cave.

becomes bigger and finally the roof collapses– the cave has come to an end.

A sheltered spot The shape and size of a cave very largely determines the sort of wildlife that can survive there. For example, a small cave opening out into deep water has all the environmental harshness of an open cliff, and if it is being actively eroded then few forms of wildlife can survive the regular pounding by the waves. But a mature cave system, parts of which are now beyond the reach of eroding wave action, is a very special place. If such a cave is filled by the sea when the tide is in but exposed to the air during low tide then it becomes a similar habitat to that of a rocky shore. But there is one important difference– the rocky walls and roof remain damp, even

on the driest day, and they are sheltered from the frosts and snow of winter, and from the heat of the summer. The result is a particularly rich fauna with sea anemones, sponges, hydroids, sea mats and tubeworms forming a colourful, closely carpeted array on the cave walls. In the damp environment predatory snails and worms are able to remain mobile for long periods, even when the tide is out. Cracks and crevices in the cave walls provide a refuge for crustaceans such as the sea slater.

Plant life Deep inside the cave the air is moist and still, but there is little or no light. Therefore plant life is restricted to algae–slimes on the roof and walls and seaweeds in the water of the cave floor. The lack of light means that only the low-water red seaweeds, such as *Lithothamnion*, *Odonthalia dentata* and *Plumaria elegans*, can survive there, since they are better able to absorb the blue-green light needed for photosynthesis than are the brown and green seaweeds.

By contrast to the almost total lack of plant life within a cave, the entrance supports the same level of seaweeds as that found on a rocky shore. The entrance arches above the waves often have luxuriant displays of thrift, rock samphire, seabeet, plantain and campion, according to the season. Here these plants can flourish, situated as they are on a site quite inaccessible to foraging cliff-top rabbits.

Seals in a cave The shelter and security offered by a sea cave make them particularly attractive places for seals. The grey seal needs shelter from the pounding seas and minimal disturbance from man when it is breeding. Although the majority of the British population congregate on remote open beaches to drop their pups some seals regularly use caves in the Welsh islands such as Skomer for this purpose.

Above: A grey seal pup at the entrance to a cave. For a seal the ideal cave is remote with a patch of dry sand at the back, out of reach of high tide. It also has some underwater exits and entrances via which the seal can leave and enter the cave unobtrusively.

Below: Given a weak point in a cliff face the pounding of the sea will gradually wear away the rock at that point and begin the formation of a sea cave.

To be suitable such a cave needs to be extensive enough to offer a patch of dry beach inside–and it has to remain dry even at high water. This is where the pup will be born and perhaps stay for up to a month, suckled by the mother. At birth the fluffy, creamy-yellow pup weighs about 15kg (33lb) but after suckling for a month or so on its mother's extremely rich milk it is likely to weigh close to 50kg (110lb). The blubber-clad youngster then leaves the safety of the cave and its mother and heads out to the open sea. A cave system that has a deep water entrance as well as a patch of dry sand is particularly attractive to seals, for it provides them with secret escape routes safe from human disturbance–man

The history of a sea cave

The first step towards the formation of a cave is the sea undercutting the cliff face at a weak point, for example a vertical fault at the base of the cliff (**1**). The sea continues to erode the rock and the cave expands (**2**). As it does so the overlying fault becomes weaker and the roof of the cave starts to disintegrate (**3**). Eventually part of the cliff top may collapse (**4**), leading to the formation of a blow hole. If the cave lies near a headland it may develop into an arch (**5**), which may in turn become a stack (**6**) if the roof collapses. The stack is then slowly eroded away (**7**).

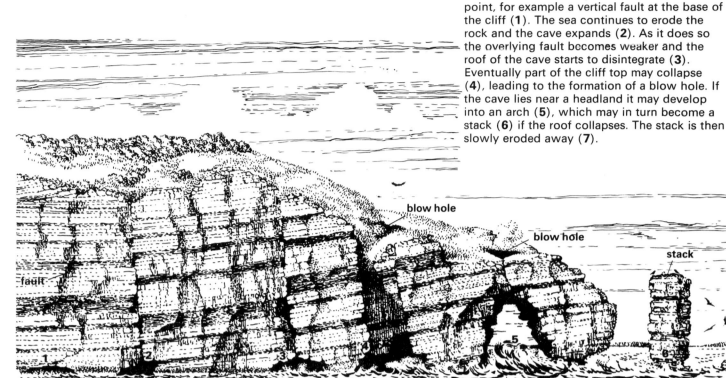

1 Cliff is undercut at base of fault	2 Erosion increases size of cave	3 Fault is further weakened and fault collapses	4 Cliff top subsides creating a blow hole	5 Continuing erosion creates an arch	6 Roof of arch collapses leaving a stack	7 Stack is weathered away

being their only enemy in Britain.

Bird residents The young seal born in a cave lies in almost total darkness deep within the cliff, but the birds that choose to roost and breed there do so close to the entrance. As with seals, birds are attracted by the security, shelter and remoteness of caves.

Once, rock doves were the typical residents of sea caves, but now they are by far our rarest species of pigeon, surviving only on remote coasts and islands in Scotland and Ireland. These birds rear their young on rocky nesting ledges. Because they can feed these fat squabs on pigeon's 'milk' they do not need to rely on the seasonal availability of food and so are able to produce offspring throughout the year. The young squabs were once gathered by coastal people as a valuable source of meat during the winter months.

Today almost all the pigeons lining the cave ledges to breed and roost are feral birds, many being ex-racing pigeons still bearing their rings. Sunny south-facing ledges, with foraging on the cliff-top and nearby shelter of the cave when necessary, is an easier prospect than the rigours of long-distance racing, and many opt for this more natural life-style and are now flourishing. The success of the feral pigeons is now being checked somewhat by the resurgence of the peregrine falcon, whose main source of food around the coast is seabirds and pigeons.

Another cave breeding bird, the chough, is

Below: One of the ways in which a cliff face can be weakened, and thus become susceptible to erosion, is by the action of a creature called the common piddock. This bivalve has sharp teeth on the edges of its shell. By twisting itself from side to side it slowly drills a hole into the rock. Several holes can be seen in this picture. By the time a piddock reaches maturity it will have drilled itself as far as 30cm (1ft) into the rock.

now a rarity. The remote coasts of Ireland, Wales, the Isle of Man and the Inner Hebrides are today its only remaining strongholds in the British Isles.

Fingal's Cave One of the most famous sea caves in the world, and certainly the most spectacular in Britain, is Fingal's Cave on the Isle of Staffa in the Inner Hebrides. At its mouth it is 13m (40ft) wide and 20m (66ft) tall, from sea level to roof. It also extends about 8m (25ft) down into the sea and goes back into the cliff for a distance of more than 60m (200ft). Fingal's Cave–immortalised by the composer Felix Mendelssohn who named an overture of 1829 after it–is aptly known as the Cathedral of the Sea.

ISLANDS: ISOLATION AND INDIVIDUALITY

The offshore islands of Britain and Ireland and, indeed, these two islands themselves, were separated from the Continent by rising sea levels after the last Ice Age. Among the effects of this isolation on our flora and fauna are the development of distinct island races and the survival of 'relict' species.

Above: View of the Isle of Samson, one of the Scillies, at low tide. The Scillies and the Channel Islands have a number of species of plants and animals not found anywhere else in Britain.

Opposite page: The cliffs of Herma Ness on Shetland's Unst, a paradise for seabirds.

Below: Manx Loughtan sheep—one of several surviving hardy breeds of island sheep in Britain.

We live on an island, a Continental one which has not long—in geological terms—been separated from the rest of Western Europe. For the last two and a half million years changes in climate and sea level have occurred together as the ice sheets advanced and retreated over the north European landmass. During the many (probably 20 in all) interglacial periods the climate and sea level were much as they are now, and ten thousand years ago, as the ice sheets from the last glaciation retreated northwards, Britain became separated from the rest of Europe.

As the climate improved, birch and pine, then hazel, oak and alder all spread northwards and with them a whole assemblage of

other plants and animals. During the glaciations much of northern Britain was under a thick blanket of ice, which swept over western and northern Scandinavia. Consequently it is unlikely that many organisms survived in these regions and the great bulk of Britain's present flora and fauna is derived from further south.

The most notable feature of an island is its isolation. As soon as Britain separated from Continental Europe a barrier to further movement by animals and plants arose. Some species, such as strong-flying birds and some wind-dispersed plants, would not have been deterred by this barrier, but those with low powers of dispersal were likely to remain on the Continent of Europe. Furthermore, the more distant a region is from the climatically favourable lands of southern and eastern Europe, the fewer the species which will

Above: Puffin Island, off the coast of County Kerry in Ireland. By no means all the plant and animal species colonizing Britain after the Ice Ages managed to reach Ireland. Species absent from Ireland include woodpeckers and such warblers as the reed warbler and nightingale (probably because of the earlier lack of suitable woodlands), the common shrew, weasel, slow-worm, adder and palmate newt.

Below: A white-toothed shrew—two species of these shrews are found on the Scillies and Channel Islands but occur nowhere else in Britain.

colonize it. It is partly for this reason that of the 260 flowering plants of Continental affinity that entered Britain, less than half continued on to Ireland. Many of the Irish species we see today entered via the land bridge that connected Ulster with Galloway, although the country was not very hospitable for wildlife following the glaciations.

Ten thousand years ago a stretch of land existed linking the promontories of southwest Ireland, south-west Wales, Cornwall and Brittany. This, called Armorica, forms an important link between the flora and fauna of these regions. As the sea levels rose, much of this land was drowned to form the waters of the Celtic Sea, and the land bridge from the Mediterranean up the west coast of Europe was broken. Some species, for example the strawberry tree and a shore-living bug *Aepophilus binnairei*, managed to travel the full length of the route to the islands of Lough Gill in Sligo, but many clearly did not make it. Less than half of the 105 flowering plants of Mediterranean/Atlantic affinity that reached Britain succeeded in reaching Ireland.

Isolation and relict species Although much of Britain was glaciated during the Pleistocene era, we should not imagine a continuous sheet of ice without any form of life. During much of this period there was probably a tundra landscape, with birch and willow scrub spreading during the interglacials. This has resulted in what are termed relict distributions for a number of species. An example is mountain avens which is at present almost confined to certain mountain tops—on Ben Bulben (western Ireland), in Snowdonia, the

Lake District, the Grampians and the Scottish Highlands. Elsewhere it occurs in Scandinavia and the alpine areas of Europe.

Mountainous areas such as those mentioned above may be regarded as 'ecological' islands. Although not isolated by water, they are separated by areas of apparently unsuitable habitat. Other species with relict distributions are dwarf birch and least willow.

Of the species or races on 'geographical' islands (that is, sea-girt areas of land) around Britain, virtually none can be considered as Pleistocene relics. For instance, *Koenigia islandica*, a member of the dock family, occurs in Britain only on the Isles of Skye and Mull off western Scotland, where it was discovered only 40 years ago. Elsewhere it is found in the Arctic as far north as 80°N in Spitsbergen. South of the main ice sheets, the rise in water levels created the Isles of Scilly and the Channel Islands. The fauna and flora of these include a number of species which do not occur elsewhere in Britain though they are not uncommon on the Continent. For example, two species of white-toothed shrew in Britain are confined to these two groups of islands, while a species of bird's-foot trefoil, *Ornithopus pinnatus*, and of meadow grass, *Poa infirma*, are also all but restricted to them. The island of Jersey has a number of named plant species, for example Jersey forget-me-not (*Myosotis sicula*), Jersey buttercup (*Ranunculus paludosus*), Jersey toadflax (*Linaria palisseriana*), Jersey cudweed (*Gnaphalium luteoalbum*), and Jersey club-rush (*Scirpus americanus*).

Size and climate Isolation is but one characteristic of islands. The size of an island determines to a large extent the variety of habitats it possesses. The small island of Bardsey off the Lleyn Peninsula of North Wales, for instance, primarily consists of heathland and rough pasture, whereas the nearby but larger island of Anglesey has a much wider range of habitats, including moorland and woodland, freshwater marshes, lakes, dune slacks, pasture and cereal crops. Where there is a greater variety of habitats, there are also more species of animals, since each has its own particular ecological require-

Right: The Glanville fritillary butterfly is a species which occurs on one of our islands–the Isle of Wight–but not elsewhere in Britain

Below: A Shetland starling. One interesting feature of island populations is a reduction in the clutch size of birds. The race of starling on Fair Isle, for example, lays on average five eggs, one less than its mainland Scottish counterpart.

Below: The grass snake is yet another of the species found over most of England, Scotland and Wales–but is absent from Ireland. To balance this lack, Ireland has some species–the strawberry tree for instance–not surviving anywhere else.

ments. Thus Bardsey Island has 37 species of land birds breeding on it, while Anglesey has three times the number with over 100 species. Although land area and number of habitats are correlated, recent studies suggest that it is the latter which is most important in determining the number of animal species on an island.

Britain, Ireland and their offshore islands have an oceanic climate, lying as they do on the edge of the North Atlantic. This results in equable temperatures with warm summers and mild winters (with little or even no frost). Animals that are sensitive to harsh winters (such as wrens) may therefore often be found on islands where otherwise they might succumb.

Independent evolution As soon as an island is formed and routes of entry for migrating animals and plants are cut off, populations and communities of organisms start to evolve independently of their neighbouring relatives.

Some species will become extinct–the more so if the island is small and able to support only a small population, or isolated so that it

receives few colonists, or if climatic conditions are variable so that when they become unfavourable the species cannot seek refuge elsewhere. Other species, however, will arrive –depending on a combination of chance, their powers of dispersal and a neighbouring source population (or assistance by man). However, even if a species finds its way to an island, its chances of colonizing that island are by no means assured. If a species with similar ecological requirements already exists on the island, the immigrant may not be able to compete with it. Likewise, if the ecological requirements of the immigrant species do not suit the habitat(s) in which it finds itself, extinction may follow.

Population size and genetic drift Small population size is often a feature of island species. This has two important consequences. First, it leaves the species vulnerable to extinction. The song thrush, for example, can be found all over the British Isles as far north as the Orkneys but is absent from the Shetlands. It did establish itself on the Shetlands around 1906 and by the 1940s there were about 24 breeding pairs. However, after the severe winter of 1946-7 the population declined and then became extinct.

The second consequence is a genetic one. When there is only a small founding population, the members are more likely to have a non-typical set of genes, different from those of the source population–and so appear different in size, colouring etc. This is known as the Founder Effect, a form of random genetic drift. There is still much argument as to the relative importance of this against local adaptation from selection pressures in the absence of movement elsewhere. At present there is no good evidence to support one argument rather than another for a particular island population.

Differences in island races Many island races or species of birds and small mammals are larger than those on the adjoining mainland. Examples are the Orkney and Skomer voles, the field mice of Great Blasket, Fair Isle, St Kilda and Foula, the house mice of Skokholm, the Shetland starling (on Fair Isle, Shetland and the Outer Hebrides), and the wrens of Fair Isle, Shetland, St Kilda and the Outer Hebrides.

A number of theories have been advanced to account for this general increase in size. It may be that the founding populations were of larger size, although for the birds at least this seems rather unlikely. It may be that the lack of ground predators–a feature of all these islands–has lowered the predation rate and hence reduced selection favouring small size, but again this seems unlikely to apply to the large races of birds. However, perhaps the most likely explanation is that the local climate plays an important role, with large size favouring the ability to retain heat and to store food as fat to withstand unfavourable conditions from which there is no escape.

Above: A view of Fair Isle (sited between the Orkneys and Shetlands). Mammals have poor powers of dispersal and it is probable that most island populations derive from accidental introductions by man. For instance, the Scottish island races of field mouse on Fair Isle, Foula and St Kilda show some resemblance to Norwegian mice, from which they may have come in the 8th and 9th centuries during the Viking raids and subsequent colonizations.

Left: Mountain avens is one of the 'relict' species found in Britain. Such species, widespread in the lowlands of Britain during the late glacial period, are now found only on some mountain tops and in other limited areas.

Britain's island wildlife

Different kinds of organisms do not disperse at anything like the same rates; this partly explains the differences in shortfall in numbers of species found between Ireland and Britain. For instance, only 68% of the native British flora is found in Ireland, but 77% of British native birds can be seen there. Similarly, only 44% of mammals, 33% of amphibians and just 25% of British native reptiles appear in Ireland. It is clear that birds with their powers of flight and plants with wind dispersal techniques find colonization easier than other types of organisms.

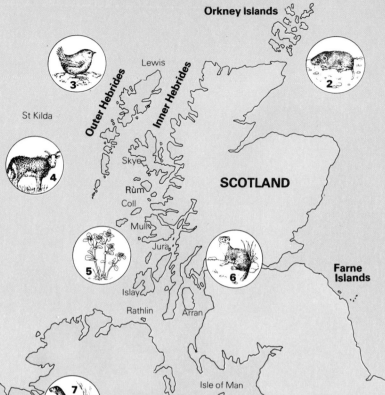

Key to species

1 Shetland wren; 2 Orkney vole; 3 St Kilda wren; 4 St Kilda Soay sheep; 5 Skye & Mull dock; 6 weasel (none in Ireland); 7 Irish stoat; 8 Great Blasket field mouse; 9 spotted Kerry slug; 10 strawberry tree; 11 Skomer vole; 12 nuthatch (none in Ireland); 13 adder (none in Ireland); 14 palmate newt (none in Ireland); 15 Skokholm house mouse; 16 nightingale (none in Ireland); 17 Jersey meadow grass; 18 Jersey toadflax; 19 Isle of Wight Glanville fritillary; 20 Jersey buttercup.

ATLANTIC OCEAN

NORTH SEA

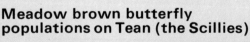

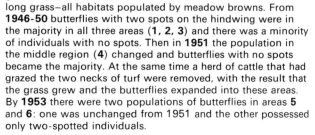

ENGLISH CHANNEL

Meadow brown butterfly populations on Tean (the Scillies)

1946-50

1951

1953

Isolation can take the form of a fairly narrow belt of unfavourable habitat. On Tean two necks of short turf separated three areas of gorse, bracken, bramble and long grass—all habitats populated by meadow browns. From 1946-50 butterflies with two spots on the hindwing were in the majority in all three areas (1, 2, 3) and there was a minority of individuals with no spots. Then in 1951 the population in the middle region (4) changed and butterflies with no spots became the majority. At the same time a herd of cattle that had grazed the two necks of turf were removed, with the result that the grass grew and the butterflies expanded into these areas. By 1953 there were two populations of butterflies in areas 5 and 6: one was unchanged from 1951 and the other possessed only two-spotted individuals.

FRANCE

STEEP HOLM ISLAND

Lying mid-way between the English and Welsh coasts, the small island of Steep Holm has developed an exotic ecology which includes giant blue slow-worms and wild peonies.

The island of Steep Holm lies 8km (5 miles) out from the seaside resort of Weston-super-Mare in the Bristol Channel. Scheduled as a *Site of Special Scientific Interest* (SSSI), it was acquired as a nature reserve in 1976 in memory of the author, broadcaster and naturalist, Kenneth Allsop, who died in 1973.

Geologically, Steep Holm is an outlier of the Mendips and thus, despite being only 1km ($\frac{1}{2}$ mile) long and $\frac{1}{2}$km ($\frac{1}{4}$ mile) wide, dramatic cliffs of Carboniferous limestone, rising to a height of 75m (250ft), ring the island. Surmounting the cliffs is a 20ha (50 acre) plateau which, for much of the year, is covered by a surprisingly lush jungle of vegetation. Nurtured by Steep Holm's own micro-climate,

which is warmer and drier than that of the mainland, growth is further assisted by the guano from thousands of sea-birds.

With its commanding position over the Bristol Channel, Steep Holm has, in the past, attracted Viking raiders, Augustinian monks, pirates, smugglers and, more recently, the military. This unusual history of human occupation is evident from the ruined buildings and coastal batteries which litter the island and in the exotic species of plants and animals which now complement the native flora and fauna.

Today, Steep Holm only attracts naturalists and tourists, who take the regular Saturday ferry across from Weston-super-

Above: A view of Steep Holm from the south-west, showing Rudder Rock and the searchlight post (far left).

Below: Steep Holm's famous wild peonies, almost certainly introduced by monks in the 12th century, bear single, scented, deep pink blooms in early May and large handsome seed pods in September. This species is from southern Europe and, in its wild state, is found nowhere else in Britain.

Mare to spend a day–members of the Kenneth Allsop Memorial Trust can stay overnight– between the months of April and November. Visitors are generally landed on the small beach at the eastern end of the island, from where they set off on foot.

A suggested nature-trail From the beach, steps lead up to a cliff-path which climbs northwards past the ruins of an inn which, in its Victorian heyday, briefly claimed exemption from licencing laws. Flanking the path, a variety of plants more usually encountered on old walls in West Country lanes grow here in their natural situations. The most conspicuous of these is red valerian whose bright red (and sometimes white) flowers favour the sunnier places from May onwards. A familiar plant of hedgerows, the cuckoo-pint abounds among the tangle of ivy below the path, but it is found in greatest profusion around the ruins of Cliff Cottage. Its bright coral-red berries are poisonous.

Beyond Cliff Cottage, the nature-trail doubles back along the track of an incline railway, built in 1941 to transport ammunition. At one time many of the island's wild peonies grew in this area, but their place has been taken by a thicket of sycamore which shows a remarkable tolerance of salt-spray.

Before the summit of the railtrack is reached, a path diverts to the rugged beauty of Tower Rock from which, looking down and across the cliffside towards South Landing, a considerable quantity of rock samphire can be seen clothing the rock. The thick grey leaves of this bushy, yellow-flowered umbellifer were once pickled and eaten by islanders. South Landing itself is reached via a steep but attractive path which follows the route of another incline railway a short distance past Garden Battery. The stone-built jetty and hoist platform provide an alternative landing to the beach, the well-preserved limekiln having been used to provide mortar for the Victorian buildings and batteries. Grey seals from the Welsh colonies are sometimes seen here. If the visitor is patient and avoids sudden noises or movements, they will frequently come close out of sheer curiosity. It is down in the splash zone at this point that the rare wild leek grows. A robust plant with long, greyish-green, strap-like leaves, its round purplish head of flowers appears in July or August. Possibly introduced by the 12th century monks, it is believed that the Steep Holm colony represents the only genetically pure wild stock of the cultivated species. Even the commoner plants on Steep Holm display exaggerated features. The common sea-lavender, for instance, which grows nearby, is distinctly larger than its mainland counterpart. This larger than mainland life quality applies to many of Steep Holm's animals, too –snails, slow-worms and even woodlice are all larger on the island.

Steep Holm Centre Returning to the summit, the trail leads on to the Victorian

Above: Hedgehogs, a fairly recent introduction to the island, can often be seen round and about Steep Holm Centre.

Right: The curious wall pennywort is to be found along the route of the nature trail leading up the cliff path from the landing stage. It is a plant that prefers damp, shady crevices, sending up tall spikes of greenish tubular flowers from a base of round fleshy leaves that are characterised by a small central dimple.

Below: Steep Holm harbours an amazing population of about 5000 purse web spiders (*Atypus affinis*), which lie in wait under stones, concealed within their silken sheaths or 'purses'. Insects unfortunate enough to alight on the sheaths are stabbed with poison from within before being dragged in to be consumed at the spider's leisure.

Left: Great black-backed gulls at their nest site at Tower Rock on Steep Holm.

Right: The slow-worm is the island's only reptile and it inhabits burrows beneath the loose scree, although it may be encountered all over the island, especially under pieces of rusting World War II corrugated iron. Illustrating the phenomenon of 'island evolution', the slow-worms of Steep Holm are much larger than those on the mainland (they have been claimed at up to 1m/3ft in length, although the largest specimen caught by a scientist was half this, at 48cm/19in; this is still long enough, however, to qualify as the second longest ever found in the British Isles). They are typically blue in colour, with shades ranging from pale sky blue to a deep ultramarine.

barracks which have been converted into the Steep Holm Centre, providing dormitory accommodation for those staying on the island as well as offering shelter, toilets, snacks and refreshments to the day visitor. The island has its own natural supply of water which would appear to be fed, in part at least, from the mainland, fresh water having been observed to bubble up off the beach following prolonged rains.

Immediately to the west of the Centre, a path leaves the trail to cross the breadth of the island. Not far from here is to be found the wild peony, for which the island is famous. Another probable introduction is the caper spurge which grows nearby. Continuing west along the nature-trail, the visitor soon enters a dense scrub of wild privet and elder, which is home to the small Chinese muntjac deer, a pair of which were presented to the Kenneth Allsop Trust in 1977. Feeding on bramble leaves and privet berries, the muntjac have

Above: Along the paths of the island you may well encounter a poisonous duo of plants—the evil-smelling henbane (shown here) whose sticky foliage supports creamy white flowers, and hemlock with its purple-blotched stem. Avoid touching these plants—both are extremely poisonous and both have a most unpleasant foetid smell. Henbane is in flower from May to September and hemlock from June to August. Apart from the danger of picking these poisonous plants, visitors to the island are warned not to try rock climbing since the cliffs are very unstable, and also not to swim in the sea because of the very powerful currents.

prospered, yet are more likely to be heard 'barking' than to be seen.

Meadow of alexanders Across the centre of the island an even more dense jungle of alexanders dominates the spring landscape. By mid-summer, nettles begin to take over the leafscape of the 'alexanders meadow', only to be ousted in their turn by the lighter green of annual mercury in October.

The alexanders meadow is a favoured haunt of the rabbit, which finds protection from the voracious gulls in the dense cover. Introduced into Britain by the Normans, rabbits were first released on to islands and promontories from which it was difficult to escape. It is significant that one of the earliest documented rabbit warrens in Norman Britain was on Brean Down, the nearest point of the mainland to Steep Holm and a mere 4km (2½ miles) away. What is so interesting about Steep Holm's rabbits is that since their introduction to the island in the late 12th or early 13th century, they have become noticeably and uniquely reddish in colour, illustrating just how rapidly evolutionary change can come about in an island context.

Steep Holm's other mammal, the hedgehog, also makes use of the protection afforded by the alexanders and the scrub. Likely to be a recent introduction, hedgehogs are frequently seen around the Steep Holm Centre.

Each year hundreds of herring gulls take over the west end of the island between Split Rock and Rudder Rock in early summer. An average of three eggs are laid from the end of April onwards and these can vary in colour from olive to brown but with the characteristic black-brown blotches. The nest is usually lined with strips of alexanders, together with any available grass, both parents undertaking the incubation. After about 28 days, hatching occurs but the chicks remain close to the nest for up to eight weeks, by which time they are fledged. However, from a clutch of three, only one immature bird is likely to leave the island alive. In addition, some 400 pairs of lesser black-backed gulls add to the noisy spectacle, preferring the more open areas and even nesting in trees. Somehow the bright pink clumps of thrift manage to survive the gulls, while lower down the cliffs a forest of bright purple testifies to the presence of the tree mallow and a splash of yellow to the biting stonecrop. Before leaving the west end of the island, the fine view of the Exmoor and Quantocks coastline, best seen from Rudder Rock, should not be missed.

The northern coast The trail now returns along the more exposed northern coast. Close to the foot of sheer cliffs, beneath Summit Battery, about 70 pairs of cormorants have their nests. They can be seen flying back and forth on fishing expeditions. A flight of 208 steps leads down to a 1941 searchlight post, now used by birdwatchers. From here you can look out towards the lighthouse on the smaller island of Flat Holm. Other Steep Holm birds which like to nest within the sound of the sea include the great black-backed gull, stock dove, rock pipit, shelduck and the oyster-catcher, while visiting species include the raven and peregrine falcon.

Plant life along the north of the island is less varied, with bramble and nettles dominating the plateau. Common scurvy-grass favours the drier slopes while the buck's-horn plan-tain, which grows from cracks in the cliff wall, boasts a sub-species that is unique to the island of Steep Holm.

Passing Laboratory Battery, where the movements of migrating birds and the dis-tribution of the island's large banded snails are the subject of study, the trail leads on to Tombstone Battery, above which an excep-tional view can be had of the entire Bristol Channel–shattering, if only briefly, the illus-ion of Steep Holm's isolation.

Plunging once more into elder scrub, our circuit of the island ends at the ruined 12th century priory, to which so much of the island's unusual wildlife owes its origin, the processes of nature having ensured that the activities of these long distant monks live on in the ecology of this island of curiosities.

Above: Banded snails (*Cepea nemoralis*) are the subject of a special study being made on Steep Holm.

Right: Alexanders just coming into bloom. This tall, leafy, green umbellifer was grown as a pot-herb by the monks of the island and has subsequently benefited from the many thousands of gulls whose guano provides an ideal fertiliser. One of the sights of the island in spring is the 'meadow of alexanders' which covers more than 8 hectares (20 acres) of ground with a lush green carpet.

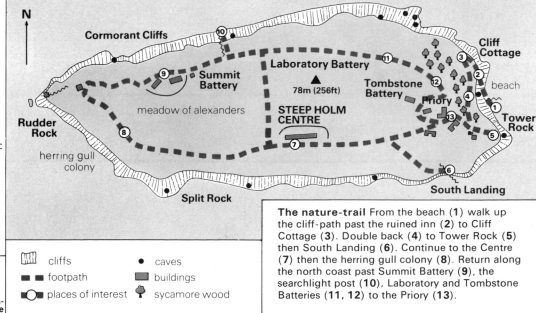

Visiting Steep Holm
The island can be visited from the beginning of April to the end of November by means of boat trips from Weston-super-Mare. These are day trips. Trust members–details below–may stop over for a weekend or even a whole week. For general information: Kenneth Allsop Memorial Trust, Knock-na-Cre, Milborne Port, Sherborne, Dorset DT9 5HJ, tel 0963 32583. Accommodation: tel 01934 632307.

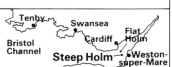

The nature-trail From the beach (**1**) walk up the cliff-path past the ruined inn (**2**) to Cliff Cottage (**3**). Double back (**4**) to Tower Rock (**5**) then South Landing (**6**). Continue to the Centre (**7**) then the herring gull colony (**8**). Return along the north coast past Summit Battery (**9**), the searchlight post (**10**), Laboratory and Tombstone Batteries (**11, 12**) to the Priory (**13**).

JERSEY'S SAND DUNES

Said to be the fourth richest sand dune system in Europe for its plants, Les Quennevais on Jersey is a naturalists' paradise of rare and fascinating species.

Les Quennevais covers some 100ha (250 acres) at the southern end of the St Ouen's Bay, which is on the west coast of Jersey. Approached from one of the fringing car parks, or by one of the regular bus services along the coast road, the peculiar topography of these dunes is immediately impressive. The small coastal primary dune (the youngest in the system) parallels the beach, but east of the coast road lies an enormous flat plain underlaid by sand, which itself lies on top of Neolithic remains. The 'real' dunes, inland from the plain rather than lying conventionally behind the primary dune, are blown up and over the old granite cliffs.

To the visitor, what is special about Jersey is its abundance of southern European or

Above: The edge of the plateau dunes at Les Quennevais, looking west over the plain to Le Rocco Tower and the sea. A distinctive feature of the plain, especially on its northern side, is the scattering of holm oaks.

Below: The harvest of fruits produced by the many different plants attracts birds like this goldfinch. Other species to be seen include blackbirds, thrushes, bullfinches, tits and greenfinches.

Mediterranean species which reach their northern limits on the Channel Islands and only just manage, or fail entirely, to reach the rest of the British Isles lying so much further north. It is an incongruous sight to see these southern species growing alongside our own familiar ones.

The coastal dunes On the beach only a few species, like the common and frosted oraches (the latter with whitish, mealy leaves) and the succulent sea-rocket, find a foothold in the fine sand. Once on the dunes, sand couch-grass knits the loose material together with its complex root mat, though the dunes themselves are largely the creation of marram grass.

Above: A gatekeeper butterfly. This and many other butterfly species are attracted in particular to the sea holly found at Les Quennevais. In some years there may be an influx of clouded yellows or painted ladies from abroad.

Lizard rarities

Jersey has two species of lizard, both of which are essentially south European in distribution. Neither can be found in the UK. The **green lizard** is the larger, at more than 13cm (5in) long, and is a striking bright green. The female tends to be browner, with faint stripes or blotches. The **common wall lizard** prefers wall and rock faces to sand dunes and is found mostly on the north east part of the island. It is much smaller and grey or brownish, usually with conspicuous dark and pale markings. Both of these animals have small home ranges.

The number of other plants capable of tolerating the dry, mobile sand and the salt-laden winds are few. Sea-bindweed creeps over the sand surface under the protection of the marram, and sea holly, with its prickly greyish leaves, is also found here.

The inland dunes The paucity of species on the coastal dunes is in marked contrast to the situation inland across the coast road. With more shelter, stable sand, a build-up of organic matter in the soil, and less salt spray, the variety of flowers and insects found here becomes prodigious. On the low dunes on the southern edge of the plain, there are extensive areas with a thin vegetative cover, and plenty of space for the winter annuals which are such a feature of this dune system. These are plants which germinate in autumn and winter, flower and set seed early in spring, and avoid the dry summer conditions by lying dormant as seeds. They are mostly tiny and can only be separated one from another by going down on hands and knees.

Two of the more conspicuous species here are grasses: hare's-tail grass, with its soft grey, fluffy fruiting heads, and the greater quaking grass with large pendulous fruits. Both introductions from the Mediterranean, they can also be found (though rarely) in southern or south-western England. These are only a

few of the grasses in these very rich areas. Added to these are many other small annuals: rue-leaved saxifrage and thyme-leaved sandwort, both with white flowers; tiny forget-me-nots, the dwarf pansy (another southern European species), and sand catchfly. The last of these, a rare British plant, has small, dark pink flowers and an inflated, conical, green-ribbed calyx.

The key to this great diversity of species is the alkaline shell sand. In such limey, dry, infertile sand, growth is restricted, and so the impact of competition between species is minimal–thus, hundreds of different species can co-exist without a few becoming dominant.

The situation is rather different on the flatter dune plain. Here, leaching of the lime, and the gradual accumulation of dead leaves and their transformation into soil material, has reduced the alkalinity of the soil and increased its fertility. This is particularly noticeable where rabbits are less populous and the level of grazing is too low to maintain an open sward intermingled with small patches of bare sand. Instead, dense grassy areas have developed, especially since the reduction of the rabbit population from myxomatosis. Set in a matrix of the beautiful cream-flowered burnet rose, perennial grasses like hairy-oat grass, sweet vernal grass, red fescue, cock's foot and common bent grow alongside kidney vetch, sand sedge and the slender shoots of wild onion. The richest areas for plants tend to be the fringes of the many small paths where a light level of trampling restricts growth rates and maintains a less competitive environment.

The main dunes Pock-marked with bare sand, the main dunes are a fascinating mixture of blow-outs (collapsed warrens dug by rabbits), stabilising swathes of marram, rich open vegetation and scrub. On the bare sandy areas the early colonizers appear again, which is unusual so far from the sea. Thus, sand couch-grass, sea holly and Portland spurge help to stabilise the mobile sand. However,

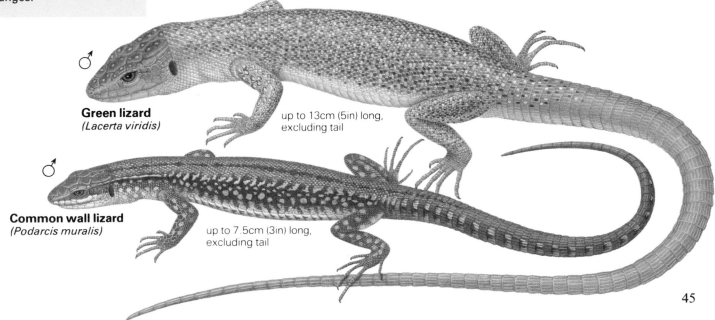

Green lizard
(Lacerta viridis)

up to 13cm (5in) long, excluding tail

Common wall lizard
(Podarcis muralis)

up to 7.5cm (3in) long, excluding tail

away from the worst of the salt spray, the yellow flowers of the fragrant evening prim-rose provide a dramatic display in early summer.

Among these plateau dunes there are also extensive patches of burnet rose, into which some of the dune annuals have invaded. These signify areas where sand blow from adjacent blow-outs or paths has covered up old surfaces, and only the rose has had the ability to extend up through the deposited material. In some of the blow-outs you can identify two, three or more old dune surfaces which have been repeatedly covered by blowing sand. To some extent, the constantly changing land surface is natural in a dune system, but until a few years ago this was exacerbated by too much trampling and pressure from cars and horses which had open access to much of the plain, and even beyond.

Bees, bugs and butterflies The mass of flowers, warm sand and sheltered hollows provides ideal habitats for a range of small animals. Ground beetles scuttle quickly across the sand in search of prey, while leaf-

Above: Nottingham catchfly can be seen growing at the edge of the scrubland on the main dunes. A rare plant of restricted English distribution, its perfumed flowers curl back their petals after dusk to attract night-flying moths for pollination.

Below right: Jersey thrift (*Armeria arenaria*) in bloom. This plant, a species unique to Jersey, is found on the plain near the small paths which undergo light trampling. It can be seen in company with the childling pink, which like the thrift is of southern European origin, and with the flat greyish rosettes of buck's-horn plantain.

Below: Kestrels can be watched hunting over the dunes and scrubland.

sucking bugs, ladybirds and other beetles stalk over the plants. On a warm summer's day the air is a cacophony of sound as grasshoppers and crickets advertise for mates; hoverflies dart to and fro between the flowers searching out the nectar or pollen, while pollinating many flowers in passing; and bumble bees buzz heavily, their legs laden with pollen. Sand wasps excavate their burrows in the loose sand, furnishing their larvae with paralysed prey; and butterflies swarm round the flowers. Sea holly seems to attract more than its fair share of butterflies. Common blues (the female browner than the male), small heaths, the larger, orange-brown gatekeepers, small skippers, walls, peacocks and small tortoiseshells – each appears in its own period throughout the summer.

The scrub It may be coincidence, or it may be the result of environmental factors, but it is noticeable that much of the scrub lies on north or north-west facing slopes on the plateau dunes. It is here that leaching would be expected to be higher and exposure to the sun's rays lower. In such circumstances, it is tempting to hypothesise that the acidification of the soil is higher, and species preferring acid conditions, like gorse and bracken, can then invade.

There seems to be a generalised pattern of scrub development (although it does not always follow this progression). First, gorse colonizes the gaps among the grasses. It has nitrogen-fixing bacteria in the nodules on its roots (as do all legumes) and, together with

Les Quennevais Dunes

Most of the interesting plants and animals are found on the dunes inland from the road where the sand is more stable and there is more shelter from the wind.

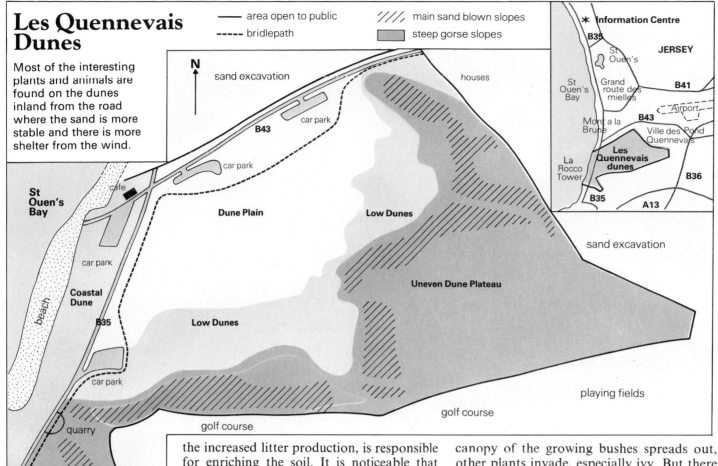

Map legend:
- —— area open to public
- - - - bridlepath
- ///// main sand blown slopes
- ▨ steep gorse slopes

N

sand excavation

houses

B43
car park
car park
cafe
car park

St Ouen's Bay

Dune Plain

Low Dunes

Coastal Dune

B35

Low Dunes

beach

Uneven Dune Plateau

sand excavation

car park

quarry

golf course

golf course

playing fields

Information Centre
B35
JERSEY
St Ouen's
St Ouen's Bay
Grand route des mielles
B41
Airport
Mont a la Brune
B43
Ville des Pond Quennevais
Les Quennevais dunes
La Rocco Tower
B36
B35
A13

Above: A map showing some of the main features of the Les Quennevais sand dunes. Some parts of the plain show signs of past disturbance. This can significantly increase the nutrient levels in the soil, and is probably the cause of the taller grasses seen in the hollows and the invading tree lupin and gorse in the vicinity.

Right: Hare's-tail grass—this grows at Les Quennevais with many other small but distinctive grasses, including sand cat's-tail, hard poa and the very rare, tiny, one-sided flower spikes of early sand grass. Not all the plants on the dunes are rare—also to be seen are lady's bedstraw, wild carrot, restharrow, bird's-foot trefoil, thyme and ribwort plantain.

the increased litter production, is responsible for enriching the soil. It is noticeable that grasses and certain other species grow much more vigorously around the gorse bushes. However, the dense shade eliminates most of the special dune plants, and as the gorse ages and its canopy opens out other bushes colonize. Nearly all those here–privet, black-thorn, hawthorn, elder and bramble– produce berries eaten by birds which could be roosting or nesting on the gorse, and thus dispersing the seeds in their droppings. As the canopy of the growing bushes spreads out, other plants invade, especially ivy. But there are also less common ones like butcher's broom, madder and gladdon.

The birds The scrub has spread substantially over the dunes and granite cliffs around Les Quennevais over the last 50 years. This has been at the expense of many of the typical sand dune plants, such as the orchids and the annuals, but to the benefit of the birds. The grassy dunes support few birds, skylarks and meadow pipits being the most obvious.

47

THE SAND DUNES OF NEWBOROUGH WARREN

Newborough Nature Reserve is an example of a successful attempt to conserve a highly vulnerable habitat threatened by seasonal influxes of human visitors. Now they are channelled safely down to the beach where they can swim or sunbathe without harming the wildlife of this fine natural area.

Above: A view of the sand dunes of Newborough Warren on the Island of Anglesey. The depredations of people in this area were, at one time, very severe. Collectors came in spring to look for the eggs of harriers and short-eared owls, and they also raided the tern colonies which used to be a feature of the Warren and may one day return. In summer, too, holiday-makers wandered all over the dunes, damaging the vegetation and causing 'blow-outs' of the sand wherever the plant cover had been eroded by too much trampling. Today the area is protected as a National Nature Reserve and the increasing number of visitors enjoy themselves on the beaches without harming the wildlife.

The sixth largest area of sand dunes in Britain is at Newborough Warren, which forms the southernmost corner of Anglesey in north-west Wales. This dune system stretches for 4.8km (3 miles) from the southern end of the Menai Strait westwards to the wide estuary of the little River Cefni. (The name 'warren' was given to these dunes centuries ago because rabbits were kept there as a valuable source of food.) On the seaward side is Caernarfon Bay and landwards is the village of Newborough (in Welsh, Niwbwrch). From the dunes there are magnificent views east to the highest peaks of Snowdonia and south across the bay to the hills of Lleyn.

As an official borough, Newborough was truly new in the late 13th century. It was created to accommodate a Welsh community transferred from the northern end of the Menai Straight because the land they occupied there was wanted by Edward I as the site for Beaumaris castle. At that time much of what is now Newborough's sandy warren was farming land with settlements. But the late Middle Ages was a period when storms were exceptionally frequent and in the course of time a succession of south-westerly gales blew sand off the wide beaches across hundreds of acres of farmlands. That the sand was still encroaching in Tudor times is shown by an instruction from Elizabeth I's government to the mayor of Newborough to punish anyone who took away the marram grass that was being planted to arrest the spread of sand.

These days about half the area of the warren is occupied by Forestry Commission plantations (mainly Corsican pine). The unplanted areas form a 607ha (1500-acre) National Nature Reserve cherished for its flora.

The sand dunes There could hardly be a better place than Newborough Warren to study how dunes develop. They are initiated by sand collecting round fore-shore plants such as sand sedge, saltwort, sea rocket and various oraches, and are then built higher by lyme-grass, marram and other grasses. Further inland they are stabilised by a completely closed mat of vegetation. You can also see how some of the dunes have remained as hills of loose sand and have had to be protected from the wind by planting marram or by covering them with brushwood. The outermost dunes have been wave-cut into vertical cliffs by recent gales, and on the Cefni estuary, too, great changes are in progress as sands and mudflats build up high enough for sea meadowgrass to spread widely as verdant saltings.

The ecological interest of the warren comes

Above: The beautiful sea bindweed can be seen on Llanddwyn Island (this island is cut off from the mainland only when the tide is really high). Llanddwyn has both sedimentary and volcanic rocks and hence its flora is very varied.

Right: Grass of Parnassus is a plant to look for on the inland dunes.

Below: Sandwich terns on rough grassland near the coast. Terns used to nest on Newborough but do so no longer.

from the great variety of its habitats. The beaches and outer dunes experience the full force of the winds and sometimes of the waves, and are drenched with salt-laden spray which few species can tolerate. But the fixed dunes inland are a quite different, more sheltered world and most of their plants can also be found in districts far from the sea—species such as thyme, lady's-bedstraw, rest-harrow, bird's-foot trefoil, kidney vetch, brookweed, bog pimpernel and various grasses and sedges. Some dune plants, however, are strictly maritime, among them seaside centaury, sea spurge, sea holly and sand pansy.

Many of these plants flourish in the damp

sandy hollows called dune slacks, which are at their best in June when you can see the rich dark purple of northern marsh orchids along with the brick-red spikes of the early marsh orchids (which also have a distinctive flesh-coloured variety). At the same season the nearby slopes have bee orchids and the miniature fern called moonwort. In July come two helleborines: the marsh helleborine is abundant in the slacks while the drier slopes are favoured by the dune helleborine, which is known elsewhere in the British Isles only on the coast of Lancashire. Autumn brings a fine array of toadstools and other fungi.

A crucial element in the ecology of these dunes comes from the fragmented shells of sea molluscs. In these lime-rich areas there are communities of calcicole plants that are typical of chalk or limestone grassland. There are not only many orchids but also such lime-lovers as fairy flax, blue fleabane, plough-man's-spikenard, carline thistle, field gentian, autumn gentian, viper's bugloss, grass of Parnassus and lesser clubmoss.

Because it is such a striking example of rapid colonization, one of the most remarkable plants of these dunes is the maritime sub-species of the round-leaved wintergreen. Until about the middle of this century it was known in Britain only in the dune slacks of Flintshire and Lancashire. Then it began to spread elsewhere and one of the places it soon reached was Newborough Warren. When the Nature Conservancy Council began to warden these dunes in the late 1950s, this wintergreen was among the reserve's closely guarded rarities. But now it is one of the commonest plants, its round or oval, dark green, glossy leaves forming carpets on the sand, often among the great spreads of creeping willow in the slacks. Evidently the decay of millions of willow leaves every winter produces just the right humus to meet its

Above: Round-leaved wintergreen blooming in a dune slack on Newborough Warren. Extremely rare on the dunes in the 1950s, this plant is today one of the area's commonest plants.

Below: You may spot the long-tailed duck in winter.

needs.

Lake plants and birds On its eastern edge the reserve has a small lake called Llyn Rhos-ddu, the margins of which are deep in aquatic vegetation, including wild iris which, in June, forms an almost uninterrupted band of yellow all around the water's edge. Floating in the shallows are pink spreads of amphibious bistort.

From a hide on the lake shore birdwatchers can observe many wintering waterfowl and in summer they may see mallard, tufted ducks, coots, moorhens and great crested and little grebes which nest there. Elsewhere on the warren other small pools have been excavated to encourage wildlife.

Other birds and insects The commonest breeding land birds of the reserve are probably the meadow pipit and skylark, and there are smaller numbers of stonechats, whinchats and linnets. Nesting waders include a few pairs of lapwings, curlews, oystercatchers, redshanks and ringed plovers. Until recent years there were large herring gull colonies, but these have declined for unknown reasons.

These days, the warren's main birdwatching interest is outside the breeding season, when the Cefni estuary is frequented by passage and wintering waders, wildfowl, gulls and terns. A pylon hide overlooks the scene from the edge of the pine plantations near the main road. Along this road at the northern tip of the reserve is Malltraeth Pool, a shallow

brackish water rich in invertebrate life and famous for its visiting waders.

The fragrant and colourful plants of this reserve are attractive to many beetles, bees, ants, hoverflies and other insects. Among several commoner grasshoppers, there is the short-winged conehead, here close to the northern extremity of its range. The most numerous butterfly may well be the common blue which, on summer days, is on the wing wherever you go among the fixed dunes. The small heath butterfly is also abundant, and in July the dark green fritillary dashes wildly by. Conspicuous among the moth caterpillars in June are the gaudily striped lackeys, which feed colonially on webs they make among twigs of hawthorn bushes. In August you may spot the green, spike-tailed larvae of the poplar hawkmoth feeding on the creeping willows.

Grazing experiments Naturalists who knew the warren over 30 years ago remember the vegetation of the fixed dunes as being much shorter than it is today, when so many tall grasses are dominant. In those days rabbits were abundant and kept the turf nibbled short. But since myxomatosis reached here in the mid-1950s, rabbits have become far fewer and this has allowed the grasses to grow – a change that could eventually lead to the development of scrub. As this would be undesirable in a reserve whose great interest is a fauna and flora of open habitats, the

Newborough Warren

If you wish to gain access to parts of the Nature Reserve away from the foot paths, you must obtain a permit from the Countryside Council for Wales, Ffordd Penrhos, Bangor, Gwynedd LL57 2LQ. An information sheet is also available from this address (enclose sae).

Map legend:
- NNR
- FC plantations
- estuarine flats
- vehicle access
- footpaths
- P parking areas

Map labels: Warden's House, N, Malltraeth Pool, Cefni Estuary, FC office, P, Cefni Saltmarsh, A4080, B4421, Newborough, Llyn Rhosddu, Penlon, Newborough Forest, Braint Estuary, Llanddwyn Bay, P, P, Newborough Warren, Menai Strait, Ynys Llanddwyn, Traeth Melynog, Abermenai Point

Anglesey inset: Holyhead, Anglesey, Newborough Warren, Bangor, Caernarfon

Below: The golden samphire, seen here in full flower, is one of the many plants to be found on Llanddwyn Island. One of the most striking of all is the bloody crane's-bill, which is locally abundant.

Countryside Council for Wales is conducting grazing experiments with sheep.

Llanddwyn Island Newborough Warren is crossed from north-east to south-west by a low spine of Pre-Cambrian rocks that end in the sea to form Llanddwyn Island, which covers 24ha (60 acres) but is an island only briefly when the tide is really high. Llanddwyn's rocks are a mixture of sedimentary and volcanic materials, including some limestone, and the flora is varied in consequence. There are small cliffs whose many plants include rock sea-lavender, golden samphire, rock samphire, sea-beet, rock spurrey and sea-spleenwort. There are also several beaches with yellow horned poppy, sea-rocket, sea-milkwort, sea-sandwort and sea-bindweed.

Rocky islets close to Llanddwyn are occupied in summer by a breeding colony of cormorants; and with them are a few pairs of shags of unusual habits, for in some years they have been found nesting in mid-winter. In autumn and winter flocks of turnstones and occasionally purple sandpipers may be seen on Llanddwyn's shores.

Access to the reserve The Forestry Commission's plantations mainly occupy the central area of the warren and it is through them that three routes lead from the main road down to the shore, a distance of about 3.2km (2 miles). One of the routes is motorable and has parking, picnic and toilet facilities close to the beach. From there you can walk a mile west along the shore to Llanddwyn. In the forest there is also the Hendai ('old houses') Trail, along which visitors can learn about the work of the Forestry Commission and see the remains of houses long buried by sand but now excavated. The National Nature Reserve has three tracks for walkers. Access away from the tracks is by permit only.

HEBRIDEAN MACHAIR

In the Hebridean Islands, particularly North and South Uist, can be found the machair–an extremely localised land form consisting of a shell-sand based (and therefore lime-rich) stable grassland that is exceptionally rich in wild flower species.

The highlands of Scotland usually bring to mind wild, heather-clad hills populated by golden eagles and red deer, but less than 80km (50 miles) west of the mainland highlands lies the archipelago of the Outer Hebrides, comprising well over a hundred islands. The largest are Lewis, Harris, North and South Uist, Benbecula and Barra. While the eastern sides of these islands show their connection with the mainland hills, the western seaboard, especially from North Uist southwards, is in brilliant fertile contrast to the acid moorland. Waves rolling in from the Atlantic break endlessly against long, white, shell-sand beaches, behind which lies the Hebridean machair–stable grassland

Right: The longest and best developed stretches of Hebridean machair are to be found on the western seaboard of the islands of North Uist and South Uist in the Outer Hebrides. On these two islands there are estimated to be over 6000ha (15,000 acres) of machair land. Machair also exists on the Inner Hebrides, Orkney, Shetland and the northernmost mainland of Scotland, but not to the same extent as in the Uists. By contrast, the eastern seaboard is hilly.

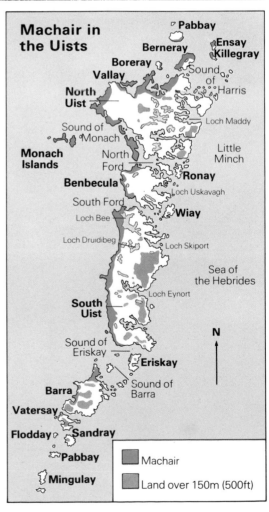

Machair in the Uists

Pabbay
Berneray
Boreray
Ensay
Killegray
Valley
North Uist
Sound of Harris
Sound of Monach
Loch Maddy
Monach Islands
North Ford
Little Minch
Benbecula
Ronay
Loch Uskavagh
South Ford
Wiay
Loch Bee
Loch Druidibeg
Loch Skiport
Sea of the Hebrides
South Uist
Loch Eynort
N
Sound of Eriskay
Eriskay
Sound of Barra
Barra
Vatersay
Flodday
Sandray
Pabbay
Mingulay

■ Machair
■ Land over 150m (500ft)

based on the shell-sand and supporting an abundance of wild flowers.

Machair formation Machair has developed in areas greatly exposed to north and north-westerly winds which, since they are inevitably salt-laden, play a considerable part in determining the flora. With the annual rainfall exceeding 1000mm (40in), the climate is cool and humid but comparatively mild.

The exact method of machair formation is unknown, but it has been suggested that the basis was the erosion and re-deposition of broad, high coastal dunes over a long period of time, probably beginning almost 6000 years ago. The long, high back-slope of these dunes was eroded out to the water-table and the sand re-deposited landward. Initially the point of erosion was just behind the dune summit, but the dune scarp forming the point of erosion gradually moved eastwards too. In some cases re-deposition was on firm ground, in others it was in depressions formed by lochs and marshes. Where these were sufficiently shallow, organic soils formed. The end product was the shell-sand grassland as we know it now.

The lime content from the shells gives the soil its fertility and lightness; in some places the calcium carbonate content of the sand is over 80%. The plain is up to 1.5km (one mile) wide, low-lying (usually less than 5m/16½ft above mean sea level), and has an extremely gentle gradient. It floods during

Left: Wild flowers are a feature of Hebridean machair; the harebell is one of the characteristic species.

Opposite page: Shell-sand beach at Seilbost, Harris.

Below: Stooked corn on machair, South Uist. Ploughing on machair takes place late, in April, traditionally with a shallow-bladed plough which turns a narrow crested furrow. Harvesting, too, is late, little being cut before September, and even then the grain may be green in the ear. The smaller areas may be cut by hand, but the usual method is by binder-reaper, a piece of equipment hard to obtain in Britain nowadays. The sheaves are put together in stooks to dry, after which they are collected together into ricks, either on the machair or adjacent to the croft buildings, and well tied down against the winter storms. Threshing either takes place during the winter or the grain is fed to the livestock in the sheaf. However, the livestock animals also tend to help themselves from the ricks. This, together with damage to standing and stooked grain from wild birds, especially greylag geese, means that the harvest is often a scanty one.

the winter.

The method of formation means that if one walked in a straight line from the west to the east coast one would pass through a succession of habitats which, in the classic situation, run parallel to the coast. Moving inland, these are: open shell-sand beach, dune, dry machair, wet machair, marsh and fen, eutrophic (nutrient-rich) loch, blackland (acid moorland improved by adding shell-sand), and moorland with myriads of acid lochs. (The townships are built on the blackland.)

Agriculture on the machair Because of its relative fertility, the machair is the most important part of the croftland for agriculture. It is seasonally grazed by both cattle and sheep, although for much of the year the sheep are on the moorland hills. In the past the blackland was extensively cultivated but the dry machair is the main area cultivated today. Each croft, or small farm, has an associated area of the township machair, which is cultivated in strips on a rotational basis. The length of this rotation varies from township to township; in some a strip is cultivated for two years and left fallow for two years, while in others the rotation is over three years, or some other combination. The important consequence for both plant and bird life is a closely integrated mosaic of small strips of cultivated and fallow land forming a very diverse habitat.

The main crops are cereals – small oats, rye, bere (barley) – and potatoes, but in recent years there has been a marked decline in the cropped acreage. Traditionally seaweed, mainly *Laminaria* species, cast upon the shore during winter gales, was used as a fertiliser. Latterly chemical fertilisers, which put no organic material back into the soil, have been used.

The flowers of the fields After the long, wet and windy winter, spring comes late to the Outer Hebrides, with little plant growth prior to May. However, by mid-June the contrast is complete for the machair is then at its best–a magnificent sight ablaze with colours of virtually every hue. Most machairs contain similar plant species: dove's-foot crane's-bill, common stork's-bill, red and white clover, bird's-foot trefoil, daisy and harebell are all widespread, together with many more species. In addition to the diversity, the sheer abundance of the flowers is breathtaking for those accustomed to modern monoculture farmland. On the machairs of the Monach Isles alone, off the west coast of North Uist, about 220 species of flowering plant have been recorded. The individuality of a machair is brought about by the dominant species; one of the most famous is that at Eoligarry in Barra, where the dominant species is the primrose. Here primroses carpet the ground so closely that it is difficult to walk without treading on them.

One of the most fascinating aspects of such rich grassland is the changing of the flowering sward as the season progresses. The red of crane's-bill and stork's-bill, together with the yellow of bird's-foot trefoil, are among the first to appear. The latter is replaced in mid-July by lady's-bedstraw which, in parts of South Uist, can be so dense as to recall the colour of an old buttercup meadow. Among the later flowers are the blue harebell and the whitish-purple eyebright.

Some plants, especially those on arable land, are scarce on the mainland as a result of the pressures of modern farming. In few places are corn marigolds and bugloss still as common as they are on machair. In late

Above: Arctic terns breed regularly in the Outer Hebrides. They frequently nest on machair.

Below: Harebells, red clover, ragwort, daisies, buttercups and wild carrot on machair.

summer corn marigolds can be found on both fallow and arable land and, in places where there is little control by herbicides, they may be the most frequent weed of cultivated areas.

Winter feed for stock is an important commodity in the Uists and many of the damper machairs are cut for hay. Some of the meadows have been re-seeded in the recent past with agricultural grasses, but a number of natural hay meadows still remain. Here again, the floral richness is impressive. Ragged robin, buttercups, red rattle, clover, even horsetails and several species of orchid, make a startling comparison with the uniformity of agricultural grasses normally cut for hay elsewhere. On the mainland many of the ancient hay meadows still existing are jealously guarded and managed to maintain their interest, often as Nature Reserves.

Wetland flowers Orchids do occur in some of the lower lying areas of dry machair, but they grow most profusely in the damper areas. Early marsh, northern marsh, common twayblade, frog and the speciality of the Hebrides, the Hebridean variety of the common spotted orchid, are all widespread. In common with many Hebridean plants, one of the characteristics of the Hebridean spotted orchid is its diminutive size (15-30cm/6-12in high) compared with its mainland counterpart. It is also stockier than the typical variety, with darker flowers, and it is more heavily spotted on the leaves.

At the edge of the eutrophic lochs these wet grasslands may merge into fen communities dominated by reeds, bulrushes, club rushes, marsh marigolds and marsh cinquefoil. The deeper open waters also support luxuriant vegetation, which forms rich feeding grounds for wildfowl. Close to the coast many of these lochs are under maritime influence, resulting in the formation of saltmarsh at the loch edges. This grades into the wet machair. On such a sandy substrate the saltmarsh tends to be species-poor – a sward of thrift associated with sea milkwort and sea plantain, sometimes with 10cm (4in) high sea aster. Parsley water dropwort and brookweed are among the scarcer species which may be present.

Birds of the machair The biological interest of the machair cannot be measured in terms of the plants alone. The wealth of birdlife is just as remarkable. As with the plants, the birds are best seen in spring and summer. Although many waders and gulls frequent the Outer Hebrides during winter, they spend most of their time feeding among the seaweed on the beaches. From February onwards the machair becomes increasingly alive with the displays, songs and alarm calls of the birds moving back on to their breeding grounds. Probably the most important of these, and the ones for which the Outer Hebrides are most famous, are the waders – oystercatchers, ringed plovers, dunlin, redshank, lapwing and snipe.

The most important species of the dry machair is the ringed plover, with over 2,200 pairs nesting in the Western Isles. This is far more than in any other part of Britain and represents about 25% of the entire British and Irish breeding population.

The scarcest of the breeding waders is the red-necked phalarope, a bird that frequents marshy, heavily vegetated lochs. At the turn of the century there were probably at least 40 or 50 pairs in the Outer Hebrides, but now there are only one or two pairs.

Another scarce bird found on the Hebridean machair is the corncrake. Like the red-necked phalarope, it is strictly protected by law; it is illegal to disturb either species

Above: Eyebright on Lewis. Eyebrights are small plants, but throughout the machair they compensate for their lack of size by their abundance. Common eyebright is the usual machair species, but another nine have been found to date in the Outer Hebrides, including some rare and endemic species.

Below: Running parallel to the coast, from west to east across the machair islands, is a succession of habitats: open shell-sand beach, dune, machair, marsh and fen, eutrophic (nutrient rich) loch, blackland (acid moorland improved by the addition of shell-sand), where the townships are built, and moorland with myriads of acid lochs.

during the breeding season. Only two or three decades ago the corncrake was widespread and common on the mainland both in Scotland and England. Now it is virtually restricted to the Hebrides and Orkney.

The future The machair has evolved under traditional land use practices, without the rigours of modern agriculture. The wealth of plant and bird life proves this, but agriculture in the Outer Hebrides has fallen behind the rest of Britain. In the 1980s the EEC and Britain initiated a plan for modernisation. With its emphasis on hay and silage production, the programme began to upset the diversity of traditional crofting and damage the machair. In response, Scottish Natural Heritage has piloted its own scheme which recognises the machair, and four other Scottish districts, as 'Environmentally Sensitive Areas'. Crofters living in an ESA are entitled to grants provided that they use methods which enhance the conservation value of the land. It is hoped that the scheme will satisfy the needs of both man and wildlife.

Characteristics of the machair

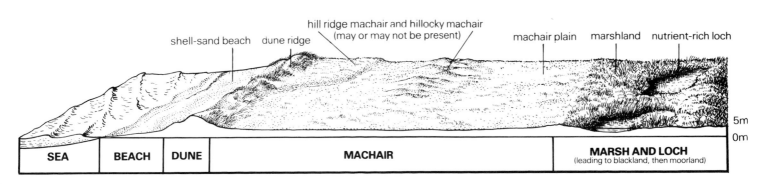

shell-sand beach   dune ridge   hill ridge machair and hillocky machair (may or may not be present)   machair plain   marshland   nutrient-rich loch

5m

0m

SEA	BEACH	DUNE	MACHAIR	MARSH AND LOCH (leading to blackland, then moorland)

THE REMOTE ISLAND OF UNST

Leaving aside the Shetland mainland, Unst is one of the larger of more than 100 islands that together comprise the Shetland Isles. For many people the attraction of Unst lies in its remoteness– the fact that it is the northernmost place in Britain.

Unst, which lies further north than Leningrad and Labrador, and on the same latitude as the city of Anchorage in Alaska, is about 16km (10 miles) long and 8km (5 miles) wide, but it has such an irregular and indented coastline that no part of the island is far from the sea. Although the Atlantic Ocean is on one side and the North Sea on the other, the island nevertheless enjoys–thanks to the Gulf Stream–a remarkably mild if rather windy climate.

There are great contrasts to be experienced in the atmosphere of the island. In winter violent Atlantic gales can lash the west coast and send spray over the top of the Muckle Flugga lighthouse, while in summer come the long twilights of the 'simmer dim', when nothing disturbs the calm beauty but the cries of birds and the bleating of sheep.

A glance at a geological map of Unst reveals a relatively simple picture. From Burra Firth (which partially divides the north end of the island) southwards from Herma Ness, the west side of the island is predominantly gneiss. Most of the eastern half is greenstone or serpentine, the latter being one of the principal rock types on Unst and extending in a broad band from near Clibberswick in the north-east to Gallow Hill in the extreme south-west. Apart from an outcrop of granite around Lamba Ness, the north-east headland around the hill of Saxa Vord is composed of schists which extend southwards in a narrowing band to a short distance south of Baltasound.

The Keen of Hamar From the natural history point of view, one of the most fascinating areas on Unst is the National Nature Reserve of the Keen of Hamar. Although attaining only 88m (289ft) above sea level, this hill has a unique combination of geological and botanical features. It supports the best-known and largest single area of serpentine fellfield habitat in the whole of Britain. On the north-west slope of the hill, stone lines or stripes can be seen–they are typical examples of solifluction (soil flowing) processes in a sub-arctic climate. It is believed by some authorities that this fellfield has persisted since the retreat of the last ice sheets.

Right: Fulmars–they nest in almost every suitable spot on Unst.

Opposite page: Arctic skuas, summer visitors to Unst, defend their nests with savage physical attacks.

Below: It is impossible to travel on Unst without encountering the sturdy little Shetland ponies. Those seen running on the hills and moors of Shetland today are the descendants of ponies which have been present on the islands for thousands of years, but there is a certain amount of conjecture as to how they reached the islands in the first place. Traditionally the ponies were used as pack animals, particularly for bringing home peat, but now they are bred for riding and export.

A noticeable feature of much of the Keen of Hamar is the shattered nature of the rock and a sparse plant cover which in places can be as little as 5%. This particular habitat is known as serpentine debris and is associated with a high rate of weathering of the bedrock, and probably also with a significant nutrient imbalance since the rocks and the associated soils are poor in potassium, nitrogen and phosphorus (nutrients essential to plant growth), but rich in nickel and chromium, which are toxic to some plants.

It was on the Keen of Hamar that Thomas Edmonston discovered the Shetland mouse-ear chickweed nearly 135 years ago. Other species found here include arctic sandwort, northern rock-cress and moss campion. These all have an arctic and sub-arctic distribution, and their occurrence together at such a low altitude is unique in Britain.

Other plants on Unst The sparse vegetation of much of the Keen of Hamar is not characteristic of all the serpentine areas, where the main vegetation type is in fact

The Island of Unst

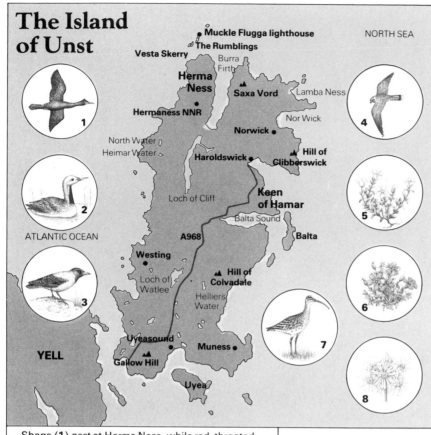

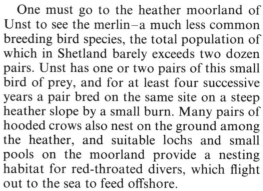

Shags (**1**) nest at Herma Ness, while red-throated divers (**2**) breed on lochs inland; the hooded crow (**3**) breeds among heather on the ground, and one or two pairs of merlin (**4**) may occasionally be seen. Arctic sandwort (**5**) and moss campion (**6**) grow on the Keen of Hamar and the whimbrel (**7**) may be found among the sparse vegetation there. An alien plant—Magellan ragwort (**8**)—can be seen near the quay at Uyeasound.

One must go to the heather moorland of Unst to see the merlin—a much less common breeding bird species, the total population of which in Shetland barely exceeds two dozen pairs. Unst has one or two pairs of this small bird of prey, and for at least four successive years a pair bred on the same site on a steep heather slope by a small burn. Many pairs of hooded crows also nest on the ground among the heather, and suitable lochs and small pools on the moorland provide a nesting habitat for red-throated divers, which flight out to the sea to feed offshore.

The cliffs of Herma Ness The outstanding feature of Unst is the variety of its nesting seabirds. In various spots around the island you can find colonies of arctic terns, gulls and fulmars, but one locality above all the others stands out—the National Nature Reserve of Hermaness, the north-west extremity of the island. To reach the superb cliffs of Herma Ness—without doubt one of the finest seabird localities in Britain—you must walk uphill from Burrafirth and then head westwards across the blanket peat. This route has its own excitement since it is impossible to avoid the territories of hundreds of breeding pairs of great skuas (known as bonxies in Shetland)

grassy heath. The southern portion of the Unst serpentine supports a rich heather/bell heather community with some three dozen species of flowering plants, ferns and club-mosses, and at least 15 species of mosses and liverworts. In contrast, the gneisses and mica-schists of the western and north-western parts of the island are mostly covered with blanket peat.

Wild flowers are very much a feature of Unst. The summer visitor cannot miss the fine specimens of northern fen orchid growing on some roadside verges, while the heath spotted orchid is even more abundant and wide-spread. Some of the meadows around Muness are bright with a variety of wild flowers in summer, and brilliant splashes of colour are provided by the rare blood-drop emlets.

Birds of the serpentine The birdlife of Unst is perhaps of even greater interest than the plants. Here again, the serpentine areas have a special interest since it is among the short vegetation growing on them that most of the whimbrel nesting on the island are to be found—on the Hill of Colvadale south of Baltasound, for example. The whimbrel is at the southern edge of its range in Britain and almost all of the British breeding population is in the Shetland Isles.

Right: Shetland mouse-ear chickweed—one of several arctic or sub-arctic plants on Unst that are unique in Britain for growing together at such a low altitude.

Below: A common seal cow and her pup basking on a rock off the coast of Unst.

and the less abundant but even more aggressive arctic skuas.

The mobbing attacks of the skuas are a fitting prelude for what follows for, quite suddenly, you come to the cliffs and the vast expanse of the Atlantic. Just off the northern tip of Herma Ness lies the Muckle Flugga reef where the sea pounds relentlessly on the rocks below the lighthouse. The rock stacks (The Rumblings and Vesta Skerry) that form the southern end of this reef are white with nesting gannets, and more can be found on other stacks just off the main cliffs, and on the ledges of the cliffs themselves at The Neap. All told, Herma Ness supports around 7000 breeding pairs of gannets. The scene at Herma Ness is one of beauty and constant activity. Away to the south on a clear day the dome of Ronas Hill (Shetland's highest point) can be seen on the horizon, and down below the cliffs common seals dot the sea and haul out on to the rocks.

Seabirds are everywhere. Puffins by the thousand dot the grassy slopes, where their burrowing causes considerable erosion. The dominant species on the cliff ledge is undoubtedly the guillemot, some of whose colonies contain hundreds of birds. Razorbills, too, are present on the cliffs but are much less numerous. Towards the base of the cliffs are colonies of kittiwakes, the most attractive of our breeding gulls. Finally, lowest of all, are the scattered pairs of shags nesting among the great jumbles of boulders at the base of the cliffs. It is justly said that the seabird cliffs of Herma Ness are the crowning glory of Unst.

Above: You can see the comical-looking puffins by the thousand on Unst—they are possibly the most abundant bird at Herma Ness.

Right: Just behind Norwick on Unst is an area of fen and stream with many wild flowers, including the brilliantly coloured blood-drop emlets.

Below: Coastal scenery near Westing on Unst—only the cries of birds and the bleating of sheep disturb the tranquillity here.

Fishes of
the open sea and sea-bed

Fishes have always been important in man's diet, but the fishes we eat, although varied enough, are only a small part of the great range of species which occur in the sea. The ones we know most about are those which are commercially exploited.

The fishes of Britain's coasts and offshore waters are well adapted to life in the wide range of habitats available to them. Offshore, the open waters provide a rich source of planktonic food for ocean-dwelling fishes, while on the sea-bed sediment communities of invertebrate animals living in the mud and sand provide food for the bottom-living fishes. Near the shore live fishes whose diet includes the small crustaceans and worms that inhabit rocky coves and gullies.

These varied habitats influence the form and colour of our fishes. Those living in the open water are torpedo-shaped strong swimmers, often with silvery scales and patterns which blend in with the shimmering sea surface. They live in schools which offer a degree of protection to the majority at the expense of the outliers, which are picked off by predators such as sharks. Departures from this streamlined shape are found on sediments, where the fishes have bodies which are generally flattened, enabling them to lie obscured under a sprinkling of sand. These include plaice, sole and dab, all of them having spots and mottled colouring that give them some protection by camouflage. Solitary large fishes swim among the kelps of nearshore waters, while hidden among the crevices of rocks are fishes ranging from the large conger eels to small gobies. Some fishes have adopted spectacular shapes or exhibit a range of colours. Most notable around British coasts are the male dragonet with its striking blue colour and long dorsal fin, the blue and orange cuckoo wrasse and the monstrous angler fish with a rod-and-line lure suspended above its cavernous mouth.

Below: The mackerel — easily recognisable from the black wavy stripes on its back — has gained popularity as a food fish since the herring fishery declined. Mackerel can reach 70cm (28in) in length, but most of those caught are 30-50cm (12-20in) long.

CHECKLIST

This checklist is a guide to some of the fishes you can find in the sea. Although you will not see them all in the same place, you should be able to spot many of them in a range of habitats from sea-bed to open water. The species listed in **bold** *type are described in detail.*

Angler fishes
Ballan wrasse
Coalfish
Cod
Conger eel
Cuckoo wrasse
Dogfish
Grey mullets
Gurnards
Gobies
Haddock
Hake
Halibut
Herring
Mackerel
Pilchard
Plaice
Pollack
Rays
Rockling
Sand eel
Sharks
Skates
Sole
Sprat
Whitebait
Whiting

Left: A school of scad (also known as horse mackerel) — this species, found all round the British Isles, is more common offshore than inshore. It is not a prime food fish but is important for seabirds such as gulls.

61

HARVEST FROM THE SEA

Britain's fishing fleets land several hundred million pounds' worth of fish—nearly three-quarters of a million tonnes in weight—each year; but throughout European waters, this increasingly efficient industry is in grave danger of taking too many fish from the sea.

Britain is one of Europe's major fishing nations and our fishing industry provides about 60% of British fish and shellfish supplies. In 1992, landings of all types of fish (excluding salmon and trout) by British fishing vessels totalled 613,700 tonnes, valued at £405 million. This diverse industry, which is spread all round the 9600km (6000 mile) coastline of the United Kingdom, forms an important source of employment and income in a great number of ports.

Fish caught Over 50 different species of fish and shellfish are taken in the waters around Britain. Demersal fish (caught on or near the bottom of the sea) such as cod, haddock, plaice and rays, account for about half the weight of the total British catch. As in previous years, cod was the most important demersal species in 1992 but others, such as haddock, plaice, whiting and monkfish, formed important catches at many ports and found a ready sale. Pelagic fish such as mackerel, herring, sprat and pilchards live and are caught near the surface and formed 40% by weight of our landings. Shellfish, which included lobsters, oysters, scallops and scampi, only represented 15% by weight of the British catch but their value in 1992 was just under £100 million.

Main fishing methods Most of the fish we eat is caught in a trawl net made from nylon and dragged along the sea-bed by a trawler. Large trawlers can be over 42m (140ft) long but today some 70% of the British catch is taken in fishing boats less than 24m (80ft) long. They still have similar equipment to the larger trawlers, including special echo sounders to locate the fish and powerful winches to haul the nets back aboard, when the skipper decides he has a good catch. As well as by trawling, fish are also caught by 'long lines', which carry several hundred baited hooks; by drift or tangle nets; by seine netting, which is a form of trawling used to catch concentrations of fish on or close to the sea bottom; and by purse seining, which catches surface shoals.

Poorer catches We often read that certain fish species are in danger because too many of them are being caught. Fish such as cod, haddock and herring are indeed being over-

Purse seining

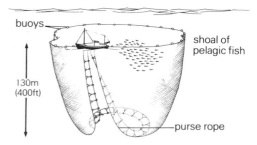

buoys

shoal of pelagic fish

130m (400ft)

purse rope

The ship sails round laying the net in an arc, hoping to enclose a shoal of fish. The purse rope is hauled in to bring the catch aboard.

fished—the result is poor catches, often including a high proportion of young fish—a situation which presents a grave threat to the future of the stock, and of the industry itself.

Among the distant water stocks traditionally exploited by UK fishermen, the first to suffer in this way were the various cod populations of the North Atlantic. As Europe's deep sea fishing industry modernised itself and used large freezer-equipped stern trawlers capable of towing huge trawls, the cod catch from the north-east Atlantic by all nations, including the Russians, rose to over 2 million tonnes. Cod stocks around Iceland were badly depleted by overfishing and fell from a peak of 547,000 tonnes in 1954 to 345,000 by 1967.

Conservation needed When catches fall as they did in the cod fishery in the north-east Atlantic, the stocks must be protected by conservation measures. Fisheries management can be implemented in various ways, such as by restricting the type of fishing gear, limiting the length of the fishing season or the size of the fleet, and by controlling the total allowable catch (TAC). A widely used conservation method is to restrict the size at which fish can be landed; another is to enforce the use of larger meshes in trawls or other nets.

In the attempt to conserve fish stocks, countries have extended their fishing limits. In 1971 Iceland extended her limits from 19km (12 miles) to 80km (50 miles); this was a serious blow to our industry because as much as 90% of the British catch came from this coastal zone. Poaching took place and the story of the Cod Wars is well known. In October 1975, when the Icelandic limits were pushed out even further to form a 310km (200 mile) zone, there was further conflict as British trawlers ignored the new limit and fished inside it, guarded by the Royal Navy.

Since 1977, Britain's fishery limits, like those of other EC member states outside the Mediterranean, have extended to 310km (200 miles) or else to a median line or agreed boundary if the countries are close. Certain countries have the right to fish up to Britain's

Drift netting

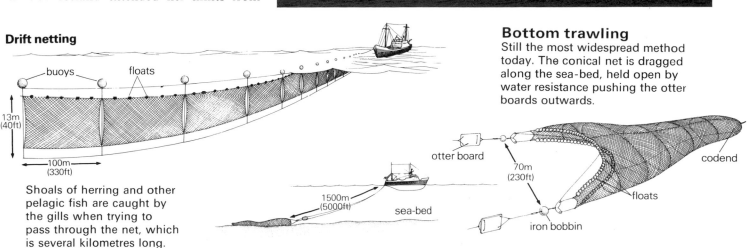

buoys   floats

13m (40ft)

100m (330ft)

Shoals of herring and other pelagic fish are caught by the gills when trying to pass through the net, which is several kilometres long.

Bottom trawling

Still the most widespread method today. The conical net is dragged along the sea-bed, held open by water resistance pushing the otter boards outwards.

otter board

70m (230ft)

1500m (5000ft)

sea-bed

iron bobbin

codend

floats

Above: Lobsters are caught close inshore in pots. The European lobster is one of our most sought-after species, and catch levels have fallen because of the intensity of fishing. Stocks have to be protected by a minimum landing size.

Left: Sorting oysters at Helford oysterage in Cornwall. In the background is the dredge, made of ropes and a wooden spar. Besides dredging for 'wild' oysters, oyster cultivation is now a prospering business. Even scallops and mussels can be cultivated—all these species being grown on trays, ropes or nets suspended in the sea.

Below: A mixed catch of bottom fish, still on board a trawler in Plymouth.

9.6km (6 miles) limit, but to date no foreign vessel has the right to fish any closer to our shore than this.

Shellfisheries In the fishing industry and generally in fishmongers' shops, crustaceans are included among shellfish, and so the term shellfish includes lobsters and crabs, which are caught in baited traps on the sea-bed. The most important crustacean for British fishermen is the Norway lobster (*Nephrops norvegicus*), which is found on soft muddy bottoms around the north-east and west coasts of Scotland, in the Irish Sea and the western approaches to Ireland and Cornwall. These lobster-like creatures are caught in large numbers, mainly in trawls, and are then landed fresh at processing factories where they are washed, peeled and frozen ready for sale. Sold as 'scampi' they are found in most supermarkets and are probably one of the most favoured seafoods.

Shellfish farming is growing in importance. This includes the cultivation of oysters, mussels and clams in certain parts of our coasts. Oysters sold in Britain fall into two main groups—the flat oyster and the cupped oyster, the latter being the Pacific oyster (*Crassostrea gigas*) which was introduced into Britain in 1965 by the Ministry of Agriculture, Fisheries and Food (MAFF) from British Columbia in western Canada.

Cockles and mussels are mainly taken from natural beds but there is a rising business in growing mussels on hanging ropes, or in nets which are suspended from buoys or rafts.

The future of fishing The decline of the British deep sea trawler fleet and reduced landings at major ports such as Hull and Grimsby has brought better fish prices and higher wages to our inshore fishermen, but there is mounting concern that the available stocks of both fish and shellfish are being over-exploited. Britain's fishermen fear that they will also be compelled to share stocks within our limits with fleets from the other EC countries. To add to the problem, Spain and Portugal have recently joined the Community, both countries having large fishing fleets desperate for fishing grounds.

Will fish farming help? Fish farming does appear to have a growing place in the production of our national fish supply, and is an expanding business, although still mainly concerned with the production of salmon and trout, and of course oysters and mussels. Even so, Britain's production of farmed marine species is dwarfed by the UK consumption rate of nearly a million tonnes of fish a year, about a third of which is imported. We are still a long way from the stage when fish farming can be seen as an alternative to catching fish in the sea. So the future of our harvest from the seas still rests on conservation and the need to rationalise fishing so that all who participate in this valuable industry can be assured of sustained yields of a variety of fishes in the future.

Fishing in the British Isles

Fleets from our main ports select their fishing grounds according to the catch they seek. The maps show our main national fish resources.

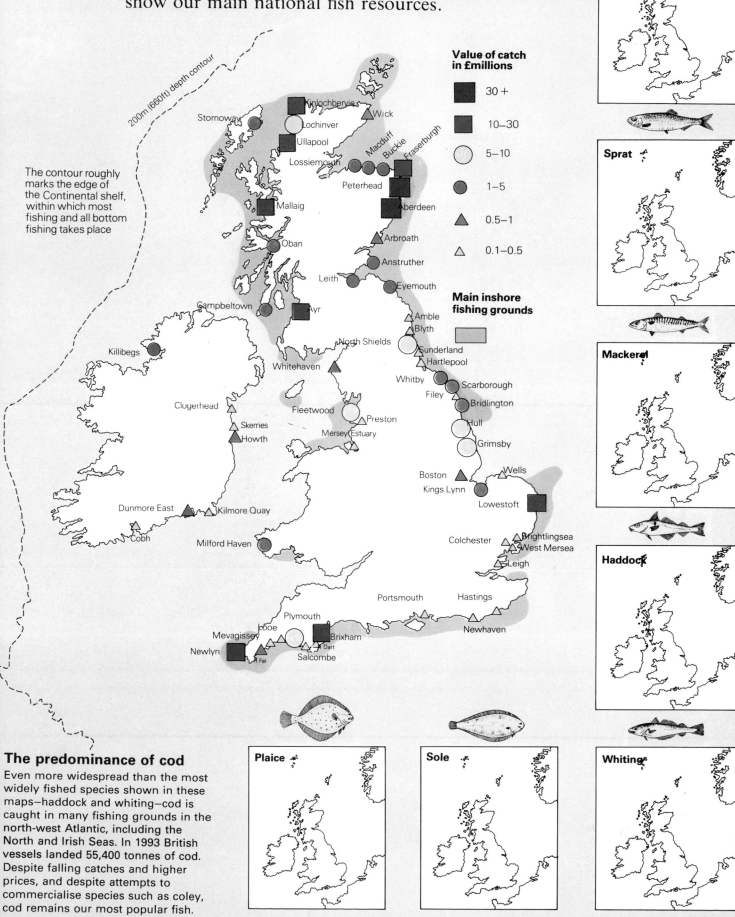

The contour roughly marks the edge of the Continental shelf, within which most fishing and all bottom fishing takes place

200m (660ft) depth contour

Value of catch in £millions

- 30 +
- 10–30
- 5–10
- 1–5
- 0.5–1
- 0.1–0.5

Main inshore fishing grounds

Stornoway · Kinlochbervie · Wick · Lochinver · Ullapool · Macduff · Buckie · Fraserburgh · Lossiemouth · Peterhead · Aberdeen · Mallaig · Arbroath · Oban · Anstruther · Leith · Eyemouth · Campbeltown · Ayr · Amble · Blyth · North Shields · Sunderland · Hartlepool · Killibegs · Whitehaven · Whitby · Scarborough · Filey · Bridlington · Clogerhead · Fleetwood · Preston · Hull · Skerries · Mersey Estuary · Grimsby · Howth · Boston · Wells · Kings Lynn · Lowestoft · Dunmore East · Kilmore Quay · Brightlingsea · West Mersea · Colchester · Cobh · Leigh · Milford Haven · Portsmouth · Hastings · Plymouth · Newhaven · Mevagissey · Looe · Brixham · Newlyn · Salcombe · Dart · Fal

Norway lobster · Sprat · Mackerel · Haddock · Plaice · Sole · Whiting

The predominance of cod

Even more widespread than the most widely fished species shown in these maps—haddock and whiting—cod is caught in many fishing grounds in the north-west Atlantic, including the North and Irish Seas. In 1993 British vessels landed 55,400 tonnes of cod. Despite falling catches and higher prices, and despite attempts to commercialise species such as coley, cod remains our most popular fish.

THE OVER-FISHED HERRING

Herrings were once called 'silver darlings' by fishermen, and whole communities depended for their livelihood on catching and processing them. Today, however, mainly as a result of over-fishing, the economic importance of the herring is much reduced.

The herring belongs to a large family of fishes which includes sprats, pilchards, sardines and other less well known species found in many parts of the world. All of them are important as food for man and his domestic animals, or as part of the food chain of economically valuable fishes. Herrings are larger than sprats, pilchards and sardines, and when fully grown can attain a length of 43cm (17in) and a weight of 680g (1½lb), though they are often caught by fishing boats before reaching this size. The fishes are flat-sided, with a silvery colour on the belly and sides, darkening to a deep blue-green on the back.

Herrings are widely distributed in northern seas, and there are two important species. *Clupea harengus* is found in the North Atlantic from Newfoundland to Scandinavia and Northern European coasts, while a closely related species, *Clupea pallasii*, extends from Japan to Canada in the North Pacific, and also occurs in the western North Atlantic. There are two main populations of *Clupea harengus*: oceanic herrings, which are found around Iceland, the Faeroes and Norway, and shelf herrings (or European herrings) which live in the shallower European waters.

Life history The shelf herrings are divided into distinct stocks, some of which spawn close inshore in spring, and some in deeper waters in summer and autumn. Sticky eggs form a mat over gravel and stones on the sea-bed or are attached in clumps to seaweed. The eggs hatch in about 10 days at a water temperature of 10°C (50°F), or longer in colder water. The larvae that emerge are about 7mm (just over ¼in) long; these are thin, scaleless, transparent creatures, furnished with a prominent yolk-sac which forms a food reserve until they start to feed actively.

At this stage of their life, the larvae are planktonic–they float rather than swim, but can make short, darting movements to catch smaller planktonic organisms for food. Many larvae are themselves eaten by arrow-worms, sea gooseberries, young fishes and other sea creatures.

As the survivors grow, they are carried by currents into sheltered bays and inlets where, by early summer, they develop scales and true fins so that they look like small versions of their parents. They shoal in large numbers, sometimes in company with young sprats. Such mixed shoals may be caught and sold. These small fishes, some 4-6cm (1½-2in) long, are known as whitebait.

In the next 18 months they usually undertake complex feeding migrations before joining the adult shoals as 'recruits'. Young herrings spawned from different stocks may be mixed together on the feeding grounds, but it is believed that they separate as they mature and go back to their own spawning areas at an age of two or three years or more, when they attain a length of at least 20cm (8in).

Eat and be eaten Herrings eat plankton, particularly copepods, all their lives; as they grow older they are able to select and catch individual larger planktonic organisms. Adult herrings have a varied diet which includes copepods, other small crustaceans and young fishes such as sand eels. They feed in the

Above: These trawlers at Ballycotton in County Cork, Ireland are multi-purpose vessels: they fish for herrings when in season, and are refitted at other times to catch different fish species, such as mackerel or plaice.

Features of a herring

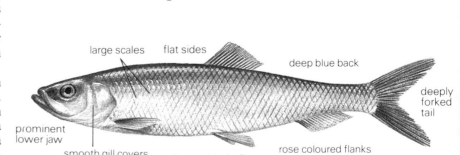

large scales flat sides deep blue back

prominent lower jaw

smooth gill covers silvery white belly rose coloured flanks

deeply forked tail

Herring *(Clupea harengus)*

upper waters and are known as pelagic fishes (as opposed to demersal fishes which feed mainly at or near the sea-bed). Herrings move upwards towards the surface at night, and down towards the sea-bed during the day. They are preyed upon by many carnivorous fishes, by whales and also by seabirds; but by far the most serious predator is the fisherman.

Fishing methods For centuries, the traditional method of catching herrings was by drift net. In this method, flat sheets of netting, weighted at the bottom and buoyed at the top, are linked together in 'trains' which may be several kilometres long. The nets are shot (lowered into the sea) at dusk and the ship then drifts with the nets to await the 'swim', when the herrings move up towards the surface water and are caught as they try to swim through the net. The advantage of this method is that the mesh size can be chosen to take only the larger herrings, leaving the younger fishes to grow heavier and more valuable, as well as breed new recruits to the shoals.

After 1945, with the advent of sophisticated instruments for fish detection, drifting gradually gave way to more active pursuit of the herring. Shoals located by echo sounders and sonar equipment can be swept into large trawls operated by one boat or a pair, with the gear adjusted to catch the fishes near the bottom or in mid-water. Purse seine nets, large enough and deep enough to enclose a cathedral, can be laid around a shoal and closed by tightening lines at the lower end to form a 'purse' completely surrounding many tons of fishes, which are then transferred to fishholds or refrigerated seawater tanks.

Processing the catch Relatively few herrings are retailed fresh. They may simply be salted whole, or they may be salted and smoked (kippered) or marinated with spices. Young herrings of about 10cm (4in) in length are canned in oil or sauce. Frozen fillets prepared from fresh or kippered herrings are packaged for quick and easy cooking. Herring roes, too, are considered to be a delicacy.

Management of herring fisheries Herring stocks have always fluctuated in size. Changes in natural conditions affect spawning success and viability of larvae and young fishes, so that recruitment to the adult shoals can vary dramatically from year to year. It was believed for a long time that the influence of fishing was small in relation to environmental effects, but recent events have shown this to be wrong. More fishes were caught than could be replaced by recruitment, and stocks began to dwindle. The need for management was recognised and conservation measures were applied – too little and too late in many cases. The herring catch in the North Sea and in the Skagerrak declined from around one million tons in the late 1960s to less than 50,000 tons in 1977.

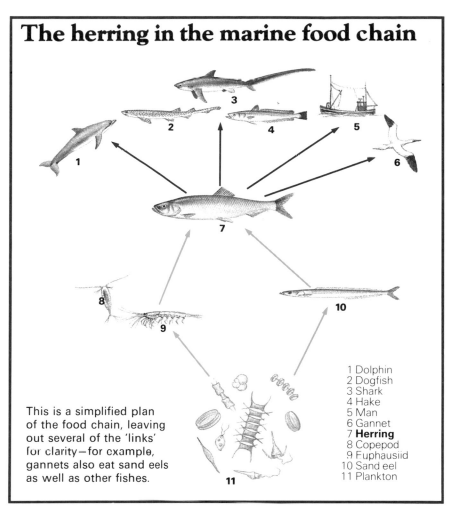

The herring in the marine food chain

This is a simplified plan of the food chain, leaving out several of the 'links' for clarity – for example, gannets also eat sand eels as well as other fishes.

1 Dolphin
2 Dogfish
3 Shark
4 Hake
5 Man
6 Gannet
7 **Herring**
8 Copepod
9 Euphausiid
10 Sand eel
11 Plankton

The main methods of fishery management are scientific assessment of the size of present stocks, projections of the effect of various levels of fishing, and regulations designed to ensure an appropriate fishing level. Various regulations have been made to control the number of ships fishing, and to set limits on the quantity and minimum size of herring that may be caught. There has been a reduction in catches allowed for 'industrial' use (the manufacture of meal and oil to make animal feeds and fertiliser) and, as a last resort, direct herring fishing has been prohibited in certain areas of the sea. In those areas which have been closed for a period of three years, the herring stocks are recovering.

Below: Herrings fresh from the sea, in a tub aboard the research ship that landed them on a voyage on the Irish Sea. Herring scales are very loosely attached, and rub off easily: here some scales can be seen on the wooden boards beside the fish. When they are caught in trawls or seine nets, herrings rub against one another a great deal and lose virtually all their scales. This is why, when bought in shops, they often appear to be completely scaleless.

MACKEREL: A FISH IN DEMAND

The mackerel, a popular sporting fish for seaside holiday makers, has in the past few years assumed a new level of importance. Since the decline of herring stocks, it has become the object of the largest single-species fishery in Britain.

Mackerel are firm-bodied fishes with a striking appearance. They are streamlined in shape and patterned with dark wavy markings on their greenish-blue backs. Their bellies are white, with tinges of pink and gold. These features tell us something about their habits, for they are fast-swimming fishes that live in shoals in midwater, their camouflaged upper coloration undoubtedly contributing to their defence against large predators such as gannets, sharks, dolphins and the smaller species of whales.

Off the coasts of the British Isles, mackerel are near the northern limit of their range, for the mackerel family (Scombridae) as a group are mostly subtropical in their distribution.

Above: Mackerel can grow to a large size, specimens approaching 70cm (28in) in length having been reported. The normal size for mackerel caught off our coasts, however, is from 30-50cm (12-20in) and this is the size of the fishes shown here. The weight of an individual mackerel increases with age and varies with the time of year, but the average weight of fishes caught around Britain is about 260g (10oz). The age of most mackerel caught is 2-4 years.

Mackerel in British waters In the north-east Atlantic mackerel spawn in spring from about March to July, each female spawning from 100,000 to one million eggs in batches, the total number depending on her size. The spherical eggs, which are 1.2mm in diameter, and which contain an oil globule for buoyancy, are spawned over deep water (120-500m/60-250 fathoms or more). They drift for three to six days depending on the ambient temperature, until they hatch into transparent larvae about 3.5mm long.

Separate stocks Spawning of mackerel is concentrated in two areas: one in the central part of the North Sea, the other in the south-western approaches, from the Bay of Biscay along the edge of the Continental shelf to the west of Ireland. Although these two populations of mackerel are similar, if not identical, in their biology, they are considered to be separate stocks: there is no evidence that a significant proportion of mackerel from one area ever spawns in the other.

Small mackerel Young mackerel are distributed over large areas, mainly closer to land than the spawning areas. Important nursery areas are the Celtic Sea south of Ireland and the eastern part of the North Sea. At about two years of age, when they are about 25cm (10in) long, they are commonly found close to the British coasts. In particular, they congregate in winter off the coast of Cornwall, where they are caught by local fishermen

Mackerel identification features

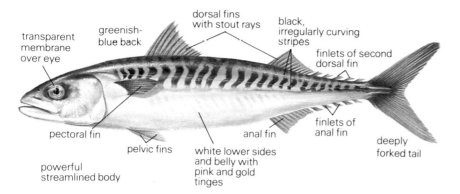

operating from small boats close inshore.

Fully grown fishes Mackerel mature into adults at an age of 2-4 years, and the adults are migratory. In spring those that spawn west of the British Isles move offshore to the spawning areas. After spawning, they migrate northwards, the larger mackerel apparently travelling faster and further than the smaller ones. Considerable numbers reach the Norwegian Sea north of the Shetlands, and some continue into the northern part of the North Sea. In some years small numbers even reach Iceland. During the summer, from about June to August, the two stocks of mackerel mix in the feeding areas to the north of Britain and in the northern North Sea.

Mackerel have a reputation as scavengers, living on waste or dead material. Nothing could be further from the truth, however, for they actively seek living food, mostly feeding at considerable distances from land. Their food consists of planktonic animals such as euphausiids (small relatives of krill), while recent research has shown that small fishes (mainly sand eels) form a larger proportion of their diet than was hitherto thought.

Returning south In the period from late August to October the adult mackerel of the western stock cease feeding and migrate south along the coasts of western Scotland. These well-grown fishes form the basis of the important Minch fishery, which is based at Ullapool and, to a smaller extent, at Mallaig and Stornoway. As the autumn progresses, the mackerel are caught progressively further south, reaching the west of Ireland about November, and in midwinter some join the overwintering shoals of younger mackerel along the Cornish coast.

Increased catches Fishing for mackerel around the coasts of Britain has increased rapidly in recent years, largely as a result of the fishermen's need to find an alternative to herring as the stocks of that species declined. At first, the home market for mackerel was slow to develop, and the catchers had to rely mostly on visiting factory vessels (known as 'klondykers') from the eastern bloc countries to buy their catches. There is now, however, a considerable demand–especially for smoked

Below: A simplified map of the main distribution and migration of mackerel in the north-eastern Atlantic. While the overall pattern is shown, individuals may occur at almost any point around Britain at the 'wrong' time. The two stocks overwinter and spawn in their respective areas, moving north in summer to feed; the stocks are partially mixed in summer. No wintering area is shown for the North Sea mackerel, as less is known about the migrations of this stock.

mackerel, which has come to be an excellent alternative to the high-priced smoked salmon in hotels and restaurants.

Landings of mackerel in Britain (including landings trans-shipped to the 'klondykers') rose from 9000 tonnes in 1972 to 350,000 tonnes in 1979. Since then, landings have steadily dropped with the introduction of limits on the total catch allowed and in 1992 only 151,000 tonnes of mackerel were caught by UK fishermen. In addition, vessels from several European countries fish intensively for mackerel. This has resulted in depletion of stocks. The North Sea stock in particular has declined considerably, since a peak catch of 930,000 tonnes was taken in 1967. The decline in the stock since the early 1970s is partly due to fishing and partly to the poor survival of young mackerel from each year's spawning since 1969.

While the western stock is in a much healthier state it, too, is decreasing in size, and only effective catch limitation seems likely to halt the decline.

Besides controlling the total level of the catch, other conservation regulations which have been introduced are designed to reduce the catching of small, immature mackerel. An area off the Cornish coast, for example, has been closed to most types of mackerel fishing for that part of the year when the fish caught tend to be small. There is some hope that such measures will halt the decline.

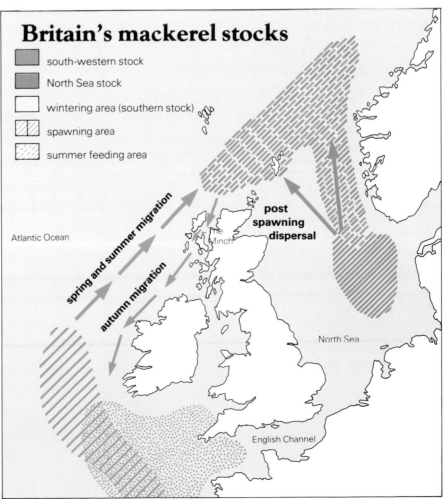

Britain's mackerel stocks

- south-western stock
- North Sea stock
- wintering area (southern stock)
- spawning area
- summer feeding area

spring and summer migration

autumn migration

post spawning dispersal

Atlantic Ocean

The Minch

North Sea

English Channel

VORACIOUS COD

The cod has been an important food fish in Britain for centuries. Its role today in the commercial fishing industry has made it one of the most sought-after fish in our seas.

The cod is one of several abundant food fishes that are found on both sides of the North Atlantic. Along with the herring, mackerel, haddock and halibut it is the basis for an industry that has contributed greatly to the wealth of the Atlantic maritime states. It is a wide-ranging fish, as the distribution map shows. However, it is not evenly distributed throughout its range. In the Bay of Biscay it is a rare fish, and on the south coast of England, while not uncommon, it is far from being as abundant as it is in Scottish waters.

Winter and summer homes Migration plays an important role in the cod's distribution. The North Sea populations tend to move southwards with the approach of winter, so that more cod than usual are found on the Suffolk, Essex and Kent coasts in the winter months. A similar migration occurs on the west coast, causing cod that may have spent the summer off the north-west coast of Scotland and Ireland to appear in the western English channel during winter.

To some extent, these migrations are linked with the breeding season and also with the success of spawning. In the 1970s, a series of highly successful spawning years increased the number of cod in the North Sea considerably, and they spread to colonize areas where they are not usually seen.

Spawning migrations around the British Isles are usually northwards towards the cooler, deeper water, but on the Norwegian coast an immense migration occurs from the Arctic regions southwards to the Lofoten spawning grounds, which has made this region famous for its fishing industry. Such dramatic movements are not seen on British coasts; instead the fish migrate southwards in winter to feed, and northwards in early spring to spawn.

The spawning season In the North Sea, the main spawning period is from February to April and may even extend to May or later. The spawning grounds lie at a depth of around 100m (330ft) but as the eggs are slightly less dense than normal sea water, they rise towards the surface. They are very small—only 1–1·8mm in diameter—but they

are produced in considerable numbers, possibly an average of one million eggs per female, although large fishes may produce many more.

The eggs require about nine days at 10°C (50°F) or seventeen days at 6°C (43°F) to hatch. The larva produced is about 4mm in length, the egg's yolk forming a prominent bulge on the underside. After the yolk is used up, the young fishes become progressively more pigmented, and from a size of about 20mm (¾in) they have the typical fins of a young cod. As they develop, their habitat changes slightly. From swarming at the surface in great numbers as newly hatched larvae, they drift with the currents into shal-

Above: A small inshore cod trawler. The cod caught commercially today are smaller than those caught on lines in years gone by, because heavy fishing of our waters does not allow the cod to grow to any great age or size.

Below: The wide-ranging distribution of the cod, from Greenland south to the Bay of Biscay.

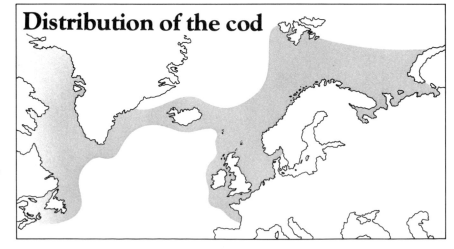

Distribution of the cod

Cod *(Gadus morhua)*

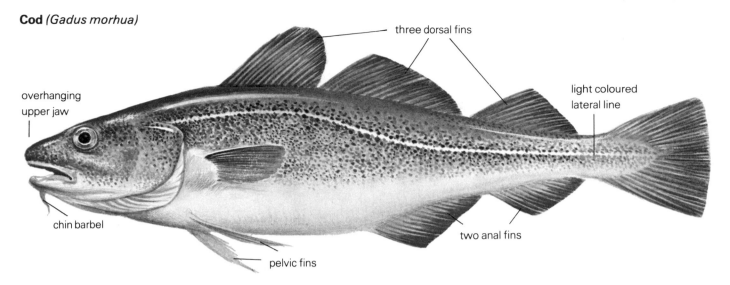

three dorsal fins

overhanging
upper jaw

light coloured
lateral line

chin barbel

pelvic fins

two anal fins

lower water and then gradually disappear from the plankton to take up life near the sea bed at an age of perhaps two months, measuring about 2·5cm (1in) in length.

Growth rates vary from area to area but on average a year-old cod would be about 18cm (7in) long, at two years about 36cm (14½in) and at three about 55cm (22in). Before our seas were fished so heavily, huge cod of about 22·7 to 34kg (50 to 75lb) and of an estimated age of 25 to 40 years were frequently caught.

Greedy feeders The young cod feed almost entirely on the minute crustaceans called copepods. When they are older and living near the sea bed their diet is less restricted, but still includes copepods (although of different species) and other kinds of crustaceans, as well as worms.

Adult cod have a very varied diet, which includes almost any animals living in numbers in its vicinity. Quantities of shell fish of various kinds, such as clams, razor shells, cockles and mussels are swallowed whole. Hermit crabs, lobsters, prawns and shrimps, brittle-stars, sea urchins and large numbers of lugworms and ragworms also form a part of the diet. More active prey such as squid and fishes of all kinds, but especially sprats, herring, flatfishes and small cod are commonly taken. The cod has a large appetite; in the winter of 1980–81, when sprats were extremely abundant on the North Sea coast, cod were stuffing themselves with them. Anglers found it difficult to catch the cod, but the stomachs of those fish that were caught sometimes contained up to 30 sprats. After eating so much, it was surprising that the cod still had the appetite to take the angler's bait!

Cod communication At night and in deep water individual fish keep in touch by sounds. Sound production is most noticeable as a preliminary to spawning and during the spawning season. The noises have been described as 'thumps' or 'growls' but they are in fact loud, low-frequency grunts, repeated three or four times. Noises are made by both sexes, for a variety of reasons, including

warning off rival males before and during spawning, and attracting females towards the males. The noises are produced by contraction of the muscles that are attached at one end to the front ribs and to the swim bladder at the other. The swim bladder acts rather like a drum, amplifying the noises made by the muscles on its surface.

Camouflage colours Cod need camouflage to protect themselves from predators such as dolphins, seals and halibut. Those caught over sandy bottoms, on which they are most common, have pale yellowish-brown backs. Cod taken among seaweed in shallow water on northern coasts are dull green on the back, mottled with brown, while areas where the ground rocks have a reddish hue yield reddish-coloured cod. All, however, have a conspicuously light, creamy coloured, lateral line. So constant is the colouring of the fish that experienced fishermen can often judge where a fishing boat has made its catch by the colour of the cod on board.

Above: The cod, with its chin barbel, the wealth of sensory pores on the underside of the head and the sensitive pelvic fins, is ideally equipped for living and feeding close to the sea bed where, in shallow water, it is mostly found. However, it is equally at home in deeper water.

Below: In water of 61m (200ft) or more, cod form schools which usually swim some 30m (100ft) off the bottom. In daylight hours the school is compact, but with twilight, or in even deeper water, the fish tend to break up into a much looser school.

MUD-LOVING GREY MULLETS

Grey mullets are common fish of our southern coasts. They have an unusual feeding method, swallowing mud to digest the plant and animal life it holds.

Above: By August, young grey mullets, some 3-4cm (1-1½in) in length, can be seen in rock pools and close inshore on our coasts, swimming in closely packed, fast-moving schools. They grow for 8-10 years, making offshore migrations in winter to avoid the cold, before they return south to their spawning grounds.

Below: The chief feeding method of grey mullets.

Grey mullets are streamlined fishes with broad heads, solid-looking bodies and forked tails. They have large, tough scales on the body and over most of the head, a single anal fin and two dorsal fins. The first dorsal fin contains four slender but strong spines. The mouth is wide and set at the extreme upper surface of the head, and the lips are hard, fringed with fine external teeth. In colouring, all species are dull green or blue-grey above, with silvery sides. There are six or seven grey stripes running lengthways along the body, and the undersides are dead white.

Distinguishing grey mullets The most common and widespread of the three British species is the thick-lipped grey mullet (*Chelon labrosus*). It is the largest British species, growing up to a length of 75cm (30in) and a weight of nearly 4.5kg (10lb). The lips are broad and thick, and they are covered with coarse, blister-like features called papillae along the forward edge. There are also close-packed, small teeth.

Neither of our other two species is so abundant or so large as the thick-lipped grey mullet, and neither has the distinctive broad lips. The golden grey mullet (*Liza aurata*) has narrow lips with moderately large teeth on the edge of the upper lip. Its colouring is the same as that of other grey mullets, but it has a conspicuous golden spot on the cheek and gill cover, which gives it its species name. Also, its pectoral fins are moderately long and, if folded forwards, reach as far as the pupil of the eye.

The third species is the thin-lipped grey mullet (*Liza ramada*); it has a narrow upper lip, but with tiny, bristle-like teeth on its edge. It lacks the conspicuous golden patch on the side of the head, but it may have a gold tint—which often leads to confusion. However, it always has a distinct dusky spot at the base of each pectoral fin, and this proves to be one of the most useful diagnostic features. The shortness of the pectoral fin also helps in identification, for if the fin is folded forwards, the tip does not even reach the near edge of the eye.

Where they are found However, if appearances are confusing, the habitats of the fishes sometimes offer clues to their identity. The thick-lipped grey mullet occurs all round the British coast, usually preferring shallow inshore waters along sandy or muddy shores, in harbour mouths and the extreme outer part of the estuaries. The thin-lipped mullet is less widely distributed, and is rare off the northern coast of England and off Scotland. It too occurs in shallow inshore waters, but also shows a strong liking for fresh water. If a grey mullet is caught far up-river in fresh water, then it is virtually bound to be a thin-lipped grey mullet. The golden grey mullet is the least common of the three species, and is found only on our south and south-western coasts.

Watching grey mullets Because they live in

How grey mullets feed

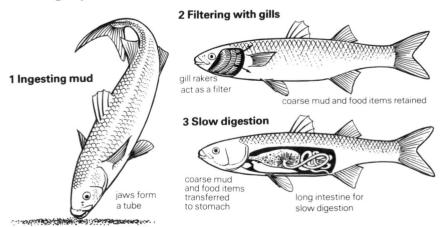

1 Ingesting mud

jaws form a tube

2 Filtering with gills

gill rakers act as a filter

coarse mud and food items retained

3 Slow digestion

coarse mud and food items transferred to stomach

long intestine for slow digestion

shallow water, grey mullets can sometimes be seen from the shore. A typical habit is to move over the sea-bed with their heads turned down towards the bottom, in a close school in which all the fish are of about the same size. Equally as often, they can be seen in small groups working their way over the pilings of piers, breakwaters or harbour walls, and sometimes along rock faces under water. This behaviour suggests that they are grazing on the fine green algae that cover such surfaces in shallow water. On the sea-bed, they feed in a different way, protruding their jaws to form a tube through which they suck up the surface layer of the mud or sand.

A gutful of mud Examination of the gut contents of grey mullets suggests that they feed very largely on mud, and in a sense this is true. The surface mud of inshore waters is a rich environment in which many minute worms, algae and other organisms live.

However, feeding indiscriminately on such minute organisms poses problems, as they are mixed up with the mud and soil that the mullet sucks in. The finer particles of mud can pass through the fine mesh of the fish's gill rakers and are puffed out with the water through the gill openings. Coarser mud, and the small animals and plants, are retained on the gill rakers and mixed with mucus, and are eventually swallowed.

The stomach of a grey mullet has a thick, muscular wall to grind the soil and food to a smooth consistency, making digestion more efficient. The mud-eating habit provides the explanation for the very long gut. On average, there is less than 15% organic matter in the food a mullet eats, so the fish has to take in a large volume of material and be able to retain it for long enough to digest the small amount of nutritive matter it contains.

Summer visitors At the onset of winter, grey mullets seem to disappear from our coasts. Young fishes swim out to sea to avoid the cooling of inshore waters, while mature ones migrate to their spawning grounds.

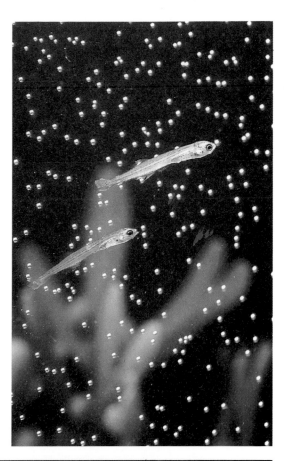

Right: Very young fry of grey mullet. These are planktonic creatures that drift with sea currents. Grey mullets spawn in late spring. One spawning area has been identified off the Isles of Scilly, and others may be in the Channel area; but most British grey mullets probably originate far to the south.

Below: An adult thick-lipped grey mullet. While the thickness of the upper lip may seem a clear enough identification feature on paper, this feature varies confusingly with the size of the specimen. As a result, it is often extremely difficult to identify small grey mullets. This picture also shows the unremarkable colour scheme of these fishes. The worldwide variety and abundance of the fishes suggests that it is successful as a form of camouflage.

Three grey mullets

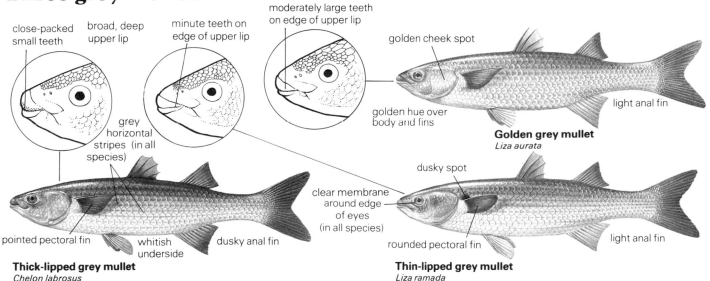

close-packed small teeth

broad, deep upper lip

minute teeth on edge of upper lip

moderately large teeth on edge of upper lip

golden cheek spot

golden hue over body and fins

light anal fin

Golden grey mullet
Liza aurata

grey horizontal stripes (in all species)

dusky spot

clear membrane around edge of eyes (in all species)

pointed pectoral fin

whitish underside

dusky anal fin

rounded pectoral fin

light anal fin

Thick-lipped grey mullet
Chelon labrosus

Thin-lipped grey mullet
Liza ramada

GURNARDS: SPINY 'SINGERS'

Six species of gurnards occur in our coastal waters. All bear numerous sharp spines, and are remarkable for their unparalleled 'singing' ability.

Above: A grey gurnard on a sandy sea-bed off Orkney. Like other gurnards, it feeds mainly on bottom-living crustaceans and fishes.

Below: The bulky outline of a tub gurnard. There is an excellent view of the flat belly and massive head. The smaller fins are the pelvic fins. The larger pectoral fins each have three separated rays, which are clearly visible. Underwater lighting conditions have affected the colouring here.

Gurnards are very distinctive fishes, with large eyes set high up on the head and hard, bony plates, often with strong spines, covering the top and sides of the head. Some species even have tough bony plates running along the back and sides. Another characteristic feature is the pair of large fan-like pectoral fins, the lowest rays of which are separate from the main fin and form stout feelers beneath the throat. Gurnards skim slowly over the sea-bed probing for food with these long fin rays, which are well equipped with sensory cells.

Two uncommon species Fortunately, the two least common of the gurnards in our waters, the long-finned gurnard and the piper, are the easiest to identify. The former has an exceptionally long spine in the first dorsal fin, its length being twice that of the other spines. The fin bearing this spine is itself noticeably elongated. The fish has a series of large and flexible scales along the length of its lateral line. Its colouring is reddish on the back and sides, shading to pinkish underneath; the lateral line is pearly pink in colour. The reflecting colour of the lateral line has earned it the alternative names of the lantern or shining gurnard.

The piper, too, is bright red, the sides being rosy, while the belly is pinkish, but it is characterised by the two prominent bony lobes that jut out from its snout. Its head is remarkably spiny: one massive spine juts backwards over the pectoral fins. The back, too, carries numerous sharp spines, all pointing backwards. Sorting a trawl catch of pipers (almost all pipers are caught in trawls as they live mainly on the lower edge of the Continental shelf in depths of 300m/164 fathoms and deeper) can be a very painful activity on account of their spiky nature.

Tub gurnard This is the most widely distributed and abundant of all our gurnards; it is certainly the largest, and is possibly the most colourful. Its head is relatively large and its eyes are small (for a gurnard), and the spines on the head are only moderately large. Most significantly, the lateral line is smooth, and its pectoral fins are extremely large. Its back and upper sides vary from brownish to bright red, and its sides are mostly pink. The top surface of the pectoral fin is brilliantly coloured: it is peacock blue spotted with green, with red at the edge.

The adult tub gurnard lives in relatively shallow water (20m/11 fathoms or sometimes even deeper) but young ones live in much shallower water. It is usually most common on muddy or sandy bottoms, and feeds on a wide range of bottom-living animals, especially fishes and crustaceans–sand eels, small flatfishes, gobies and dragonets, swimming crabs and brown shrimps. It is the largest of our gurnards, growing to a length of 75cm (29½in) and a weight of 5.2kg (11½lb).

Red gurnard The size and predominantly red colouring of the tub gurnard cause anglers

Gurnard identification

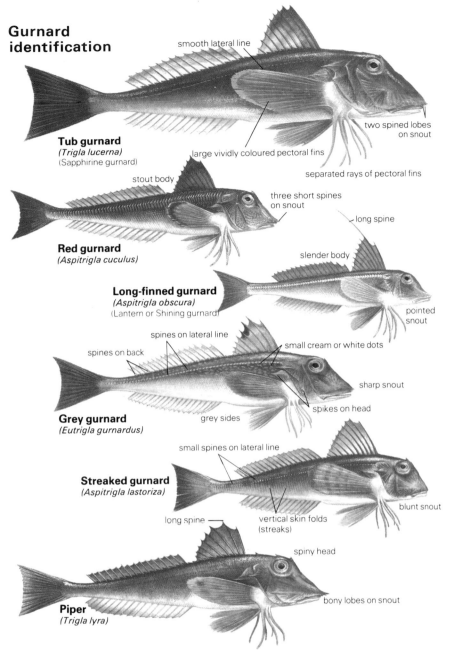

Tub gurnard
(Trigla lucerna)
(Sapphirine gurnard)

smooth lateral line

two spined lobes on snout

large vividly coloured pectoral fins

separated rays of pectoral fins

Red gurnard
(Aspitrigla cuculus)

stout body

three short spines on snout

long spine

Long-finned gurnard
(Aspitrigla obscura)
(Lantern or Shining gurnard)

slender body

pointed snout

spines on lateral line

spines on back

small cream or white dots

sharp snout

Grey gurnard
(Eutrigla gurnardus)

grey sides

spikes on head

Streaked gurnard
(Aspitrigla lastoriza)

small spines on lateral line

blunt snout

long spine

vertical skin folds (streaks)

spiny head

Piper
(Trigla lyra)

bony lobes on snout

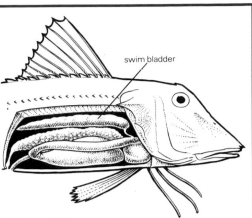

swim bladder

Loud 'singers'

Gurnards are probably the noisiest fishes in our coastal waters. Each species has a large and very muscular swim bladder. This is vibrated by the muscles running along its sides to make what have been described as single, vibrant squawks or barks, growls and a series of rapid clucks'. Research into the sound made by fishes has shown that gurnards are noisiest when many of them are present, and also when there are other noise-making fishes close by. They are also especially noisy at dusk in the spawning season. These observations suggest that their sounds are produced to warn off competitors and possibly aggressors, and during the excitement of spawning when they must keep in close company with each other. Being bottom-living fishes which feed by stirring up the mud, it is a great advantage to them to keep in touch by sound rather than sight in what must be murky water. These sounds can be heard clearly in shallow water from a quietened boat, particularly at night when there are not so many other noises.

frequent puzzles. The true red gurnard is a much smaller fish, rarely growing to a length of even 40cm (16in) and a weight of 900g (2lb).

The red gurnard is a rather deep-bodied fish, with a moderate sized head and a large eye. Along its back lie two rows of sharp spines, one each side of the dorsal fin, but the lateral line is smooth although covered with large, expanded scales. As its name suggests, it is bright red, but the pectoral fins are pinkish with a dark edge, totally different from those of the tub. The red gurnard is most common on our southern and western coasts and lives on sand or gravel bottoms in depths of some 20m (11 fathoms).

Grey gurnard This is similar in size, growing to a length of 45cm (18in), but is very widely distributed all round the coasts of the British Isles. It tends to live off-shore in depths of 20-50m (11-27 fathoms), and is only locally caught in shallower water, and mostly in Scottish waters at that. It lives mainly on sandy bottoms, but is also found on mud and shell grounds.

Above: Six gurnard species are found in the coastal waters of Britain and Ireland. Three are relatively common: the tub gurnard, the grey gurnard and the red gurnard, their abundance and breadth of distribution round our coasts being in this order. The streaked gurnard has a somewhat local distribution, being moderately common in the western English Channel and to the south-west of Ireland, while the piper is relatively common in deep water to the west of the British Isles. The long-finned gurnard is rare; it has been found only in the western Channel, and then from very occasional captures. A seventh species, the armed gurnard, was reported last century.

The grey gurnard is dull coloured, brownish on the back with grey upper sides, fading to pale grey. The body is liberally spotted with small cream or white dots, and there is a rounded black spot on the edge of the first dorsal fin. It has sharp spines along the back as well as on the head.

Streaked gurnard The sixth, and one of the less common gurnards (of the species described here, only the long-finned and the piper are rarer), is the streaked gurnard. This is a dumpy, heavy-bodied fish with a blunt snout and small, deep head. A small species—not often exceeding 36cm (14in) in length—its most obvious feature, which gives it its name, is the series of skin folds that run vertically along the length of the body, originating from the lateral line. It is a dull red in colour.

It is rare in British waters except in the western English Channel, although it is not abundant there. It lives in moderately deep water of 40m (22 fathoms) and sometimes even deeper than this.

THE BALLAN: OUR LARGEST WRASSE

The ballan wrasse is the largest and probably the most common of the British wrasses–a group of saltwater fishes. Like many others of its family, the ballan wrasse has the bizarre trick of changing its sex halfway through its life.

Wrasses are among the most colourful of all our saltwater fishes, and the ballan wrasse is no exception. The young are usually a beautiful emerald green and the adults are mostly either green or brown, though reddish specimens are not at all unusual. As with other wrasses, the body of the ballan wrasse is fully scaled, but on this species each scale has a paler centre and a darker rim, giving the fish a spotted appearance. The fins are also often spotted, especially during the breeding season, and sometimes a ballan wrasse is found with a white line running the length of its body.

The ballan is a very slow-growing species that lives to a great age. Fishes as old as 25 years have been caught and it is probable that, if left alone, they would grow older still. A length of 45cm (18in) and a weight of 1½kg (3½lb) are common, but specimens can attain 60cm (2ft) and 3½kg (8lb), making this species the largest British wrasse.

Rocky refuge The favourite habitat of the ballan wrasse is rocky areas, particularly cliffs and reefs, which provide a safe refuge. It can be found all around the coasts of Britain and Ireland, except for parts of the east coast. The ballan wrasse is very much a creature of habit and in some instances the same fishes, recognised by particular deformities, have been found in the same territory for several years at a stretch. At night the wrasse can often be found sleeping, wedged between rocks of hidden in seaweed; it can even be picked up before it swims off.

Being an inshore species, and common, ballan wrasse are a familiar sight to both divers and sea-anglers. Divers most often see them singly or in small groups, swimming through a kelp forest with a characteristic jerky rowing action of the pectoral fins. Adults venture down to at least 30m (100ft) but they can also be found right up to the intertidal zone. Indeed, young ballan wrasses are very often found in rock pools, particularly those providing plenty of cover in the form of green seaweed (their green bodies blend in very well); occasionally, adults are also trapped in rock pools when the tide recedes.

Omnivorous feeders The ballan is omnivorous and eats almost anything available, though its food is composed mostly of animals, particularly molluscs and crustaceans. It also takes brittlestars, barnacles and, very rarely, small fishes or pieces of seaweed.

The ballan wrasse feeds by sucking in prey through its fleshy lips and then macerating it with powerful throat teeth–the teeth in its jaws are used to dislodge food from the rocks.

Anglers often find that they can catch very few ballan wrasses during the winter. This is partly because wrasses are less active, and so feed less, when the water temperature is low. They also appear to migrate offshore in some winters into deeper, warmer water to avoid the extreme cold near the coast, which can easily kill them.

Sex change The ballan wrasse has an extraordinary life-cycle. It has long been known that there are many more female ballans than males, and also that no juvenile males have ever been found. Furthermore, most males

Above: Adult ballan wrasses are predominantly green or brown, though reddish specimens are not unusual and old males are often bright chestnut. All are spotted due to the scales having pale centres.

Aging a ballan wrasse

The age of a fish is often estimated from the growth rings on the scales, but this is not the only way. Growth rings also occur on other bony structures, including the opercular bone covering the gill chambers. In the ballan wrasse this bone, once it is cleaned and dried, shows the rings clearly and is ideal for aging. The bone shown here comes from a twelve-year-old ballan wrasse specimen.

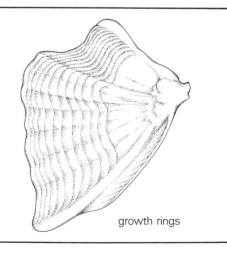

growth rings

are more than 13 years old, though some comparatively young specimens around six years old have been found, and most of the really large old ballans are male.

The explanation for this strange situation lies in the curious life-cycle of the ballan wrasse. All specimens are born as females. They become sexually mature after about six years old and then begin spawning. However, after a few years, some individuals change sex and become fully functional males. There are no external differences associated with this change, only internal ones. This phenomenon explains why no young males are ever found, why most old fishes are males, and why there are many more females than males. There is no evidence to suggest that males ever change back into females at a later stage.

Sex change in other wrasses Many other wrasses – possibly even all of them – undergo the same strange life-cycle. In the case of another British species, the cuckoo wrasse, the process is accompanied by a startling change in colour. The female is a beautiful red with three black blotches, interspersed with white, near the tail. When she turns into a male, she loses these blotches and becomes predominantly blue, with a dark head and bright blue lines running along the body. The sides and belly often become a vivid orange. The two sexes are so different that they were for a time thought to be different species.

The mechanisms controlling these changes, in both the ballan and other wrasses, are not fully understood. It is known, however, that in some tropical species of wrasse the changes are controlled by social pressures operating through a system of dominance by larger, older males. When a dominant male dies, his place may be taken by a large female, who then changes sex to become the dominant male.

Spawning and young Little is known about the spawning behaviour of the ballan wrasse. The female builds a nest of fine algae, usually wedged into the crevice of a rock, and lays her eggs in it. These are then fertilised by a male. Since there are far fewer males than females, it is likely that each male has several females nesting in his territory.

After hatching, the larvae drift for a while, then develop into young fish and settle in rock pools and in other shallow water. Small ballan wrasses can be found in rock pools from June onwards each year.

Vulnerability The ballan wrasse's strange life-cycle, and its territorial habits, make it extremely vulnerable to spear-fishermen who, by going after the biggest specimens, can soon remove all the males from an area. The problem is made worse by the ballan's great curiosity, which allows it to be quickly persuaded to feed out of a diver's hand. It is to be hoped that its curiosity does not lead to a decline in numbers of this charming and beautiful fish.

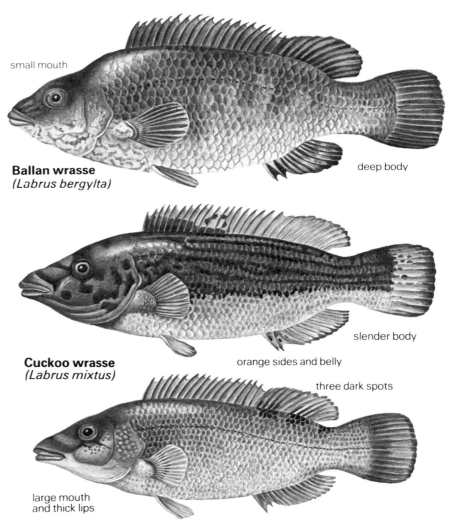

Ballan wrasse
(Labrus bergylta)

small mouth

deep body

Cuckoo wrasse
(Labrus mixtus)

slender body

orange sides and belly

three dark spots

large mouth
and thick lips

Above: The ballan wrasse remains the same colour as it changes sex, but the cuckoo wrasse undergoes a startling colour change from red to blue.

Right: The lower set of throat teeth is known as the ballan cross because of its shape. It is sometimes carried by sailors as a charm to prevent drowning.

Below: A rocky coastline with reefs to provide a safe refuge is the preferred habitat of a ballan wrasse.

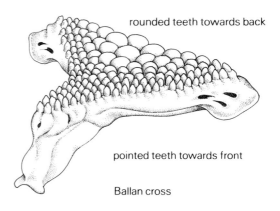

rounded teeth towards back

pointed teeth towards front

Ballan cross

ANGLER FISHES

One of the most extraordinary looking of fishes, the angler fish is also among the most highly adapted, possessing a 'fishing rod' for luring prey into its capacious jaws.

Above: The angler fish is not often seen moving about on the sea-bed, preferring instead to spend most of its time hiding in wait for prey (below). When it settles down for a period of fishing, an angler fish digs itself into the sand or stones, then raises itself up and flaps down again, spreading out the skin flaps on the sides of its body. As the loose sand and bits of weed dislodged by the digging come to rest on the angler's back the camouflage is complete.

The shallow coastal waters around Britain and Ireland are the home of two species of angler fish; they are even found in estuaries. The commoner of these is *Lophius piscatorius,* known simply as the common angler fish.

This species is a huge fish, growing to a maximum length of 2m (6½ft) and weighing 40kg (90lb). In its general shape it resembles a banjo. The head and body are flattened from above, and the tail tapers gradually to the tail fin. Just behind the head are two large fan-like pectoral fins, and there is a small dorsal fin towards the tail directly above the anal fin. The pelvic fins are tucked away under the belly and look like small legs.

The two most striking features about the angler are the size of its mouth, which occupies the whole width of the head, and the series of long whip-like rays on the head and the front of the back. The rays represent the last vestiges of the first dorsal fin. The foremost of these rays has a leafy double flap at its tip; at the base of the flap there is a small worm-like organ. This is the lure used to entice fishes towards its mouth.

The angler is a master of camouflage and can change the colour of its back perfectly to match any natural background. In contrast to the neutral colouring of the back, the underside is pure white, except for the tips of the pelvic fins, which are black, and the pectoral and anal fins, which are dusky.

A second species It was the characteristic white underside of the angler that led to the discovery, as late as the 1970s, of a second inshore species of angler fish in British waters. Occasionally an angler with a dusky underside was caught, and a close examination showed that it differs from the common angler in other ways as well. The new discovery was subsequently identified as *Lophius budegassa,* a species until then known mainly from the Mediterranean.

Later captures have shown that this species occurs fairly regularly off the southern and western coasts of Britain but it is less common than *L. piscatorius.* Because of the distinctive coloration of its underside it has been named the black-bellied angler.

Different depths As far as is known, both species have similar life-styles, but the black-bellied angler seems to live in deeper water, mainly between 100-300m (55-165 fathoms), although it has occasionally been caught at depths of 50m (27 fathoms). The more common angler fish lives mainly between 18-100m (10-55 fathoms).

The common angler lives on sandy or gravelly sea-beds, or on shell grounds; it is also often found on rocky sea-beds, usually on the edges of reefs or rocks where sand patches offer it a chance to hide. It is, however, very adaptable and is occasionally captured in muddy places such as estuaries.

The angler has a distinctly sedentary life-style, spending most of its time hidden on the

sea-bed. Yet it is occasionally seen to swim, propelling itself with its broad paddle-like tail fin.

Fishing for prey The ability of the angler fish to attract prey to itself by means of a rod and lure is one of the most fascinating aspects of its natural history. As a potential victim approaches, the angler raises its first dorsal fin ray above its back and bends it forwards, sometimes jerking the 'bait' on the rod to and fro to attract the prey. Any fish showing an interest is lured closer. It does not need to come very close, however, for the angler's huge mouth and throat can, when opened, create such an inrush of water that the prey is carried straight inside.

The angler eats virtually any species common in the area where it lives, particularly small fishes easily attracted by its lure.

Breeding habits The common angler breeds in spring and early summer in deep water well offshore. The eggs are shed as ribbon-like gelatinous sheets, usually only one egg thick. The young fishes have enormously prolonged fin rays and float near the surface buoyed up by the large surface area of these fins. During this stage they are carried considerable distances by the ocean's currents and may be swept into areas, such as the North Sea, where the adult forms are rare.

Deep-water species There are many other species of angler, rarely seen because they live in deep water. Several have been recorded in the Atlantic Ocean off the British and Irish coasts, one of which is the Atlantic football fish (*Himantolophus groenlandicus*). This species, occasionally caught by trawlers deep-fishing for hake, is almost spherical, and large specimens are the size of a football. It has sparse bony plates on its back and sides, each with a spine in the middle.

Above: The mouth of an angler is equipped with long backward-pointing teeth to prevent any prey escaping. Its diet consists mainly of smaller fishes, such as whiting, young cod and haddock, though the number of crustaceans found in its stomach suggests that, as well as taking fishes, an angler also snaps at anything else passing by.

Below: Angler fishes have a bizarre and somewhat menacing appearance.

Another deep-water species found to the west of the British Isles is *Ceratias holboeli*. These fishes have solved the problem of finding one another at spawning time in the immensity of the deep, dark sea by a device unique among vertebrates – the male, which is never longer than 6cm (2½in), is parasitic upon the much larger (1.2m/4ft) female. Immature males and females are free-swimming but when a male makes contact with a maturing female he takes a firm hold on her skin with his jaws and hangs on for the rest of his life. Eventually, his jaws fuse with the flesh of the female, his gut and gills degenerate, and the female's blood circulation provides him with oxygen and nourishment.

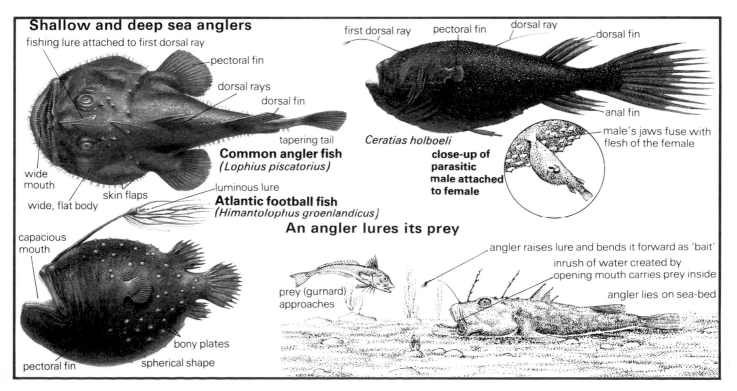

Shallow and deep sea anglers

fishing lure attached to first dorsal ray
pectoral fin
dorsal rays
dorsal fin
tapering tail
wide mouth
wide, flat body
skin flaps

Common angler fish
(*Lophius piscatorius*)

first dorsal ray
pectoral fin
dorsal ray
dorsal fin
anal fin
male's jaws fuse with flesh of the female

Ceratias holboeli

close-up of parasitic male attached to female

luminous lure
Atlantic football fish
(*Himantolophus groenlandicus*)
capacious mouth
bony plates
pectoral fin
spherical shape

An angler lures its prey

prey (gurnard) approaches
angler raises lure and bends it forward as 'bait'
inrush of water created by opening mouth carries prey inside
angler lies on sea-bed

CONGER EELS OF REEFS AND WRECKS

Conger eels lurk in crevices among rocks and reefs, hunting for smaller fishes, cuttlefishes and other marine animals. Wrecks, pier walls and the legs of North Sea oil drilling rigs also provide suitable habitats for this highly adaptable fish.

Above: The conger's method of feeding is one of stealth rather than bold action. Concealed in the half-light within a crevice in the rocks or in a wreck, it waits until unsuspecting prey comes within reach, then with a quick lunge it seizes its victim. The conger takes bottom-living fishes as well as cuttlefishes, octopuses and even crabs. At night, congers tend to leave their hideaways and forage across the open sea-bed. It is then that they are sometimes caught in trawls.

The conger eel is not a familiar fish. Little used for food, it is usually seen only by anglers and divers. It is, however, a common fish all round the coasts of Britain and Ireland, but possibly most abundant where rocks and reefs offer it shelter.

Its preference for rocks means that it is sometimes found on the shore in rock pools and in seaweed-hung crevices near the low tide mark. As it is adept at slipping deep into tiny crevices in the rock, the conger is not easy to catch, but occasionally one emerges as a result of prodding with a stick – a quite frightening experience if one happens to be barefoot, for the eel has a reputation for snapping savagely when cornered.

Two species of eel The two common species of eel in the British Isles are the conger eel and the so-called freshwater eel, which despite its name spends part of its life in the sea. In rock pools and even the shallow pools left by the tide on some sandy beaches, eels of both species are found, and so it is necessary to distinguish between the two. First, look at the jaw and fins. The conger's upper jaw is longer than the lower, while in the freshwater eel the 'chin' juts forward in front of the upper jaw. A conger's pectoral fins are rather pointed, while those of the freshwater eel are rounded, and the conger's dorsal fin begins close behind the head.

Such anatomical details may not, however, be necessary to recognise the eel: size alone may be conclusive evidence. At the stage of their lives when they are found on the shore, freshwater eels are not usually more than 50cm (20in) long, although exceptional specimens of 1m (39in) are caught. If an eel found on the shore is more than 75cm (30in) long, it is almost bound to be a conger, for they rarely occur on the shore under this length.

Hiding places Rocky shores at around low tide mark are an important habitat for young congers, although they are probably as numerous offshore provided there are rocks among which they can hide. Larger congers live in deeper water, but not necessarily very deep water, for specimens up to 2.2kg (5lb) in weight are caught from the shore. They have also adopted man-made 'reefs' (such as breakwaters), and there are few sunken ships or aircraft wrecks which do not have their populations of conger eels.

Prey of the conger The conger's jaws are lined with rows of strong, triangular teeth, as close together as the teeth of a comb. They are relatively unspecialised, leaving the conger

Right: A young conger eel in the shallows.

Below left: A sea angler 'gaffs' a conger—speedily bringing it aboard with a special hook known as a gaff. Gaffs are used in preference to landing nets when there is a danger that the angler might be injured by a large or dangerous fish. The eel seen here is a middle-sized specimen— the species can grow to a length of 2.7m (9ft) and a weight of around 68kg (150lb). The largest conger known to have been caught by an angler weighed nearly 50kg (108lb) and was caught off the Eddystone Reef in 1976. Congers of this size have a girth bigger than a man's thigh and are extremely muscular and active fish. They are also very tenacious of life, and snap boldly in self-defence with their jaws. When encountered in the sea by divers, however, they do not normally attack, despite their size and strength. This contrasts strongly with the moray eel, a far more dangerous fish.

Head of conger eel

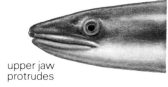

upper jaw protrudes

Head of freshwater eel

lower jaw protrudes

Above: Details of the shape of the head are useful in telling apart our two most common species of eel. Look at the mouth and jaws: the conger's upper jaw is longer than the lower, while the freshwater eel has a jutting chin.

free to feed on both hard and soft bodied creatures. The few observations that have been made on the diet of congers show that they eat large quantities of bottom-living fishes such as rocklings, dogfishes, flatfishes and pollack. Pollack are specially attracted to wrecks. Congers also catch cephalopods such as cuttlefishes and octopuses. Crabs of various kinds, particularly the edible crab, and lobsters, are also eaten by congers.

Atlantic spawning Relatively little is known about the breeding places of the conger, although like the freshwater eel it migrates to distant waters to spawn. The only known spawning area of the conger lies far to the south of Britain, somewhere between Gibraltar and the Azores, where the sea is over 3000m (1640 fathoms) deep. It is believed that all western European congers originate in that area, having developed from eggs shed in mid-summer, probably in the middle depths of the water. The larvae drift near the surface, generally taking a north-easterly course, until at the age of one to two years (depending on the direction in which they have drifted) they

reach shallow water and metamorphose into young conger eels.

Congers and man The conger is one of the few fishes to have benefited from man's domination of the natural environment. Man is responsible for the wrecks on the sea-bed, the oil rigs in deep water and the many breakwaters, harbour walls and pier pilings–all of which offer a secure habitat. Some of these, indeed, are in areas such as the southern North Sea and the eastern English Channel, where natural habitats for the conger are scarce.

A second factor is that in some harbours fishermen prepare their catch for market on board ship, throwing a considerable amount of offal and fish heads into the water. Conger eels living in the crevices of such harbour walls live well on these remains, although the species as a rule does not scavenge. Thirdly, people do not eat congers as much today as they used to, and therefore serious commercial fishing for them ended many years ago. As a result of all these factors, the conger eel is more abundant now than in the past.

Below: The larva of a conger eel. This stage of the life-cycle is followed by the post-larva, which is the first stage of metamorphosis into a young eel. The larva grows to a length of a few centimetres. The post-larva is similar, but larger.

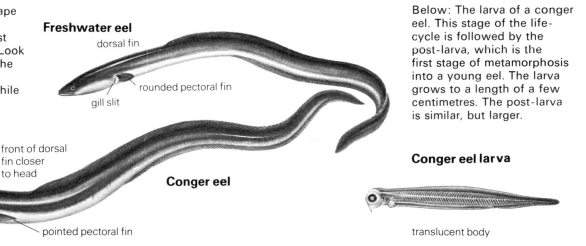

Freshwater eel

dorsal fin

rounded pectoral fin

gill slit

front of dorsal fin closer to head

Conger eel

gill slit

pointed pectoral fin

Conger eel larva

translucent body

DOGFISH: SPOTTED SHARKS

There are two species of dogfish in British waters—both harmless members of the shark family. They are perhaps better known as rock salmon on the fishmonger's slab.

Dogfish do not fit into the popular conception of sharks—fast swimming, white-bellied, surface living hunters of the open sea. However, without going into anatomical details, dogfish do have easily recognisable features in common with all sharks. The skin is covered with fine 'teeth', sharp-edged and all pointing backwards. If you were to run your hand over a dogfish from head to tail it would feel smooth; but rub it the other way and your skin would be scratched by thousands of tiny sharp teeth.

In common with all sharks, dogfish also have a series of 5-7 gill slits along each side of the head. They 'breathe' water through their mouths and emit it through these gill slits. Many also have a breathing hole behind the eye (spiracle). Their fins have no bony rays but are supported by tough cartilage (gristle) and their entire skeleton is made up of cartilage. Although it is not so rigid, this looks like real bone and is just as hard.

Sharks lack the swimbladder that is a feature of most bony fishes and which helps them to stay buoyant in the water so that they do not waste energy trying to stop themselves sinking. Many sharks compensate for this by having enormously large oil-filled livers which act in exactly the same way as the swimbladder. There is no truth in the claim that sharks have to keep swimming or they would sink to the bottom—their livers help them

Above: The dogfish has a long tapering, flexible body made up of cartilage — a firm elastic gristly tissue also found in sharks, rays and skates. It is a sea-bed scavenger searching even for scraps thrown overboard by passing ships.

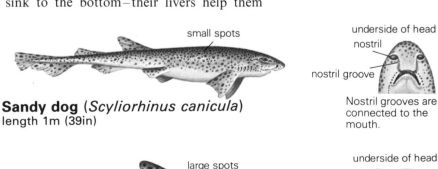

small spots

Sandy dog (*Scyliorhinus canicula*)
length 1m (39in)

underside of head
nostril
nostril groove

Nostril grooves are connected to the mouth.

large spots

Nurse hound (*Scyliorhinus stellaris*)
length 1.5m (60in)

underside of head
nostril
nostril groove

Nostril grooves are not connected to the mouth.

stay afloat. Dogfish, however, are essentially bottom-living animals and their livers are relatively small.

Two species The sandy dog or lesser spotted dogfish, and the nurse hound or larger spotted dogfish are the two species found in British waters. As their names suggest both are spotted; their backs are sandy or grey-brown with dark brown spots and their undersides creamy white. The sandy dog usually has many small brown spots in contrast to the nurse hound which has larger and fewer spots. Unfortunately the size of the spots and colouring are not infallible identification guides, because the nurse hound sometimes has numerous small spots as well. Size is a better guide for distinguishing them.

The sandy dog, which is the commoner and more widely distributed, grows to about one metre (39in) in length and weighs up to 6kg (14lb). It lives on sand, fine gravel and even muddy bottoms, and its colouring closely matches the dappled colouring of the sea bed. As an adult it is normally found in depths of 10-55m (33-180ft), but newly hatched young from 10cm (4in) upwards can be caught in much shallower water.

The nurse hound, the larger of the two species, grows to 1·5m (60in) in length and weighs 9.5kg (21lb). It is found in similar depths to its relative and it tends to live on rough and even rocky seabeds, although it is occasionally caught on sandy bottoms. The young, like those of the sandy dog, are also found in shallow water, but they are larger on hatching – about 16cm (6½in) long.

Egg cases Although most sharks are live-bearers, retaining the fertilised eggs within the mother's body until they are fully developed, dogfish lay eggs in egg cases. The females move into shallower water to lay their eggs, which are enclosed in smoothly-rounded, oblong cases with long tendrils at each corner. These tendrils, which tangle up in algae, on rough rock surfaces, on wrecked ships and even on underwater structures such as pier pilings, keep the case safely anchored for the nine months or so it takes for the egg to develop into a young dogfish. Surprisingly, since it is the larger species, the nurse hound lays its eggs in shallower water than the sandy dog; the eggs can even be found at the extreme low tide mark on rocky shores, tangled in the kelp.

Dogfish dinner Dogfish eat a wide range of bottom-living invertebrates, mainly crabs, shrimps, worms and whelks; but they also eat sand eels, gobies, and other fish which live close to the sea-bed. They will also scavenge over the sea-bed and eat all kinds of odd items, many thrown overboard from ships, including fish heads from trawlers' catches.

Dogfish are often sold at fishmongers as 'rock salmon', although the recommended trade name for the fish is 'flake'. They make perfectly good eating; the firm flesh is palatable and has no bones in it.

Born in a case

Dogfish eggs are laid in tough, leathery cases with long curling threads which anchor the cases to seaweeds and often to pier pilings. These threads are so strong that it is rare to find such cases in shoreline jetsam while the eggs are developing. The young dogfish (pups) hatch at lengths of 10-16cm (4-6¼in), depending on the species; the cases—also called 'mermaid's purses'—break away and are washed up on the shore where they become black and brittle.

In contrast to bony fishes, dogfish and other sharks produce few, but very large, eggs. The yolk which is not much smaller than that in a hen's egg, will nourish the young dogfish during its long nine month development. At the end of this stage the pup lies with its tail curled over its head, completely filling the case. For a few days after it hatches a small yolk sac can be seen on the pup's belly, supplying it with enough food while it searches for shelter.

MUCH-MALIGNED SHARKS

Despite their man-eating reputation, the majority of sharks–including all those found in British waters– eat nothing more than fishes and crustaceans. In fact, they have more to fear from man, who has caused many species to become rather scarce.

Sharks are living representatives of a group of early fishes known as the cartilaginous fishes. These have been found in fossil form dating back as far as the Middle Devonian period, 400 million years ago. Although often thought of as primitive, they are in fact highly evolved animals, living successfully in a wide range of habitats.

There are some 300 species of shark worldwide, most of which are marine although some live in fresh water for at least part of their life. They are particularly abundant in tropical and warm temperate seas as well as deep seas, but a few occur in polar regions. The Greenland shark, for example, is widespread in the Arctic but rarely visits the coasts of Britain.

Twenty-two species of shark have been recorded in British seas down to a depth of about 1000m (547 fathoms), including such unusually named species as the porbeagle, starry smooth hound, spurdog and tope.

Myth and reality Although vicious, cruel, murderous and man-eating are all adjectives that have been used to describe the shark,

Above: The sharp double row of teeth in the porbeagle's jaw enable it to grasp and slice prey.

Below: The small, star-like white spots on the starry smooth hound's back give this shark its name.

none is an accurate description of the sharks to be found in our waters. While it is true that sharks do occasionally attack men, maiming and sometimes killing, the number of occasions on which this has happened is insignificant compared to the number of harmless sharks wantonly killed by man each year.

Sharks have highly developed sensory powers and can detect the presence of a wounded fish from a considerable distance. As they are virtually weightless in water, even the larger species can be very agile when necessary. They do not attack at random among a shoal of fishes when they are looking for prey, but isolate and attack the particular fish they want. The most common constituents of their diet are small prey such as squid and a variety of fishes. Sharks' teeth are perfectly adapted for the type of food they eat, differing in structure from species to species, according to diet.

One common factor, however, is the replacement of the teeth in the jaws. Every shark has several complete series or rows of teeth on each jaw, the innermost row being small and still forming in the gums. As the outer teeth break or become loosened, they drop out and are replaced by others formed close behind. One species, the North American lemon shark, is known to lose a tooth every eight days.

Fast feeders A shark's teeth are equally well adapted for the type of food that the species selects. The starry smooth hound, a common British shark, feeds on crabs including the hermit crab, which it crushes together with the adopted whelk shell in which the crab lives. This species has flattened teeth, raised only into slight bumps, and as many as 12 rows are in use at any one time. With its strong jaw muscles and these grinding teeth, this small shark can crush any crab it encounters, reducing its shell to a mass of fragments.

Many of our larger sharks, including such summer-time visitors as the blue shark and the mako, as well as the resident porbeagle and the tope, have pointed triangular teeth with sharp edges. These are ideal for dealing

with soft-bodied prey. The teeth in the upper jaw of the porbeagle have a small extra cusp at the base of each side; those of the lower jaw are similar, but rather oblique. This shape gives them the effect of both a dagger—for stabbing and holding small, actively-swimming prey—and shears, for cutting up the prey. Generally, only two or three rows of teeth are in action at once, but a wide variety of fishes can be taken including herring, mackerel, pilchard, cod, pouting and whiting, as well as squid.

Razor-edged teeth The spurdog and its relatives have cutting teeth that are even more efficient, being triangular or oblique with a razor-sharp edge. The spurdog, which takes its name from the long spine in front of each dorsal fin, is common in shallow water where it feeds on such fishes as herrings, sprats, sand eels and whitings. It can chop chunks out of its prey. The velvet belly, its deeper-water relative found off the west coast of Britain, has vertical, razor-edged teeth in both jaws. It attacks large fishes, biting a circle of flesh out of their back or sides, which is sometimes found intact inside the shark.

Reproduction Male sharks have a pair of structures called claspers on the inner side of their pelvic fins, which they use to transfer sperm to the female's cloaca. Fertilisation takes place internally in all the species, but there are major differences in the way the young develop.

In some species, such as the shallow water dogfishes, the eggs are protected by a horny case and laid in shallow water. Most sharks, however, retain the fertilised egg within the mother's body and the young are born alive, looking like miniatures of their parents. Live-bearing British sharks include the porbeagle, tope, blue shark (which gives birth rarely in our waters), the smooth hounds and the spurdog.

Advantages and drawbacks Live-bearing clearly offers one major advantage to the young shark, in that it is protected inside its mother; but there are disadvantages as well. The female shark is naturally limited in the number of young she can carry. The maximum litter of the spurdog, for example, is 11 pups, depending on the size and age of the mother. This is very few in comparison with the 350,000 eggs laid by fishes such as the plaice, although of course this number is reduced by a variety of hazards and only a small number may hatch.

A more obvious disadvantage of live-bearing in sharks is the damage caused to population numbers by heavy fishing. Sharks such as the spurdog have gestation periods lasting between 18-22 months; so if the stock is at all heavily fished, large numbers of pregnant females will probably be caught. Population numbers are further limited because many sharks are slow-growing and may not become mature—and thus breed—until they are ten years of age or more.

Some facts about sharks

A shark differs from a bony fish in a number of ways. Its skeleton is composed of cartilage, sometimes with a calcium deposit, making it almost as hard as the true bone of a fish's skeleton. Its tail is much more rigid than that of a fish since its backbone extends up the upper lobe of the tail fin.

More obvious visible differences include the 5-7 gill slits found just behind the head on each side of the shark's body, while the gills of a bony fish consist of a single external opening on each side, overlaid by the gill cover. Also, a shark's skin is covered with tiny 'teeth' rather than scales, giving it a smooth appearance but a rough texture if rubbed from tail to head.

Finally, a shark can swim all its life without fatigue and, although it does not possess a swim bladder, it has an enormous oil-filled liver which serves a similar purpose to the swim bladder in other fishes, as well as providing it with a store of food.

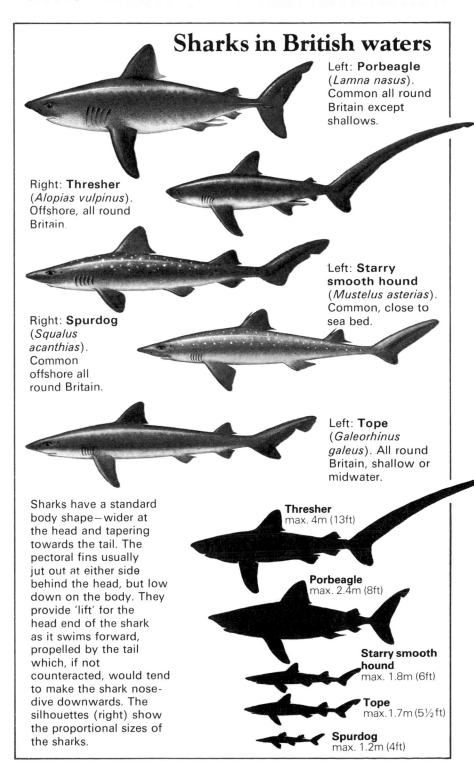

Sharks in British waters

Left: **Porbeagle** (*Lamna nasus*). Common all round Britain except shallows.

Right: **Thresher** (*Alopias vulpinus*). Offshore, all round Britain.

Left: **Starry smooth hound** (*Mustelus asterias*). Common, close to sea bed.

Right: **Spurdog** (*Squalus acanthias*). Common offshore all round Britain.

Left: **Tope** (*Galeorhinus galeus*). All round Britain, shallow or midwater.

Sharks have a standard body shape—wider at the head and tapering towards the tail. The pectoral fins usually jut out at either side behind the head, but low down on the body. They provide 'lift' for the head end of the shark as it swims forward, propelled by the tail which, if not counteracted, would tend to make the shark nose-dive downwards. The silhouettes (right) show the proportional sizes of the sharks.

Thresher max. 4m (13ft)

Porbeagle max. 2.4m (8ft)

Starry smooth hound max. 1.8m (6ft)

Tope max.1.7m (5½ft)

Spurdog max. 1.2m (4ft)

BASKING SHARKS

The best time to sight basking sharks – the second largest species of fish in the world – is on calm sunny days as they swim around the British coast. The shape of their fin above water is unmistakeable.

Observant holidaymakers at west coast resorts of the British Isles may often see the dorsal fin of a basking shark cutting through the water. The name 'basking' relates to the fish's habit of swimming near the surface. The Irish used to know the shark as sun fish. In summer, a basking shark will come remarkably close inshore – within 1-2m (3-6ft) of rocky shore lines, if the water is deep enough.

As the shark swims through the water, its dorsal fin tends to flop from side to side. The upper lobe of the tail fin is often visible above the water, moving with an S-wave motion 2m (6ft) or so behind the dorsal fin. When the fish swims well up in the water, the whole of the dorsal fin up to 1m (3ft) high is visible, and the snout sometimes projects above the surface. You can occasionally row right up to the shark and touch the dorsal fin when you will notice the body is surprisingly wide as it looms large beneath the bottom of the boat.

Slimy, scaly skin The skin above the water looks dark black; but the underwater parts of the body appear to be mottled in shades of grey and brown. The body exudes a vile, black slimy mucus, which can strip certain kinds of paint off metalwork, stain the sides of boats and cause hemp ropes and cords, as well as fishermen's nets, to rot. The black slime probably discourages many potential parasites. The skin also has tooth-like scales capable of inflicting serious grazes.

Gentle giant Following a basking shark by boat, as it swims along in absolute silence at about two knots, is not as dangerous as it sounds. For all its size it is basically a harmless and docile fish. In a five tonne specimen the brain is a mere 40g (1½oz), so the fish is not capable of any complex aggressive behaviour. Nevertheless it can dive at a terrific speed if startled, when the sweep of its tail could damage the boat. And if a basking shark met a boat head-on at full speed, it could easily hole the hull. However, it cannot sustain such sprint speeds for long without exhausting itself, and must soon revert to its normal, slow, meandering motion.

Not a mammal Nearly 9m (30ft) long and weighing about seven tonnes, the basking shark is recognised as the world's second largest fish. Its size has often led people to suppose it is a marine mammal related to the whale. It is, in fact, a fish breathing with gills which extract oxygen from the water. It has an upright tail in contrast to the horizontal tail of whales and dolphins.

The body form is just a large version of that of smaller sharks, including dogfish, and like all sharks the basking shark has a skeleton of cartilage which is more flexible than bone. Basking sharks and the whales have one thing in common – both are planktivores, feeding on vast quantities of drifting microscopic plankton in the summer months (see illustration). No large items of food are ingested as the shark has only minute teeth. Jellyfish sometimes get tangled in the gills, but no one knows whether they form a major part of the fish's diet. The stomach contents have the consistency of smooth paste, made up of millions of crustaceans.

Mating and birth Little is known about the mating behaviour of basking sharks. But, as with all sharks, the male copulates with the

Above: The crew onboard this fishing vessel – involved in a satellite tracking project on basking sharks – caught this old female fish on the Clyde near Arran. They failed to lift the fish on to the deck however, because the winch couldn't take the shark's weight (around seven tonnes), and the jib wasn't high enough to lift the 9m (30ft) long fish out of the water.

Right: The basking shark's skin is covered with little flea-like creatures called parasitic copepods. These are about 15mm (⅝in) long, but the conspicuous twin trailing egg sacs can reach 50mm (2in). The skin, where irritated, seems to produce a white chalky material which makes these otherwise dull-coloured parasites quite noticeable.

Anatomy of the basking shark

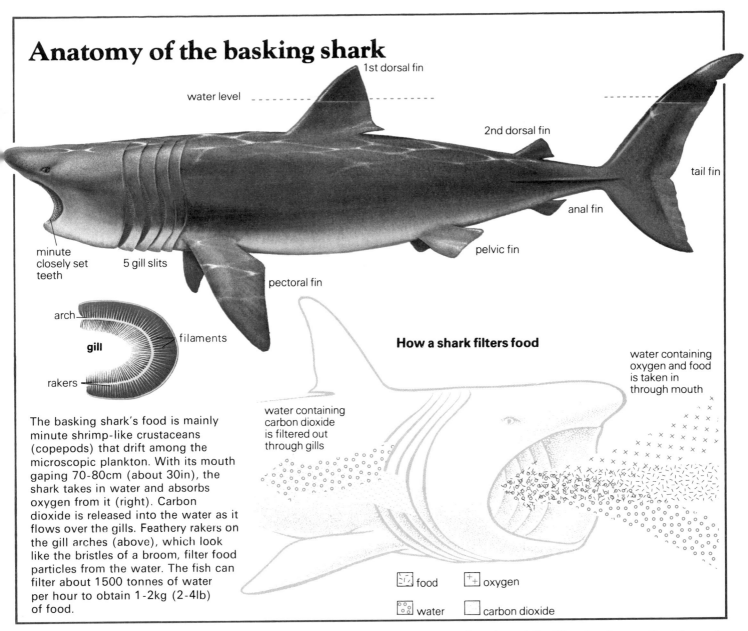

1st dorsal fin

water level

2nd dorsal fin

tail fin

anal fin

pelvic fin

minute
closely set
teeth

5 gill slits

pectoral fin

arch

gill

filaments

rakers

How a shark filters food

water containing
carbon dioxide
is filtered out
through gills

water containing
oxygen and food
is taken in
through mouth

food   oxygen

water   carbon dioxide

The basking shark's food is mainly minute shrimp-like crustaceans (copepods) that drift among the microscopic plankton. With its mouth gaping 70-80cm (about 30in), the shark takes in water and absorbs oxygen from it (right). Carbon dioxide is released into the water as it flows over the gills. Feathery rakers on the gill arches (above), which look like the bristles of a broom, filter food particles from the water. The fish can filter about 1500 tonnes of water per hour to obtain 1-2kg (2-4lb) of food.

female and fertilises her internally. The male has two claspers on the pelvic fins, either of which can be inserted into the female to transfer sperm. The clasper is equipped with hooks, and some females have been caught apparently suffering from damage caused by recent mating. It is estimated that the male produces about 50 litres of semen; the sperm is contained in translucent packets known as spermatophores.

Little is known of the development of the eggs after fertilisation. Despite the thousands of basking sharks that have been caught, no female has ever been seen by scientists with eggs or developing embryos inside her. However, in 1936 a Norwegian fisherman was towing a basking shark into harbour, when she gave birth to five live and one dead young. The fisherman caught one of the young and reported that it swam along with its mouth open, apparently feeding just like an adult. There was no sign of a yolk sac or navel cord. These newly born babies were about 1·5m (5ft) long.

Despite this evidence, the fact that basking

Right: Sea lampreys up to 60cm (2ft) long are regular passengers on the basking shark. They attach to the underside of the body with suckers, causing superficial damage and leaving circular marks on the shark's skin.

How age affects the shape of the dorsal fin

young

old

Above: You can tell the rough age of a basking shark by its dorsal fin. If the fin is quite pointed, the shark is quite young; if the fin is squarer, more worn and flops to one side, it belongs to an older fish.

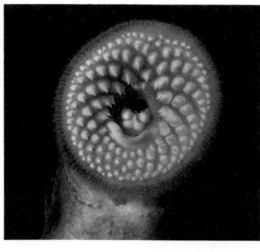

sharks give live birth rather than laying eggs was not generally recognised until the 1960s. Although some shark species do lay eggs, most produce live young, and sharks are said to have 'invented' this form of giving birth millions of years before mammals appeared on land. There is considerable argument about the length of the gestation period. Some evidence suggests a period of over three years, but other research indicates a period of less than nine months. It is remarkable that pregnant females are never caught; where they go is still a mystery.

It is unlikely that basking sharks exercise any kind of parental care towards their young, which take ten years to mature.

Migration mystery Basking sharks are seen off our coasts during the summer – from April off Cornwall, and May or June off Scotland. This suggests a northward migration in the spring followed by a corresponding southward migration in the autumn. It is now thought that such a migration pattern is a misconception caused by schools of basking sharks simply coming to the surface at different times and at varying latitudes.

Basking sharks may winter in African waters; nobody is certain. As they occur throughout all oceans of the world outside the tropics, their migrations appear to be extensive. Against this, fisherman have caught sharks in winter, at deep levels just off the coast of Scotland and near their summer feeding areas. Therefore there may well be local stocks which do not travel very far.

A few fish have been caught that did not have gill rakers (part of the fish's filter mechanism inside the mouth which traps food particles – see illustration). This led to another mystery about the basking shark. However, all the rakerless specimens were caught in winter and further catches revealed fish shedding gill rakers in the autumn and others growing new ones in spring.

The basking shark seems to stop feeding in winter when it sheds its gill rakers, and probably lies on the bottom somewhere in deep water; but the position of these wintering grounds has still to be located.

Sharks enter the space age

Scientists at Aberdeen University have recently designed a special radio package to facilitate tracking of basking sharks. The package, which looks like a yellow plastic toy boat (below right), contains a powerful radio transmitter in a waterproof casing. Each package transmits a unique identifying code, which is picked up by a special radio receiver aboard a space satellite orbiting above the earth's atmosphere. The satellite retransmits the information to a ground station, where the position of the fish is automatically calculated and relayed back to the scientists waiting at Aberdeen.

The scientists carefully approach a surfaced shark on an inflatable boat equipped with a silenced outboard motor. They then inject a special stainless steel anchorage into the base of the shark's dorsal fin and attach a towline to this anchorage. The radio transmitter is connected to the other end and floats behind the fish when it swims on or near the surface. When the shark dives deep, the transmitter automatically switches off and is easily towed underwater by the shark. The transmitter and towline are shed after a few months, without any adverse effects to the shark.

This unique collaboration between space scientists and marine biologists will enable them to learn not only more about basking shark movements, but also how all plankton-eating fish find concentrated food supplies.

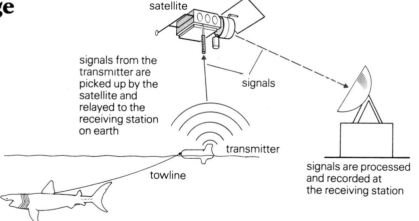

satellite

signals from the transmitter are picked up by the satellite and relayed to the receiving station on earth

signals

transmitter

towline

signals are processed and recorded at the receiving station

1103

LEATHERY RAYS AND SKATES

The most obvious feature shared by rays, skates and sharks setting them apart from other fishes is that they have tough leathery skins rather than scales. But the similarities go deeper than that, for both groups are cartilaginous fishes with pliable cartilage skeletons instead of bone. The rays and skates form a distinct group from the sharks, distinguished by their flattened shape, huge 'wings' and whip-like tail.

Ray or skate? In popular usage, the word 'ray' refers to small short-nosed species, whereas 'skate' refers to larger species with elongated snouts. The marine biologist, however, usually refers to them all as 'rays' since there is no clear biological distinction between the two groups.

Most of the species found in British waters, and all those sold in fishmongers as skate, belong to the family Rajidae. The most common British species in this family are the thornback ray or roker, the blonde ray and the spotted ray. The last two are very similar to each other and fetch a higher price in fish-

mongers than the thornback, which, as its name indicates, has a ferociously spiny back to deter predators. All rays have fine prickles on their skins, but on the thornback they are developed into large, viciously hooked spines, so that the fish can be handled safely only with gloves.

The largest species of ray found around Britain is the blue or common skate–a 2.7m (9ft) specimen was caught in Caernarvon Bay in 1960. Sadly, despite its name, this species is now extremely rare.

Sting rays and electric rays Two other families of rays are represented in British waters, apart from the family Rajidae: sting rays and electric rays. The sting ray has a large

Above: A roker gliding along on the sea-bed. All rays have prickly backs to some degree, often with large spines running down the middle, but the roker is covered with particularly large, viciously hooked spines; it should be handled only with gloves on.

Below: The underside of a typical male ray, showing the position of the claspers. In other respects, both sexes exhibit the same features, though the females tend to be larger.

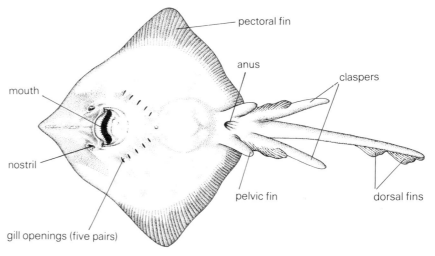

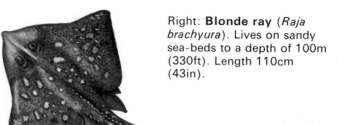

Right: **Blonde ray** (*Raja brachyura*). Lives on sandy sea-beds to a depth of 100m (330ft). Length 110cm (43in).

Above: **Thornback ray** or **roker** (*Raja clavata*). Our most common ray in shallow waters. Length 90cm (35in).

Right: **Sting ray** (*Dasyatis pastinaca*). Found in shallow water and estuaries. Length 1m (39in).

Above: **Cuckoo ray** (*Raja naevus*). Our smallest ray at 70cm (28in) long. Its back bears two distinct spots.

Above: A spotted ray being landed. The technique used, in which the fish is hauled ashore or on-board ship with a long hook, is called gaffing. This species is a relatively common British ray but is not often caught by anglers since it lives well out to sea.

Below: All rays have a hole set just behind each eye on the upper surface of their bodies. This hole is called a spiracle and allows the ray to breathe while resting on the sea-bed.

stinging spine at the base of the tail. The electric ray can deliver a 220-volt shock, with a peak current of 8 amps – enough to power a colour television set! It uses it for defence and to stun prey.

Flat from birth As with more familiar flatfishes such as plaice, the flattened shape of rays is an adaptation allowing them to lie inconspicuously on the sea-bed. Unlike these other species, however, rays are born flat; they do not metamorphose from round-bodied larvae.

The eyes lie on top of the body but the mouth lies flush with the underside, though it can be protruded for feeding. The diet of most rays consists mainly of bottom-living animals such as crab, sandeels and small flatfishes, which they detect by means of a well-developed sense of smell. They can also catch some midwater species such as sprats by enveloping them in their wings. All rays, as well as the electric ray, can give out an electric shock (usually weak), which they may use to help disturb or stun their prey. They then pounce on the food with a short burst of speed.

Rays are among the most graceful swimmers of any fishes, moving by a continuous series of undulations passed backwards along their pectoral fins.

Clasping males The reproductive cycle of rays differs in many ways from that of bony fishes. The males are born with a pair of claspers unique to rays and sharks. These are situated at the base of the tail and grow as the ray matures, so that in older specimens they can be half the length of the tail.

During mating the claspers are brought together to form a channel through which the sperm is introduced into the female. Meanwhile, the two fishes are held together by hooks on the male's claspers and, in some species, on the wings as well.

Eggs in purses Most bony fishes lay a great number of tiny eggs, but the rays (and most other cartilaginous fishes) produce a much smaller number of large eggs. Each egg of a ray is contained inside a tough protective envelope–the familiar mermaid's purse–for an incubation period of anything between

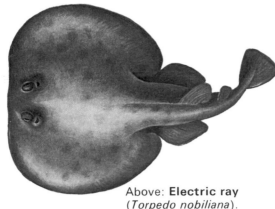

Left: **Spotted ray** (*Raja montagui*). Lives on sandy bottoms in deep water. Length 75cm (30in).

Above: **Electric ray** (*Torpedo nobiliana*). Differs from other rays in its smooth skin. Length 1.8m (70in).

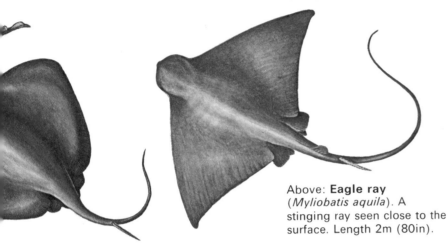

Above: **Eagle ray** (*Myliobatis aquila*). A stinging ray seen close to the surface. Length 2m (80in).

Declining numbers Over the last 80 years, the pressure of fishing has caused stocks of many rays to fall dramatically. The problem is compounded by the fact that young rays are unusually large when they hatch, and so they can be immediately caught in trawls and shrimp nets. The blue skate, for example, is 22cm (9in) long at hatching.

As its alternative name of common skate implies, the blue skate used to be a popular specimen fish for anglers, but it is now among the most threatened of all our rays. Angling organisations have removed it from their lists to encourage anglers to return it to the sea if they catch one. Unfortunately, this is unlikely to stop the decline since most of the blue skates caught nowadays are taken as bycatches in commercial trawling. As yet, there is no method of preventing this from happening.

As an example of the decline of this fish, records for 1902 state that the blue skate was abundant in all parts of the Irish Sea. Today, the annual catch for the whole of the Irish Sea is just one or two fishes.

The story is much the same for other British rays. In 1938 the total catch for all ray and skate species was 17,475 tonnes; by 1992 this figure had fallen dramatically to around 4000 tonnes. All the signs are that this decline will continue due to increased fishing pressures, and the blue skate could soon disappear altogether from our waters.

four and fifteen months. The egg-cases, usually laid in shallow water, are stuck to stones and shells, but they can often be seen washed up on the shore. They are similar to the mermaid's purses of dogfishes, except that they have a pointed horn at each corner, rather than coiled tendrils.

Egg-laying can take place any time between March and August, and the cases are most commonly seen on the shore in late summer and autumn.

For the first few days after hatching, the young ray lives on the yolk inside the egg. Thereafter, it begins feeding on small bottom-dwelling crustaceans such as shrimps.

Slow to mature Rays take an exceptionally long time to mature. This, plus the fact that they lay far fewer eggs than bony fishes, makes them extremely vulnerable to over-fishing. For example, each herring lays thousands or even millions of eggs in a year and the young fishes reach maturity in two or three years. Compare these figures with those of rays. The roker becomes sexually mature at nine years and lays about 140 eggs a year; the blonde and spotted rays mature at the same age but lay only 70 eggs a year; and the blue skate matures at eleven years and lays just 40 eggs a year.

This reproductive pattern makes rays vulnerable to over-fishing by man—as are some marine mammals, particularly whales and seals.

Right: Rays lay their eggs inside cases known as 'mermaid's purses'. The cases are laid in shallow water stuck on to shells or stones, but they are often washed up on beaches.

Below: Incubation takes between four and fifteen months. For the first few days after hatching, the young ray survives on a yolk-sac attached to itself.

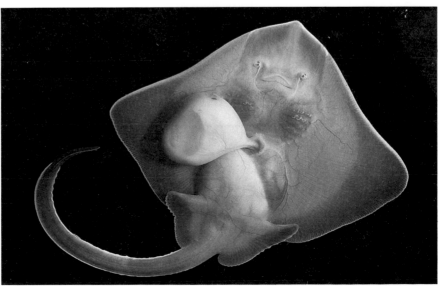

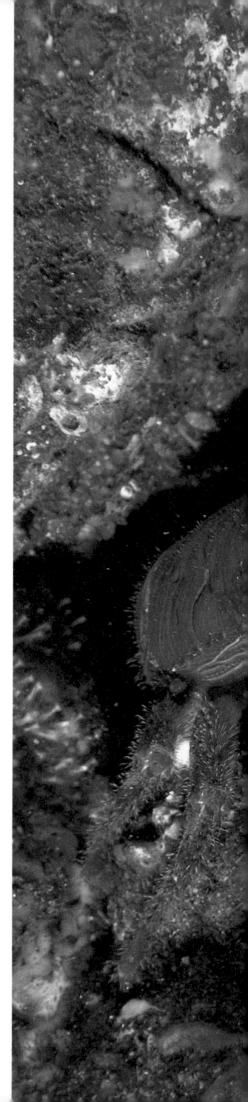

Invertebrates of the open sea and sea-bed

The great variety of life in the sea ranges from the simplest of single-celled animals drifting in the plankton to the highly intelligent and complex dolphins. In between is a wealth of different forms, most of them invertebrates (animals without backbones).

In the open ocean, surface waters teem with plankton – the term comes from the Greek meaning 'that which is made to wander'. Organisms specially adapted for life there include comb jellies, jellyfishes and many small crustaceans, as well as the young stages of bottom-dwelling creatures. When these animals come to settle on the sea-bed, they find a vast range of habitats to choose from. And they do choose – guided by gravity, light and dark, by the texture of the potential settlement surface and by the presence of others of their kind. Some, such as sponges, corals, barnacles and sea squirts, attach to a spot where they will remain for the rest of their lives – which are likely to be short if they have made a mistake in their choice. Others, such as the molluscs (snails, cockles, sea slugs and their relatives) are capable of limited migration, while the crustaceans (crabs, lobsters and their relatives) migrate considerable distances to breed or move into new habitats when mature. The molluscs include a remarkable group, the cephalopods, made up of the squid, octopus and cuttlefish.

Some of these invertebrates are commercially exploited. The crustaceans are probably the largest group to find their way to the fishmonger's slab and a great deal is therefore known about their biology. Much of that knowledge has been gained by remote sampling of the sea-bed using grabs, dredges and trawls. However, these instruments provide a poor picture of sea-bed life and cannot take samples in the rocky areas close to the shores. In recent years diving has allowed marine biologists to explore underwater areas and to study the enormous variety of marine life which occurs around our coasts. The richest sites are those with the widest range of habitats within a small area, particularly those in the south-west of the British Isles.

Below: The strange-looking cuttlefish, a relative of the octopus and the squid, is a streamlined, rapidly swimming and extremely efficient predator of small fishes and crustaceans. It can be found around much of the coastline of Britain.

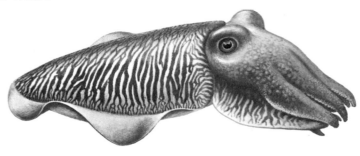

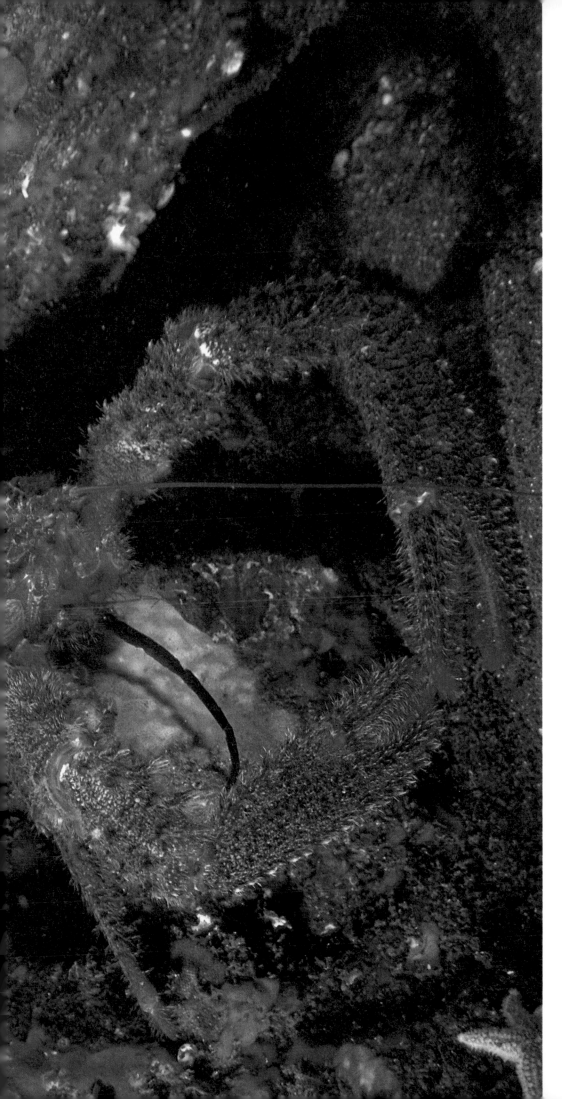

CHECKLIST
This checklist is a guide to some of the invertebrates you can find in the sea. Although you will not see them all in the same place, you should be able to spot many of them in a range of habitats from sea-bed sand and mud to open sea. The species listed in **bold** *type are described in detail.*

Arrow worms
Comb jellies
Common lobster
Common octopus
Corals
Cuttlefishes
Edible crab
Jellyfishes
Krill shrimp
Lesser octopus
Mantis shrimp
Marine plankton
Norway lobster
Opossum shrimp
Prawns
Sea anemones
Sea fans
Sea firs
Sea mats
Sea slugs
Sea snails
Sea squirts
Spider crabs
Sponges
Squat lobsters
Squid
Starfishes

Left: The squat lobster, with its luminous blue and orange markings, hides itself under crevices during the day, out of sight of predatory fishes and octopuses. It emerges at night to feed.

MARINE PLANKTON

Plankton – semi-transparent organisms – are wide-ranging and drift or float at the mercy of the sea. Viewed under a microscope, some reveal bold colours and bizarre shapes.

Plant plankton is divided into two groups – dinoflagellates and diatoms. The cell content of both groups includes the green pigment chlorophyll that is vital for photosynthesis.

Dinoflagellates are often very small single-celled organisms that bear one or more beating hair-like structures known as flagellae. The flagellae help them to make small movements in the water, but are not powerful enough to counteract currents. The phyto-plankton may be of bizarre appearance, like the anchor-shaped *Ceratium* which measures up to 0.4mm in length. The strange shapes and extensions of their bodies help the plants to float and catch the water currents which then waft them around.

The second principal group, the diatoms, are often large and may be composed of a number of cells arranged end to end to form a chain. *Chaetoceros* is a diatom with chains that may be up to 0.07mm in diameter and much longer. They also have strange extensions to help flotation, although they lack the moving flagellae of the dinoflagellates.

Buoyancy aids Phytoplankton can also have additional aids to floating; for example, globules of oil or fat stored inside the cells which make the organisms lighter than the surrounding water and therefore more buoyant. Although they cannot control their destiny in the sea, some kinds are able to adjust their vertical position in the water. The dinoflagellates are stimulated by light and

Above: This shrimp-like creature is an euphausiid, one of the larger members of the marine plankton, reaching about 15mm ($\frac{1}{2}$in) in length. Still larger euphausiids form the Antarctic krill on which the giant whales feed.

Below: Radiolaria and diatoms are beautiful but rarely seen members of the plant plankton. Radiolaria can look like miniature sputniks, with spherical bodies, sculptured shells and rods radiating outwards.

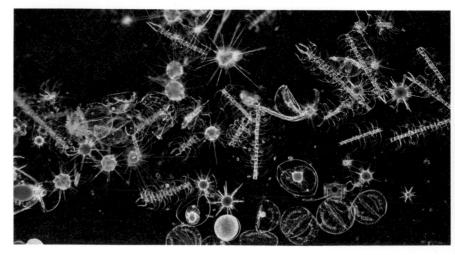

swim towards it by using their beating flagellae. Therefore, the dinoflagellates, and some other phytoplankton, move up towards the surface by day and sink down in the water at night.

Full and part-time plankton The animal plankton, known as zooplankton, is very diverse and includes representatives of many groups of animals. They range in size from microscopic to animals as large as the lion's mane jellyfish (*Cyanea*).

Zooplankton also includes temporary as well as permanent members. Many of the bottom-dwelling invertebrates, as well as the fish, reproduce by means of a larval phase, which become the temporary members of the zooplankton. The larva is generally very different in shape and life-style from the parent, and it remains with the plankton until it is an adult. This is an ideal way for cumbersome, slow-moving bottom-dwellers to disperse and for young animals to grow up without competing with their parents for food or living space.

The permanent members of the plankton include some conspicuous organisms: jelly-fishes, comb jellies, worms, sea-snails and sea-slugs, many types of crustaceans including krill and copepods, arrow worms and salps. These are diverse animals but they do all have features in common. These include mechanisms to make them buoyant, such as oil droplets, rafts of bubbles or accumulations of light substances in their bodies, and they are generally transparent or near colourless in order to make them inconspicuous to predators.

Filter feeders Phytoplankton forms the basis of the plankton food chains or food webs, and it is grazed by a variety of animals. Important grazers include the small crustacean copepods, which range from

In winter, the levels of phytoplankton in the sea drop because the plants are affected by the short daylight periods and low temperatures. In summer, the daylight hours increase and the phytoplankton levels rise sharply, providing more food for grazers belonging to the zooplankton, such as the copepod and crustacea larvae (above). As a result, the zooplankton population increases until, with the onset of winter, the whole cycle repeats itself again.

Below: A selection of the larger zooplankton found in the sea. *Beroe,* the comb jelly, may reach up to 10cm (4in) long. *Salpa democratica,* with tentacles up to 30cm (11¾in) long, is sometimes found in chains of individuals.

about 0.3 to 3mm in length. They filter the microscopic plants from the sea water as it passes between their mouthparts, which act like a sieve. Along with the planktonic larvae of barnacles and other bottom-dwelling crustaceans, they form an important group of grazing organisms.

The crustaceans are not the only filter feeders. The strange salps, looking rather like floating sea-squirts, have a sophisticated filtration mechanism. Salps such as *Salpa* and *Dolium* are able to extract the smallest plants from the phytoplankton, some of which are minute organisms less than 0.075mm in diameter.

Planktonic predators and prey All these grazing animals are, in their turn, food for the carnivorous plankton, or for the non-planktonic carnivores such as the herring which feeds largely on copepods. Salps may be snatched from the sea by birds such as terns, while krill are eaten by whales such as the massive blue whale.

The zooplankton includes a number of creatures that are effective carnivores. These range from the small medusae of the hydroids to the large jellyfish. Both these types of animals catch food with their trailing tentacles armed with stinging cells; the size of the prey can vary from copepods to fish, according to the size of the predator. Comb jellies like *Beroe,* once believed to be close relatives of the sea-anemones and jellyfish, are not equipped with stinging cells. Instead their trailing tentacles, which can be let out and hauled in like fishing lines, bear lasso cells which ensnare small swimming animals like copepods and larvae. So efficient are the comb jellies that they can compete effectively with herring for prey.

Some zooplankton have elaborate mechanisms for detecting the whereabouts of their food. The tiny arrow worms like *Sagitta* detect water-borne vibrations generated by the swimming appendages of crustaceans. Arrow worms are attracted by these vibrations and use the wave patterns as a guide for their sense organs to track down the prey which they finally seize with their minute but vice-like jaws.

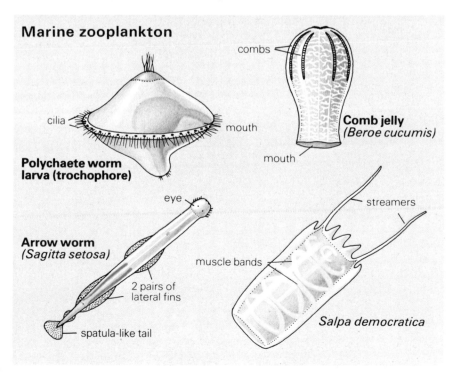

Marine zooplankton

combs

cilia

mouth

Comb jelly (*Beroe cucumis*)

mouth

Polychaete worm larva (trochophore)

eye

streamers

Arrow worm (*Sagitta setosa*)

muscle bands

2 pairs of lateral fins

spatula-like tail

Salpa democratica

STUNNING JELLYFISH

A jellyfish performs a unique dual role: it stuns prey with its stinging tentacles and at the same time harbours fish seeking protection from other predators under its umbrella-like 'bell' of jelly.

Jellyfish live in the open sea, both at the surface and at considerable depths. A few species – the stalked jellyfishes – attach themselves to rocks. About 12 species of jellyfish are recorded in British waters; the most familiar is the common jellyfish which you can sometimes find stranded on beaches.

Stinging tentacles The common jellyfish has an umbrella-shaped body fringed by short tentacles at the edges. These are equipped with stinging cells. Underneath and towards the centre of the body hang four arms which surround the mouth. The mouth is the route into and out of the body, and serves as an anus as well as a reproductive opening.

The jellyfish can extend and retract the tentacles at the edge of its body. These are smaller in the common jellyfish than in some other species (for example the lion's mane jellyfish) which also have small flap-like lappets interspersed with the tentacles.

The tentacles are used to catch prey such as small fish and swimming crustaceans which may accidentally collide with it. Jellyfish do not actively pursue their prey but depend on such chance encounters. The stinging cells give powerful stings. Even jellyfish stranded on the beach can inflict an unpleasant wound if you touch it. The tentacles stun the prey and pass it on to the central arms which then manoeuvre it into the mouth.

The mouth opens into a central gastric cavity with a complex arrangement of digest-

Above: The common jellyfish (*Aurelia aurita*) reaches 25cm (10in) or more in diameter. It has an umbrella-shaped body – a feature of many jellyfish – which is transparent with a bluish tint. It is commonly found in the English Channel and the North Sea.
Below: The compass jellyfish (*Chrysaora hysoscella*) has a similar shaped body to the common jellyfish, but it is 30cm (12in) in diameter. It is regularly found in the English Channel.

ive canals leading away from it. These may be visible through the top of the body. Fluid is pumped round the canals, distributing food to all parts of the animal.

The strange thing is that some fish – such as the young of horse mackerel and scad as well as of whiting and haddock – sometimes shelter under the bells of jellyfish, where they get some protection from their own predators. These fish appear to be immune to the stinging of the tentacles. They feed on the developing reproductive organs of the jellyfish, and may even take refuge right inside its body. Several species of small sideways-flattened crustaceans, called amphipods, may live in association with adult jellyfish, swimming about them for most of their life.

The powerful stinging cells deter would-be predators as well as catching prey. However, jellyfish do have enemies of their own. The surface floating snail catches and eats them, as does the large sun fish and the leathery turtle.

How they move Although jellyfish can swim they are at the mercy of water currents which control their distribution. All they can do by their own efforts is to move up and down in the water and control their orientation. A simple arrangement of muscles allows the jellyfish to contract its bell-shaped body to expel the water from underneath and give it lift in the water. Other small muscles control the bending and flexing of each of the small

Jelly texture

The body is composed of two layers of cells, with a thick mass of jelly (mesoglea) in between. This jelly accounts for over 90% of the total volume of some jellyfish. It also provides an important elastic framework that supports the body—a kind of 'skeleton' against which the muscles can work.

Haliclystus auricula, 2.5cm (1in) high.

Pelagia noctiluca, not more than 10cm (4in) in diameter.

Lion's mane (*Cyanea capillata*) 45cm (17in).

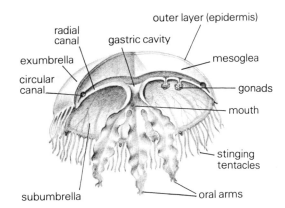

outer layer (epidermis)
radial canal
gastric cavity
exumbrella
circular canal
mesoglea
gonads
mouth
stinging tentacles
subumbrella
oral arms

lobes or lappets that lie round the edge of the body and help the jellyfish to swim.

The co-ordination of the various muscle systems rests with the jellyfish's simple nervous system. This comprises several net-like arrangements of nerve cells that stimulate muscles round the body, and individual systems such as those controlling one lappet, or those associated with the oral arms and feeding.

The animal keeps the right way up in the water with four balance organs (statocysts), and the typical regular pulsations of the body are governed by a pace-maker in the nervous system which initiates each wave of contraction.

Some common species Among the jellyfish you are most likely to come across is the compass jellyfish (*Chrysaora hysoscella*); it has brown and cream radiating marks on top of its bell which resemble the dial of a ship's compass—hence the name.

The yellow sea blubber, or lion's mane jellyfish, (*Cyanea capillata*), has numerous long trailing tentacles which resemble a lion's

mane and make it easy to distinguish. It is brick red to brown in colour. This was the species Sir Arthur Conan Doyle, author of the Sherlock Holmes stories, described in one of his tales 'The Lion's Mane'. There is also a closely related species that is bluish in colour.

The more mushroom-shaped bell-like body of the jellyfish *Pelagia noctiluca* is brownish with a slightly warty appearance. It also has luminous structures in the body which produce flashes of bright light if the animal is disturbed.

Another jellyfish, *Rhizostoma pulmo*, has a tall domed umbrella. The edge of its body carries many small lappets but no tentacles, and the eight arms round its mouth are frilly and ornamented.

Not all British jellyfish are floating, open-sea animals. There are several species which attach themselves by means of a holdfast 'foot' to a plant or rock. The body of one of the stalked jellyfish *Haliclystus auricula* is trumpet-shaped and its tentacles are gathered together into groups on the ends of eight short arms. Stalked jellyfish cannot swim, but move by 'looping' rather like a leech.

Impostors Jellyfish have often been confused with the adult (medusa) stage of their relatives the seafirs (hydroids). The medusa stage of some hydroids looks like jellyfish, but has a shelf-like membrane around the inside of the bell. True jellyfish do not have this feature. One special type of floating hydroid—the Portuguese man o'war—famous for its powerful tentacles, also looks quite like a jellyfish with its gas-filled float. It sometimes appears around British shores although its normal habitats are the waters of the Mediterranean and the Atlantic. The Portuguese man-o'-war is actually a colony of different individuals, each with its own function.

A complex life cycle

There are both male and female jellyfish, but they have no mating behaviour. The adult (1) usually has four sex organs (gonads), which in the common jellyfish are horseshoe-shaped. When the gonads are ripe, sperm is released into the sea and drawn into the female's body to fertilise the eggs in her ovary. The egg develops into a small mobile embryo (2) which settles on the seabed. Here it develops into a polyp-like structure called a scyphistoma (3). As this grows it divides by a process called strobilation (4), which produces larvae (ephyra) (5). These larvae drift with surface plankton.

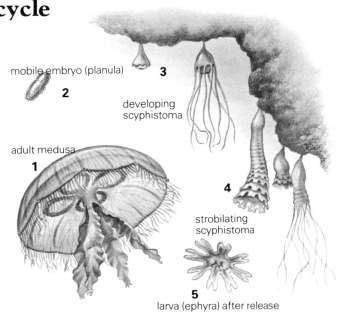

mobile embryo (planula)
2
3
developing scyphistoma
adult medusa
1
4
strobilating scyphistoma
5
larva (ephyra) after release

The coelenterates are animals with bodies composed of two layers of cells, separated by a layer of jelly. They have no anus; the mouth is surrounded by tentacles with stinging cells for food capture and defence. They are sedentary or free-swimming, solitary or colonial animals.

1 Class Scyphoza—Jellyfish. Floating umbrella-like adults, small stationary polyp stage. Marine only, not colonial.

2 Class Hydrozoa—Hydroids (or seafirs) plus allies. Adults sedentary, attached to sea or river bed as polyps. Mobile medusa (small jellyfish) stage. Mainly marine and colonial.

3 Class Anthozoa—Corals, sea anemones. Sedentary adults as polyps on seabed; no medusa stage. Solitary or colonial. Marine only.

CORALS: MARINE 'FLOWER' ANIMALS

Although most corals inhabit tropical seas and form the major part of coral reefs, a few species are found around the British Isles. Like their close relatives the sea-anemones, some corals bear a superficial resemblance to flowers.

Above: *Alcyonium glomeratum* is one of the soft corals found below the low-water mark around the British Isles. It is distinguished from *A. digitatum* by its more slender, more numerous fingers. It is typically blood-red.

The word 'coral' is used to describe several related groups of animals within the phylum Coelenterata. Until recently sea-anemones were the coelenterates which had received the greatest attention since they are the most easily found, occurring in shallower waters than corals. However, the growth of SCUBA diving has stimulated interest in British corals

and provided new information.

Almost all corals are colonial, comprising numerous individuals called polyps – each resembling a small sea-anemone – attached to a common skeleton. According to the type of coral, the structure of the skeleton varies in composition from calcareous, through keratinous (horny), to one with a fleshy nature in which limestone spicules are embedded. The skeleton gives the colony its overall shape.

A few species of coral are solitary, consisting of a single anemone-like polyp sitting on a hard skeleton. Corals remain fixed in one place as adults, and are thus less mobile than the sea-anemones, which can creep slowly about when necessary.

Although an individual coral animal closely resembles a sea-anemone, in some species it may be very small – only about 1mm in height. It has a cylindrical body with a mouth at one end leading into the body cavity. A ciliated groove (lined with fine hairs) directs a current of water into the cavity, providing oxygen and inflating the polyp by hydrostatic pressure. The body cavity is divided inwardly by partitions called mesenteries. The mouth is surrounded by a ring of tentacles which are used for catching prey and which can be retracted at the onset of danger.

Attack and defence Like sea-anemones and jellyfishes, corals are well supplied with stinging cells (called nematocysts), particularly on the tentacles. When these are touched, an elaborately coiled, often barbed, thread shoots out, penetrates the prey and injects a poison. In addition to the stinging cells being used to catch the small invertebrates and plankton on which corals feed, they may also be used for defence.

There are no corals poisonous to man in British waters, but in tropical waters care has to be taken to avoid touching the stinging fire corals, which can inflict a painful rash. A few species of coral have non-poisonous threads which ensnare prey by their sticky nature.

Coral reproduction Coral colonies increase in size by budding off new polyps. Corals can also reproduce sexually. In sexual reproduction eggs and sperm are released from the polyps into the sea where fertilisation takes place. A ciliated larva is produced which swims freely for a short time before settling on the sea bottom and developing into a new polyp. This buds repeatedly to form further polyps, and the bases of the polyps secrete the skeleton.

Types of coral There are two main groups of coelenterates containing corals. One group, the octocorals, includes the soft corals, the tropical precious corals used in jewellery, and the horny corals or sea fans. They are nearly always colonial and have small polyps characterised by eight pinnate or feathery tentacles.

The soft corals have no continuous, solid skeleton. Instead, they have limestone spicules embedded in the soft living tissue secreted by the polyps. The precious corals and the horny corals have skeletons of limestone or a more flexible horny material.

The second group, the hexacorals, includes black corals (the tropical semi-precious corals used in jewellery), and the true stony or reef-building corals. They have larger polyps with unbranched tentacles characteristically arranged in multiples of six, sometimes in large numbers. Although most species are colonial, there are also a number of solitary ones. They have stony skeletons on which the polyps sit, and in tropical reef-building species they form large branching or rock-like lumps of limestone.

Soft corals Like sea-anemones, soft corals sometimes occur locally in British waters in huge numbers. The best known is dead man's fingers (*Alcyonium digitatum*), which bears a passing resemblance to its common name when washed up dead on the beach. Under water, however, the fleshy projections are white or brown, or during reproduction a pinkish white. The feathery tentacles may be about 10mm (½in) in length. *A. digitatum* is

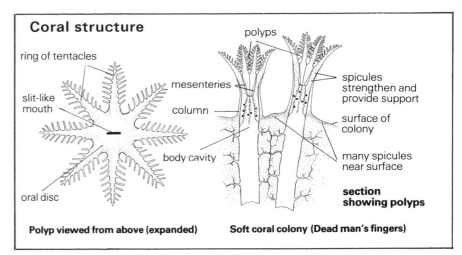

Coral structure

ring of tentacles
slit-like mouth
oral disc

polyps
mesenteries
column
body cavity

spicules strengthen and provide support
surface of colony
many spicules near surface

section showing polyps

Polyp viewed from above (expanded)　　Soft coral colony (Dead man's fingers)

often found attached to pier supports or to rocks in sheltered places on the lower shore around most of the British Isles. Colonies reach about 12–20cm (5–8in) in length.

Two other soft corals are found around the British Isles but they are limited to just a few places and occur only below the low-water mark. *Alcyonium glomeratum* is distinguished from *A. digitatum* by its relatively slender and more numerous fingers; it is typically blood-red or rust-coloured and only occasionally pale orange or yellowish. Large colonies reach 50cm (20in) in size. It is found only in sheltered, dark sites – usually quite deep (10–50m or 33–160ft) – on the south and west coasts of the British Isles, particularly in the waters of Devon and Cornwall, but also as far north as the coast of mid-west Scotland.

Parerythropodium coralloides, the second soft coral, is a species found mostly in the Mediterranean and on the west coast of France, but it also occurs locally on the west coast of Britain as far north as the Isle of Mull, occasionally in large numbers. It has small lobes and resembles species of *Alcyonium*, but

Above: Individual coral animals are known as polyps. Each polyp has a mouth at one end leading into a body cavity divided by mesenteries. The polyps of colonial corals, such as these, are linked to each other. The mouth of each polyp is surrounded by a ring of tentacles which are used to catch prey.

Below: The Devonshire cup coral (*Caryophyllia smithii*), with the polyps expanded. This species is comparatively common on the west coast of the British Isles as far north as Shetland and Orkney. The Devonshire cup coral is solitary, with each polyp resting on its own cup-shaped stony skeleton rather than being connected to other polyps.

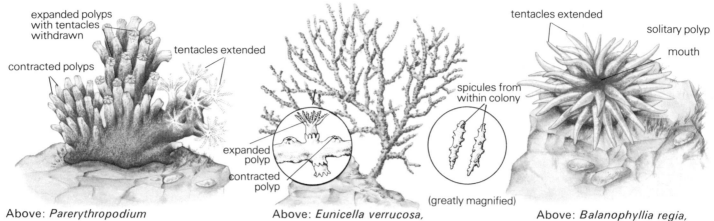

Above: *Parerythropodium coralloides*, a colonial soft coral.

Above: *Eunicella verrucosa*, a colonial sea fan.

Above: *Balanophyllia regia*, a solitary coral.

Below: *Swiftia pallida* is one of the only two sea fans (horny corals) known in British waters. The colony grows in one plane—hence its name—with the flat surface facing the current so that there is a maximum area for catching food borne by the current. The sea fans have a horny internal skeleton which grows in a branching fashion, with the polyps sited along the branches. *S. pallida* is found on the west coast of Scotland at depths of 18-60m (60-200ft).

it often grows as an encrustation on rocks, usually in deep water. Its colour varies from white to deep red, but most British specimens are pale pink, often with a ring of white on the polyp just below the tentacles which gives the colony a spangled effect.

Sea fans Sea fans or horny corals differ from soft corals in having a horny internal skeleton which grows in a tree-like branching fashion and is fastened to a rock or some other firm surface. The polyps grow along the branches. The colonies grow in one plane—which is why they are also known as sea fans—and the flat surface generally faces the prevailing current so that there is a maximum area for catching food. Only two sea fans are

known in British waters, *Eunicella verrucosa* and *Swiftia pallida*.

The better known of these is *E. verrucosa* as it is often collected, either for decorating marine aquaria or as a souvenir. When dried and mounted it makes an attractive ornament. It grows at depths of 20-100m (10-50 fathoms). Colonies reach about 30cm (12in) in height and branch profusely in one plane, although bushy forms are also sometimes found. On the west coast of Britain both pink and white colonies are found, but on the south coast colonies are pink.

The second sea fan, *Swiftia pallida*, is found at several sites on the west coast of Scotland at any depth from 18 to 60m (60-200ft). It is

The corals used for making jewellery belong to the genus *Corallium* and are well known for their spectacular delicate red or pink skeletons. *C. rubrum,* the species found in the Mediterranean, has been collected by man since the Neolithic period some 5000 years ago. Although its most important use has always been for jewellery and decorative purposes, the Romans used to grind it to a powder which was taken as medicine, and in the Middle Ages it was believed to possess various magical properties. Corals grow very slowly, and as a result Mediterranean coral, especially, has been drastically over-collected. It is now found only at great depths—more than 50m (160ft)—in such places as off the coasts of Tunisia and Sardinia. Most of the coral used in jewellery today comes from the Pacific Ocean, and it is collected and carved with great artistry and skill by the Japanese and Taiwanese before being sold all over the world.

usually whitish or pale grey and the colony is smaller and less branched than *E. verrucosa..*

In the more popular SCUBA diving areas—all around the Scilly Isles, for example—*Eunicella verrucosa* has been rather badly over-collected in the past, but scientists now think that the populations may be recovering at last, since divers are being discouraged from collecting these attractive corals as marine curios.

Stony corals Unlike tropical species, no British stony corals form huge reefs. They are, for the most part, solitary and seldom branch. One of the better known species, the attractive Devonshire cup coral (*Caryophyllia smithii*), is comparatively common on the west coast as far north as Shetland and Orkney. Unlike most stony corals, it is solitary (the polyps are not connected to each other), and it closely resembles sea-anemones, apart from the fact that the polyp sits on a cup-shaped stony skeleton. Several polyps may be found on one rock. They have up to 80 translucent tentacles varying in colour from brown, red, orange or pink to white, or a vivid emerald green. The tentacles have many stinging cells, and end in white knobs. When the soft parts are withdrawn, the skeleton, about 1cm (½in) high, can be seen with its radiating septa (walls).

Different forms of Devonshire cup coral are found at different depths. The shallower water form is found attached to rocks, shells and worm tubes in shaded places and deep pools down to about 100m (330ft) and it has a more or less cylindrical coral skeleton. The deep water form occurs down to a depth of about 1000m (3300ft) and has a coral cup in the form of an inverted cone with a narrow base.

The attractive scarlet and gold star-coral was first discovered in a rock pool near

Above: Dead man's fingers (*Alcyonium digitatum*), shown here with tentacles retracted. It is sometimes found in large numbers in the shallow waters off the coast of Britain. The common name derives from the coral's appearance when it is washed up dead on the beach with the knobbly projections and feathery tentacles no longer attached. The example pictured below shows the variable colour of this species. Here, the tentacles are fully extended.

Ilfracombe by the Victorian naturalist Philip Gosse who named it *Balanophyllia regia* because of its royal colours. Young specimens have a yellow body with yellow tentacles, but as they age they become progressively redder until they attain the rich scarlet colour found in adults. It has up to 48 tentacles without the terminal knobs of the Devonshire cup coral. The skeleton also differs in that it is finely perforated and the radiating partitions show a distinct six-rayed effect. The scarlet and gold star-coral is not very common, being found only below low tide level to about 10m (33ft), attached to rocks in caves and gullies in the extreme south-west off the coasts of Devon, Cornwall and Dyfed.

THREE SHRIMPS OF THE SEA

Many more types of shrimp live round our coast than the ones that end up on our tables. Three such are the krill, opossum and mantis shrimps.

Above: A shoal of opossum shrimps in the waters off Orkney. Like krill shrimps, they are an important food for many marine animals. One species is made into a paste called 'chervé' to be used as bait for mullet.

Below: A mantis shrimp, with its stalked eyes at the front of its head and its large spined claw, seen here folded and ready for striking. At the back of the shrimp, along its jointed abdomen, are five pairs of swimmerets.

The North Atlantic is home to six species of krill shrimp, though the layman is only likely to see them among catches of fish landed on the quaysides of our larger fishing ports. Most krill shrimps have no common name but the conspicuous eyes of one species, *Meganyctiphanes norvegica*, is well known to Scottish fishermen, who gave it the Gaelic name 'suil dhu', meaning 'black eyes'. These eyes are used chiefly for sensing changes in the light level–the species lives at depths where only blue-green light can penetrate and the eyes are, therefore, sensitive only to these colours.

Krill anatomy Just behind the eye of a krill shrimp lies the head region, which is covered with a thin shell (the carapace) that leaves the

gills beneath exposed and prominent. The front limbs are thin, lack claws and are divided into an inner and an outer branch; the outer is whip-like and used by the krill shrimp to direct water currents into a 'food groove' lying between these limbs. There are seven visible pairs of limbs, and an eighth pair which is reduced and cannot be seen. Food particles––smaller planktonic organisms and detritus derived from the sea-bed–are strained off by numerous hairs covering the front limbs and the other mouthparts.

The abdomen is flexible and consists of six segments. Five of these each have a pair of limbs called swimmerets that are used for swimming and to pass currents of water over the gills.

A particularly interesting feature of the krill shrimp's anatomy is the luminescent organs distributed on the eyes, at the base of the seventh pair of front limbs, and between each of the first four pairs of swimmerets. Except for those in the eyes, all of these organs contain a lens, light-producing cells and a reflecting pigment. The light produced collectively by the enormous shoals of krill found in the dark depths of the sea is sometimes brighter than the intensity of sunlight reaching these depths–even at mid-day.

Vertical migrations An interesting behaviour trait of krill shrimps is their habit of making regular vertical migrations. In the case of *Meganyctiphanes*, which has been well studied, the animals live near the sea-bed by day but begin to rise towards the surface of the sea as dusk approaches.

Such migrations allow the krill shrimps to vary their diet, since the food available to them differs with depth. Furthermore, the downward migration allows them to avoid predators while the upward migration allows them to spread to other areas of the sea via water currents.

Life-cycle The majority of krill shrimps shed their eggs into the sea where they hatch as minute so-called 'nauplii', looking quite unlike their parents. They pass through five larval stages, becoming progressively more shrimp-like in appearance, until in the post-larval stage all the legs are developed and the

shrimp takes on the shape of the adult.

Krill shrimps are of considerable importance in the food chains of many higher marine animals–indeed, the blue whale feeds exclusively on them. They also form the major food for a great number of commercially important fishes. Consequently the economics of many fisheries depend upon krill supplies.

Opossum shrimps This group of crustaceans resembles krill shrimps in some respects but the ones found in inshore waters are distinguished by a combination of features: the front limbs are developed for swimming rather than feeding and the roughly cylindrical abdomen bears small, hardly functional swimmerets. But the most important feature, and one that separates opossum shrimps from all others, is that the female develops a brood pouch, called a marsupium, in which she incubates her eggs.

A common inshore species is *Praunus flexuosus*, one of three species sharing the common name of chameleon prawn because of their ability to change colour. This species can be found in considerable numbers in rock pools and among beds of eel-grass. When disturbed the shrimps escape by springing backwards very quickly; the movement can be so sudden and forceful that they may be thrown out of the water.

Chameleon prawns, along with other opossum shrimps, are filter feeders but they can capture small moving animals and they also feed on carrion.

The majority of opossum shrimps are marine but a few species live in brackish water and one or two in fresh water. Of the marine forms, most occur in shallow waters, but the large *Gnathophausia ingens* (length 16cm/6½in) descends to depths of 3500m (1800 fathoms) in the Atlantic.

Breeding habits The chameleon prawn, *P. flexuosus*, mates at night, the males being attracted to females that have recently moulted. In British waters breeding takes place between February and the end of September. The eggs are incubated in the female's marsupium for about three weeks, in the summer between 27 and 40 being brooded at one time. As the year progresses, the number of eggs becomes lower and the incubation period longer. A fully grown female may produce three broods in a year, and lives for about 18 months. The young lack a larval stage and, when released from the marsupium, look much like the adults.

Mantis shrimps Mantis shrimps–so-called after their mantis-like second pair of legs–are uncommon in British waters, the majority of species being tropical or subtropical. They are predatory creatures, living in burrows or just beneath the surface of the sand, and they use their mantis-like limbs (which are equipped with sharp spines) to spear soft-bodied prey. The shrimp remains concealed until it selects its victim, which it does by sight; then it darts out with phenomenal speed and strikes

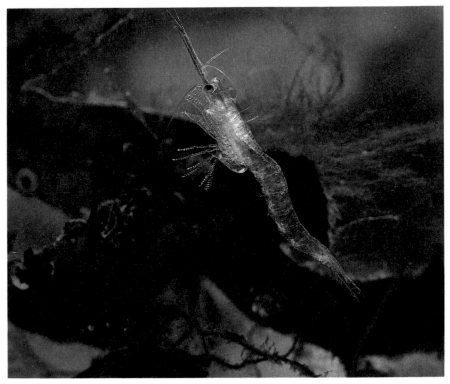

its victim with its claw. This strike is one of the fastest animal movements known, taking between four and eight thousandths of a second, so that the claw itself moves at a speed of more than 10m (33ft) a second. The impaled prey is pulled backwards into the burrow and torn apart by the mantis shrimp's mouthparts.

Above: The chameleon prawn, *Praunus flexuosus*, has a characteristic manner of swimming: it hangs almost vertically in the water. Notice the developing brood pouch on this female.

Three types of shrimps

Krill, opossum and mantis shrimps have similar body structures: two prominent eyes in front of a carapace that covers all (or most) of the thoracic or body segments, and finally a segmented abdomen. Both thoracic and abdominal segments bear limbs, which may be used for swimming, feeding or grooming. Krill shrimps can be distinguished from the other two groups by a combination of exposed gills and uniform front limbs; opossum shrimps by their extremely small swimmerets; and mantis shrimps by their distinctive large claw.

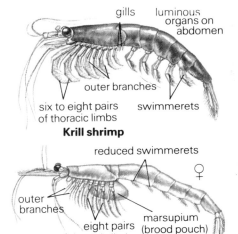

Krill shrimp

gills, luminous organs on abdomen, outer branches, six to eight pairs of thoracic limbs, swimmerets

Opossum shrimp

reduced swimmerets, outer branches, eight pairs of thoracic limbs, marsupium (brood pouch)

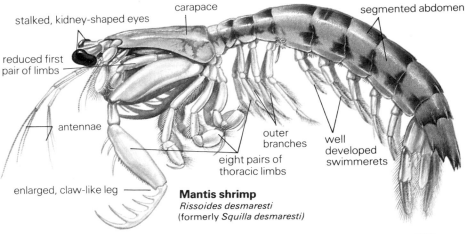

stalked, kidney-shaped eyes, carapace, segmented abdomen, reduced first pair of limbs, antennae, outer branches, eight pairs of thoracic limbs, well developed swimmerets, enlarged, claw-like leg

Mantis shrimp
Rissoides desmaresti
(formerly *Squilla desmaresti*)

EDIBLE CRABS: SEA-BED MIGRANTS

The edible crab is one of the largest marine invertebrates found in Europe. This crustacean is a relative of the lobster, and around British coasts the two species often inhabit the same areas of rocky ground, where they compete for food and shelter.

The edible crab has a reputation as a scavenger, but this is misleading, for it also feeds on living prey such as small fishes and marine worms. Shellfish, such as mussels and barnacles, are easily crushed in its powerful claws. It is extremely voracious, and has a keen sense of smell which helps it to find its prey on the sea bottom.

Moulting the shell Crabs, like all crustaceans, are covered with a hard, rigid shell known as an exoskeleton. In order to grow, crabs have to cast these outer shells, made of calcified chitin. This is known as moulting, or ecdysis. During the first few years of life, when growth is rapid, a crab moults several times a year, but by the time it becomes sexually mature moulting may occur only once a year, or even less frequently.

Immediately after moulting, the crab has a soft shell. It absorbs water and swells, increasing in size across the back by as much as 20% or 30% in one moult. On average, an 8cm (3½in) male grows to 11.5cm (4½in) in one moult, and 14.5cm (5¾in) in the next. After a moult, the new shell slowly hardens and the

Above: An edible crab on the shore. This species (*Cancer pagurus*) forms an important source of food for man, and in 1989 the shellfishermen of Britain recorded a total catch of over 14,000 tonnes of crabs, valued at £14 million.

crab's body ceases to increase in size, until after the next moult.

Summer mating The sex of a crab can be easily determined. The female or hen crab has a broad abdomen (unlike lobsters, prawns and shrimps, a crab has an abdomen that is folded flat under the body). In contrast, the male or cock crab has a narrow abdomen, which fits tightly to the body. The claws of the male are also larger than those of a female of the same body size.

Mating occurs in inshore waters during the summer, immediately after the female crab has moulted and while she is in the soft-shelled condition. Prior to the moult, and for a period of up to a fortnight afterwards, the male stays close to the female, being attracted to her by a scent or pheromone, which she gives off during breeding time.

Immediately the female has cast her shell, mating takes place, and the male's sperms are introduced into the female's two sperm sacs. One supply of sperm may fertilise two or more batches of eggs, and so may be sufficient for at least the following year.

The eggs remain attached to the 'swimmerets' on the abdomen of the mother for about seven months. A crab with eggs is sometimes called a 'berried crab', and the number of eggs varies from half a million on a 12.5cm (5in) crab to three million on an 18cm (7in) crab.

Hatching and larvae Crabs usually select a soft sea-bed for spawning (extruding the eggs), often in deep water. This occurs during November or December. In the spring and summer following spawning, the 'berried' females move inshore, where the eggs hatch. Hatching times vary for the different stocks of crabs around our coasts, but the main periods are all between May and September.

The young larval crabs which emerge from the eggs have a shrimp-like appearance, and live among the free-floating plankton in the surface water layers for about a month. This period is a dispersal phase, because the larvae, which are extremely small (less than 2mm long), can be transported considerable distances by water movements from where they first hatched.

Crab migrations Investigations in the 1960s

Three stages of moulting

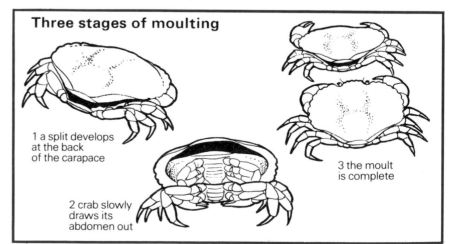

1 a split develops at the back of the carapace

2 crab slowly draws its abdomen out

3 the moult is complete

The sea-bed walk of the edible crab

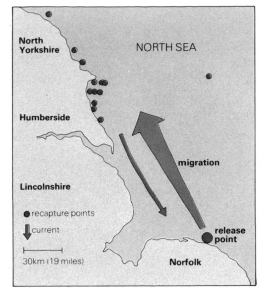

Long-distance migrations
A total of 1228 crabs were released in the Norfolk crab fisheries, known to be a good habitat for the animal. This map shows the 13 most distant recapture sites, corresponding to the longest migrations recorded in the Norfolk experiment (many other crabs were recaptured nearer the release point). This provided experimental evidence of the actual distance of the migration for the first time.

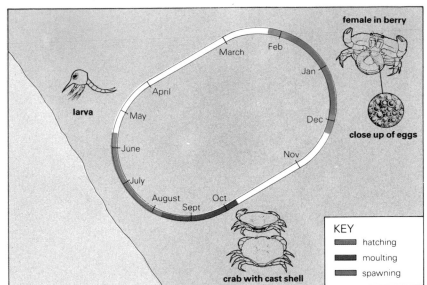

A circuitous journey
Moulting and mating take place during the autumn, when the crabs are close inshore. The female then migrates to deeper waters and softer sea-beds, since these provide a more suitable environment for the process of spawning, or extruding the eggs. With the eggs placed on her swimmerets (underneath her abdomen) she returns inshore, to arrive in time for hatching, which takes place in summer. While the young then drift back in the sea current to where the cycle began, the mother may possibly head for the deeper water to spawn a second time; it is possible that the more distant recaptures are of females that have been out to sea twice or more often, returning to a more northerly point each time.

and 1970s have revealed some interesting facts about the migration of crabs. A small tag, which is not lost when the crab casts its shell, was attached to a large number of crabs of both sexes. Each tag was numbered, and a record was kept of the size, sex and shell condition of each crab marked in this way. The crabs were then released in the sea. Fishermen who caught tagged crabs were rewarded if they returned the crabs, providing information on the date and place of recapture.

Some of the crabs, for example, were released on the Yorkshire coast. A total of 135 females were recaptured, and of these over 40% were found to have moved distances of 32km (20 miles) and over. Nearly all of these migrations were in a northerly direction, the crabs being caught in North Yorkshire, Durham, Northumberland or Scotland. The longest distance moved was by a female released near Flamborough Head, which was recaptured off Berwick (Northumberland) 16 months later, having moved 260km (163 miles). For male crabs, the results were different, and only 51 of those recaptured had moved distances of 32km (20 miles) or more.

The migration of the females can be seen to compensate for the effects of sea currents that move in the opposite direction. The mother moves northwards from a suitable habitat for crabs, so that the larvae will drift back to the same area when she has hatched them. She

thus ensures that, despite the sea current, as many as possible of her young will have a suitable habitat for their survival.

Crab fisheries In England there are three main crabbing areas—the coasts of Northumberland and Yorkshire, the south-west coast of Dorset, Devon and Cornwall, and the small but productive Norfolk fishery based off Cromer, Sheringham and Wells. Crabs are also plentiful on all coasts of Scotland, with traditional fisheries along the east coast. However, Shetland and Orkney now account for over 30% of Scottish crab landings, and catches from the Western Islands are increasing as stocks of crab, previously unexploited, are now being fished.

Below: A sizeable mature crab on a bed of seaweed. In Britain, both national and local regulations govern the size and condition of crabs that may be landed and sold. The national minimum landing size is 11.5cm (4½in) across the broadest part of the crab's back. In some areas, local regulations have raised the minimum size to 12.7cm (5in). In addition, national regulations prohibit the landing of both 'berried' and soft-shelled crabs.

WELL-CAMOUFLAGED SPIDER CRABS

Spider crabs are, to most people, the least familiar of British crabs – not because they are rare but because they are experts in camouflage, covering themselves with bits of seaweed and sponge, and 'wearing' sea-anemones.

Above: Many spider crabs camouflage themselves with organic material, some relying on plants or animals such as anemones to grow on them, whereas others collect pieces of sponge, seaweed or anything else suitable for the purpose. Here a species of spider crab, *Hyas araneus*, is gathering seaweed, which it chews before securing it in place. This species is found all around the coast of Britain. It grows to a length of 11 cm (4½in).

With their triangular bodies and, in some species, their long thin legs from which they get their common name, spider crabs form a distinct group among British crabs. In all species, the body becomes narrow towards the front and on some it extends forwards to form a 'beak'. The body shell (called the carapace), and sometimes the legs as well, are covered with spines and protuberances. These are a feature of spider crabs and may provide some protection against predators.

Sixteen species of spider crabs occur in waters around the British Isles. Most confine themselves to offshore waters, but a few extend their range into the intertidal region.

Masters of camouflage Many spider crabs are masters of camouflage, which they achieve by two methods, called active acquisition and passive acquisition.

In active acquisition, the crab gathers a covering of plant and animal growths from its surroundings, a process often known as 'masking'. Using its claws, the crab plucks small pieces of seaweed, sponge or other growths from the substrate and fixes them in place on its body or limbs, securing them by means of special hook-shaped hairs on its body surface. Often, the crab chews the pieces before securing them in place.

In passive acquisition, the crab becomes camouflaged as 'spores' of marine plants and larvae of animals settle on the shell and grow. Spider crabs are particularly vulnerable to these growths because they are lethargic, more or less sedentary animals, and also because they do not continue to cast their shells after reaching maturity; growths established on the final shell, therefore, are never discarded.

Their ability to acquire camouflage, combined with their relatively sedentary lifestyle and slow movements, make spider crabs very difficult for predators to detect.

Anemones for protection Some species of spider crab provide themselves with protection by associating with a species of sea-anemone, the snakelocks anemone. An example off parts of our coast is Leach's spider crab (*Inachus phalangium*). The crab sits with the rear of its shell against the anemone's column, which it sometimes grasps with its last pair of legs. In this position, the crab is almost totally hidden by the anemone's over-hanging and protective tentacles. Another species, the long-legged spider crab (*Macropodia rostrata*), has a similar association with the snakelocks anemone. It has been observed to tap the anemone with one of its second pair of legs; the anemone responds by raising its tentacles and expanding its column on that particular side, allowing the crab to adjust its position.

The relationship between the snakelocks anemone and a spider crab works both ways. The anemone protects the crab from preddators with its stinging tentacles, while the crab is immune to them – spider crabs have even been seen to crawl over the tentacles without harm. The anemone, on the other hand, benefits by seizing bits of food captured by the crab. In fact, the anemone often eats the greater share, with the crab feeding on the remains disgorged by its companion.

Grazers and scavengers Unlike many other crabs, spider crabs are not predators – they are too slow-moving for that. Instead they graze on algae and colonial animals such as sponges, or they scavenge.

At least one species, the long-legged spider crab (and possibly others in the genus *Macropodia*), has become specialised for feeding upon planktonic organisms. This crab attaches itself to the tips of weeds, hanging there by means of its hindmost pair of legs, which are spined and curved at the ends to give the animal a firm anchorage. Once anchored, the crab appears to sweep its front two pairs of legs through the water searching for food, which it captures with its claws.

Breeding and life-cycle The breeding habits of British spider crabs vary somewhat between different species. Females of the genus *Hyas*, for example the contracted crab (*Hyas coarctatus*), produce only one batch of eggs each year; these require 9-10 months to complete their development. Long-legged spider crabs, however, breed throughout the year and the eggs develop in just 12-15 weeks.

The eggs of spider crabs hatch into minute larvae about 2mm long. They are free-swimming and live in the upper regions of the sea, feeding on microscopic plankton. The larvae resemble shrimps and are known as zoeae. Compared with other crab species, spider crabs have a short larval life, the zoeae passing through only two stages before changing into a more crab-like stage called a megalop. This settles on the sea-bed and moults into a small crab that may show, even at this stage, some resemblance to the adult into which it will eventually grow.

Some British species Most British spider crabs are extremely small. For example, the long-legged spider crab has a body length of only 17mm ($\frac{2}{3}$in), with the scorpion spider crab slightly longer at 2.5cm (1in). Both are

Above: The largest British species of spider crab is the thornback, or spiny spider crab.
The thornback is found along southern coasts on sand and among rocks, from the lower shore down to a depth of about 50m (25 fathoms). Small specimens can be found in rock pools. The colour of its shell can vary from red or pink to white, and may be spotted. Its body length is up to 18cm (7in).

Right: Spider crabs are quite distinct from other true crabs. Their shells are triangular, narrowing towards the front, and their legs are longer and usually thinner than those of other crabs. Whereas most crabs have smooth shells, the shells of spider crabs are covered with spiny protuberances, particularly noticeable on the thornback, shown here with the common shore crab for comparison. Some spider crabs, but not the thornback, have a beak-like extension at the front.

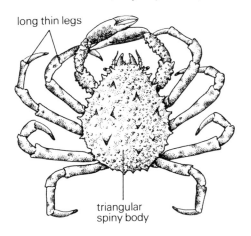

Thornback *(Maja squinado)*

long thin legs

triangular spiny body

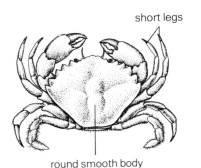

short legs

round smooth body

Common shore crab *(Carcinus maenas)*

Left: Leach's spider crab is often seen associated with a snakelocks anemone, the crab sitting with the rear of its shell against the anemone's column so that it is protected by the tentacles. Towards its front the crab has gathered pieces of orange sponge and seaweed to provide further camouflage.

Below: With a body length of no more than 17mm (⅔in), the long-legged spider crab is one of the smallest crabs found around the coast of Britain. This specimen has covered itself with pieces of seaweed, held in place with special hook-shaped hairs.

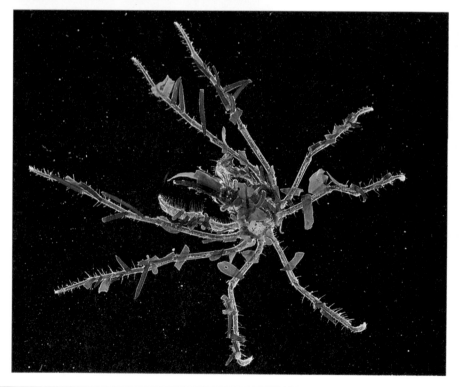

found among seaweed or rocks in shallow or deep water, though the latter also inhabits the lower shore.

The largest British species is the thornback, or spiny spider crab (*Maja squinado*), which grows to a body length of 18cm (7in). Small thornbacks occasionally occur in rock pools and large specimens are often found in shallow coastal waters, particularly during the summer. At this time of year, many thornbacks congregate in the shallows, where they form huge mounds that can contain as many as 50-100 individuals.

The purpose of this strange behaviour is probably to protect the females while they moult in the centre of the mound—after moulting, the females are soft-shelled and vulnerable. In this condition, they mate with the hard-shelled males near the outside of the mound.

The thornback is particularly well-suited to this behaviour since, unlike many other crabs, it is not carnivorous and does not attack its own kind, especially when they are soft-shelled and defenceless.

Growth of a scorpion spider crab

All spider crabs have a short larval life consisting of two zoeal stages followed by a megalop, which moults into a true crab. For the scorpion spider crab (*Inachus dorsettensis*), whose larval stages are shown here, the first crab stage appears three weeks after hatching. With this species, all three stages are about 2mm long, though usually succeeding stages are larger.

first-stage zoea
dorsal spine
rounded carapace
eye
antennae
rudimentary legs
abdomen

second-stage zoea
eye now stalked

megalop
antennae
large eye
elongating carapace
developing legs
abdomen shortens

COMMON LOBSTERS: A VALUABLE CATCH

Commercially, the common lobster is one of the most important crustaceans occurring on the coasts of Britain and Ireland. Here we look at the life of this armoured creature of the rocky sea-bed, as well as at the industry that has arisen to exploit it.

The common or European lobster is found from the Arctic Circle to Morocco and into the Mediterranean, but its main centre of distribution is around the coast of the British Isles. Lobsters are usually found on rough or rocky ground from the intertidal zone to depths of about 110m (60 fathoms).

Lobsters are territorial animals, usually living in a crevice or underneath a rock, where they spend much of their time, coming out to

Above: A common lobster leaves its hiding place in a crevice among the rocks.

Right: Although the common lobster's distribution ranges from the Arctic Ocean to North Africa, it is most abundant in our coastal waters, giving rise to important fisheries.

Lobster fishing around Britain

Shetland
Orkney
Stornoway · Wick
Ullapool · Lossiemouth
Mallaig
Oban
Campbeltown · Eyemouth
Burton Port · Ayr · Seahouses
Whitby
Bridlington
Aran Islands
Dingle · Cromer
Barmouth
Saltee · Aberystwyth
Kilmore Quay · Newquay
Milford Haven
Port Isaac
Portland · Selsey
Newlyn

■ Lobster fishing grounds

feed mainly at night, when their activity is increased considerably. They feed on fishes, marine worms, molluscs, crustaceans and starfishes.

Lobster structure The lobster is completely enclosed in an exoskeleton (outer shell) of calcified chitin. The body is composed of a combined head and thorax (enclosed in a large shield-like structure known as a carapace) and an abdomen of six articulated segments. The most easily recognised features are the large claws (chelae), used for tearing and crushing food. There are eight walking legs.

The lobster also has a long pair of antennae which are sensitive to vibrations, and shorter antennules which detect chemicals. Compound eyes lie on either side of a hard, forward-pointing feature known as the rostrum. Lobsters usually walk, but they can escape rapidly backwards if threatened, by suddenly flexing the abdomen. The sex of a lobster can be determined by the different shape of the sexual appendages, which are situated underneath the abdomen. In addition, the male lobster has larger claws and a narrower abdomen.

Moulting to grow The common lobster can grow up to 8kg (18lb) in weight, although such a weight would be unusual today. The rigid shell must be cast off or moulted at intervals so that growth can take place. Prior to each moult a new shell develops beneath the old one before it is cast. When moulting is about to take place, the lobster retreats into hiding, because after moulting it is soft-shelled and defenceless, and easy prey for such fishes as cod, dogfish and conger eel.

At the start of moulting, the membrane between the carapace and the abdomen splits; the soft-shelled lobster then 'jack-knifes' out of the old shell by a series of contractions. The first part of the soft lobster to emerge from the old shell is the portion at the back of the carapace and the top end of the abdomen, followed by the legs, claws and abdomen.

After emerging from its old shell, the lobster's new shell is very soft, wrinkled and pliable; it then swells up to its new size, mainly by the lobster taking in water beneath the shell. The new shell gradually hardens by a

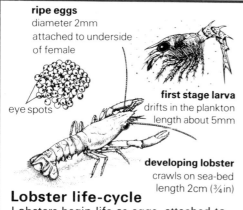

ripe eggs
diameter 2mm
attached to underside of female

eye spots

first stage larva
drifts in the plankton length about 5mm

developing lobster
crawls on sea-bed
length 2cm (¾in)

Lobster life-cycle

Lobsters begin life as eggs, attached to the underside of the mother. The larvae that hatch are planktonic creatures, floating in the sea. After the third moult they sink to the sea-bed; at this stage they begin to resemble their parents.

Above: A common lobster lies with its claws extended. Each claw has its own specific function. One has serrated edges which overlap scissor fashion, and are used for cutting and tearing. The other claw is more heavily built and the two edges meet directly together to form an efficient crusher. The first two pairs of walking legs also have small pincers, which are used to pick up food and pass it to the mouthparts. The food is cut and torn into smaller particles by the mouthparts. From here they pass into the stomach, which has special grinding 'teeth' (ossicles) in a structure known as the gastric mill.

Traps for the unwary

There are a number of local variations of lobster pot, but in general they fall into two main types. The creel (far right) has one or more side entrances, and is used mainly in Scotland and along the east coast of England. The inkwell type (right) has a single top entrance, and is used on the west coast. Fish bait is placed in the interior of the pot, gurnards, plaice and salted mackerel being the species most commonly used. Lured towards the pot by the bait, the hungry lobster climbs inside one of the entrances, but has difficulty escaping because of the constriction and shape of these entrances.

lobster enters here

entrance funnel is too high for the lobster to climb out

smooth-sided entrance funnel

west coast type

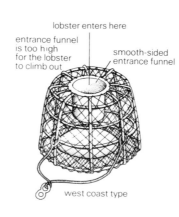

build-up of calcium salts. The shell becomes rigid within a few days, but is not completely hardened for three or four weeks.

Life-cycle Mating takes place between a soft-shelled female and a hard-shelled male. Occasionally soft-shelled males mate, but it is thought unlikely that these pairs will be fertile. The female retains sperm from the male in a special receptacle until she lays the eggs, usually about four months after mating. When it is time for her to lay eggs, she lies on her back and curls her tail forward, extruding the eggs on to her abdominal appendages or swimmerets. The eggs remain attached to the hairs on the swimmerets for approximately ten months, and a female carrying eggs in this way is called a 'berried' female. The eggs may number between 5000 and 100,000 depending on the size of the female.

The eggs usually hatch in June or July, and the young lobster larvae that emerge are released into the plankton to fend for themselves. The larvae moult three times, changing their form with each moult. After the third moult, they spend most of their time on the sea-bed, beginning to resemble their parents.

Lobster fishing Lobsters are caught all round the coast of Britain and Ireland wherever the sea-bed is rocky. Lobster and crab fisheries are usually on the same grounds, but often only one of the two species is the main catch of a particular area. Most lobsters are caught within 8km (5 miles) of the coast, but in recent years there has been a tendency to fish further offshore, particularly in the English Channel and around the Channel Islands where boats have made substantial catches up to 65km (40 miles) offshore. The main catches are made from May to October.

The type of boat employed in lobster fishing depends on the available harbour facilities and on local weather conditions. Generally there are two types: the small open boat of between 4.5 and 9m (15-30ft) and the larger, decked boats of up to 18m (60ft). The larger boats tend to be employed in the offshore lobster fisheries and work on a seasonal basis, perhaps trawling for the rest of the year.

Handling the catch When lobsters are caught, the undersized ones–those that have not yet bred and are needed to conserve the stocks in the fisheries–are returned to the sea. Lobsters big enough to be sold are stored on board. The national minimum permitted landing size for lobsters is 85mm (3⅓in) carapace length (the length measured from the rear of the eye socket to the rear end of the carapace, along a line parallel to the mid-line of the body shell). Egg-bearing females are not protected by legislation, although many fishermen believe that this is an essential conservation measure.

Large catches are normally landed and sold on the same day, but smaller catches are often held in storepots. At some ports there are storage tanks where live lobsters are kept in seawater until sold.

thin body adapted for swimming

Prawn
(Palaemon elegans, formerly Leander squilla)
length up to 5cm (2in)

Norway lobster, Dublin Bay prawn or Scampi
(Nephrops norvegicus)
length up to 15cm (6in)

flat body adapted for crawling and burrowing

main claws nearly equal in size

heavy main claws unequal in size

Common lobster
(Homarus gammarus)
length up to 45cm (18in), sometimes longer

Above: Three commercially important crustacean species.

Below: A lobster stranded in a rock pool at low tide.

TENTACLED PREDATORS

Among the most elaborate molluscs in our sea are the squid–highly advanced predators who reach out and grab their prey with long, sucker-covered tentacles.

The squid you see on a fishmonger's slab or preserved in a museum jar convey a poor impression of these highly specialised predators. Possessing only a delicate pen made of chitin to support their body, in death they collapse into a shapeless mass that reveals little of their appearance in life. The result is that squid are, to most people, among the most obscure marine animals, a circumstance that has probably contributed to their traditional science-fiction role as alien monsters.

Squid structure Squid are classed as molluscs, their closest relatives being cuttlefish and octopuses. The outer part of a squid's body, called the mantle, consists of a cylinder of muscle that tapers to a point at one end and joins on to the head at the other. A chitinous internal shell, called a pen, extends along the inside of the body attached to the upper surface. Suspended from it are the internal organs for breathing, digestion and reproduction.

Apart from the organs, the rest of the body is simply a cavity used by the squid for locomotion. When the walls of the cavity contract, water is forced out through a funnel close to the head, thus jet-propelling the squid along. The cavity is then opened to allow water in for the next thrust. Normal motion is tail-first but, by controlling the funnel, the squid can move in any direction and can perform rapid turns.

Attached to the head of a squid are eight

Above: One of the strangest squid to be found in the waters around Britain is a deep-sea species called *Histioteuthis*. This squid has one eye (the one shown here) much larger than the other, though no one is yet sure why. The dark dots scattered about its body are light organs, thought to be important for camouflage.

Below: The arms of a squid are equipped with powerful suckers for holding on to its prey while feeding.

arms and two tentacles. The ends of the tentacles thicken into clubs which are studded with suckers. To catch prey, such as fishes, the tentacles are extended and the prey grasped between the clubs. The tentacles then withdraw and pass the prey to the arms, which are also covered with suckers. These hold the prey while the squid tears off chunks of food with its sharp beak.

Colour changes An important aspect of the squid's behaviour is its ability to change colour very rapidly to confuse both prey and predators.

The remarkable feature of the squid's colour change is that it appears to happen instantaneously. Most animals that can change colour do so slowly. The reason for this is that the message to change colour is passed from the brain to special glands that secrete hormones. The hormones act as chemical messengers and travel in the bloodstream to the skin where they trigger the pigment change.

In squid, the situation is quite different: they do not need hormones to trigger the change. Instead, the brain sends a message via a nerve directly to special cells in the skin containing the pigment and a special set of muscles. When the muscles relax, the pigmented area expands and the colour shows. When they contract, the cell pigment disappears from view. Since messages can travel along nerves far faster than hormones can

Common squid (*Loligo forbesi*)

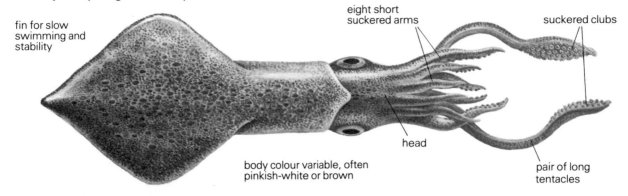

fin for slow swimming and stability

eight short suckered arms

suckered clubs

head

body colour variable, often pinkish-white or brown

pair of long tentacles

travel in the bloodstream, the squid's technique is obviously much quicker.

To see how the squid uses this ability, imagine one being pursued by a large fish. If the squid is dark at first, then becomes pale, and at the same time suddenly changes its direction, the fish is likely to be left confused and without a meal.

Inky smokescreen The squid has a further strategy to evade predators: the use of its ink. Many people think that the ink is used as a kind of smokescreen in which the squid hides, but this is not the case. The ink is used as a decoy. A dark squid ejects some ink and at the same time turns pale and darts off in a different direction, leaving a would-be predator chasing the ink while the squid escapes.

The ink is contained in a sac on the roof of the mantle cavity. When it is ejected it is passed through the funnel and mixed with mucus. The purpose of the mucus is to hold the ink together in a blob about the same size as the squid, and it also seems to act as a chemical attractant to the attacker.

Squid reproduction The general facts about how squid reproduce are much the same for all species, though there are differences in details. For the common squid, which is widespread around the south coasts of England, the breeding season starts in April. To mate, the male and female meet head on and, while their arms are interlocked, the male inserts one of his arms inside his mantle cavity and

Above: A squid lays its eggs on a rock inside masses of finger-like projections of jelly.

Below: A pair of squid just prior to mating. This takes place head-on with arms interlocked.

grasps a capsule of sperm called a spermatophore. This he inserts into the female's mantle cavity to fertilise her eggs. After the eggs are laid, the adults usually die.

The eggs are laid inside finger-like masses of jelly on rocks, or some other hard surface. They are left to hatch into tiny squid a couple of millimetres long. The young grow rapidly and, within a year or two, are themselves ready to reproduce and die.

British squid The common squid is one of our smaller species, reaching perhaps 45cm (18in) long. Its streamlined body is ideal for darting here and there, yet it is also capable of slow, refined movements by carefully undulating the fins along the sides of its body.

A faster species is *Onychoteuthis banksi*. This is a small squid that darts through the surface waters of the open sea. It catches its prey with vicious tentacles, in which the suckers have become modified into sharp, curved claws.

Among the largest squid to be found around our coasts is a group known as *Ommastrephes*. They may be several feet long and are occasionally seen stranded on beaches.

Deep-sea squid Some of the strangest squid,

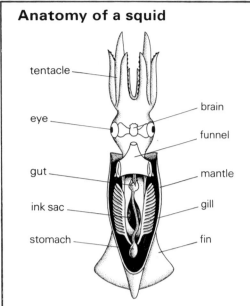

Anatomy of a squid

- tentacle
- eye
- gut
- ink sac
- stomach
- brain
- funnel
- mantle
- gill
- fin

All squid species have much the same structure. The head is attached at one end to the arms and tentacles, and at the other to a tapering cylinder of muscle called the mantle. Lying along the inside top of the mantle is an internal shell—the pen—from which hang the organs. Only a small part of the space inside the mantle is taken up with the organs. Most of it is a cavity that can be alternately filled with water and then evacuated through the funnel to provide the squid with jet-propelled motion.

Above: A squid devouring its prey. All squid are predators, feeding mainly on small fishes and crustaceans. These they catch with their sucker-covered tentacles.

Below: A species of *Loligo* stranded in a north Devon rockpool. A sight like this is rare; squid are seldom found close to the shore.

for example, *Histioteuthis*, are found in the deep sea around Britain. As a juvenile, this squid has a pair of eyes much like those of any other squid, but as it matures the right eye becomes almost twice as large as the left. This strange phenomenon has puzzled biologists for many years. Some have argued that the large eye functions in the poorly-lit deep sea and the small one is used for when the squid rises to the well-lit surface. Others have argued that the opposite is true. The problem is still not resolved, but recent observations have shown that *Histioteuthis* orientates itself with its large eye pointing up and the small one pointing down.

Most deep-sea squid are arrayed with light organs, often resembling brilliant jewels. These may be important for communication, recognising mates, or even camouflage.

How can a light organ act as camouflage? Some squid are almost transparent, apart from a few organs which are always opaque. Any creature looking up at a squid from below would see these organs silhouetted against the faint light coming from the surface. However, with light organs placed just below the opaque areas and giving off the right amount of light to balance that coming from above, the squid becomes invisible.

Squid for food Most people regard squid as being little more than curiosities, yet they could have economic importance as food.

The reason lies in the decline in numbers of one of their major predators, the sperm whale. It has been estimated that, in 1972, about 320 million tons of squid were eaten by sperm whales, compared with an annual figure of about 800 million tons some 35 years earlier. So there could be about 500 million tons of squid 'available' for human consumption each year. Since our current annual world catch of fishes is between 70 and 80 million tons, the potential of squid as a food source becomes clear. To date, however, many squid found in the stomachs of whales are unknown species that we have never been able to catch.

OCTOPUSES: MANY ARMED MOLLUSCS

The two species of these curious molluscs most likely to be encountered around Britain are the common octopus and the lesser octopus. Both hide away for most of the day but emerge to probe for prey during the hours of darkness.

Above: Although the common octopus (*Octopus vulgaris*) lives in shallower waters than the lesser octopus (*Eledone cirrosa*), divers rarely catch sight of one. It can be distinguished from the lesser octopus by the two rows of suckers along each arm and by its rough-textured skin.

Octopuses are molluscs, placed in the class Cephalopoda–the same class as the squids and cuttlefishes. Most species of octopus lack a shell, and their most obvious feature is the ring of eight arms or tentacles with suckers which surrounds the mouth. Like squids and cuttlefishes, octopuses possess a funnel, or siphon, with which they can rapidly jet propel themselves about if necessary, although they can also crawl about using their tentacles.

Inside the 'head' Internally, the bulbous 'head' contains the gills, a highly evolved nervous system, and reproductive, circulatory and digestive systems. The common octopus has been studied in great detail, and much that has been learned about it applies equally to other species.

The brain is large and complex, making it capable of learning, and allowing it to perform a range of activities beyond the scope of other invertebrates. In addition, there are concentrations of nerve cells in other parts of the body, and a number of functions, such as digestion rate and circulation of the blood, come largely under direct nervous control–in vertebrates these roles are performed by hormones.

The blood flows through vessels, as it does in vertebrates, but the oxygen-carrying green pigment–haemocyanin–does not occur in blood cells (as does the red pigment haemoglobin in vertebrates), being carried instead as part of the blood fluid. The blood is very viscous and difficult to pump around the body and, in order to maintain blood pressure, all the main blood vessels can contract to assist the flow. Despite this assistance an octopus cannot manage with one heart, and there are two secondary hearts, one for pumping blood through the fine network of vessels in each of the two gills.

Night strike Octopuses are solitary animals which spend most of the daylight hours hidden in a cavity, although they are everwatchful of events in their vicinity. They wander mostly at night, their arms carefully exploring for food such as other molluscs and crustaceans.

Vision is important, and an octopus is read-

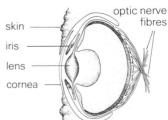

skin
iris
lens
cornea
optic nerve fibres

Above: Octopus eyes resemble those of vertebrates.

Below: The eyes always remain horizontal.

body inclined at angle
eye horizontal

ily enticed from its lair by any interesting movement. If a crab should pass by, the octopus becomes visibly alert, its eyes rising and falling on its head as its gaze fixes on the potential meal. It glides towards the crab on its arms, and waves of changing patterns and colours pass across its body as it seems scarcely able to contain its excitement. When within striking distance it shoots forward, propelled by a burst of water through the funnel, and engulfs the crab beneath the web of skin that extends down between its arms. The crab is quickly immobilised by a nerve poison secreted by the salivary glands, and the octopus returns to its home where the crab is consumed at leisure. Digestive juices are thought to penetrate the crab before ingestion, facilitating complete removal of all the flesh before the shell is discarded. When the octopus eats a hard-shelled mollusc, it penetrates the shell by slowly drilling with its radula (a tongue covered in many small teeth)

Above: The octopus can change not only its colour but also its skin texture to match its background, particularly when threatened or when lying in wait for prey.

Below: The lesser octopus can be quickly distinguished from the common octopus by the single row of suckers on each tentacle, a fin ridge which extends around the body, its smooth skin and its musky odour.

until the shell is punctured.

Mating in octopuses An octopus does not usually tolerate the presence of another octopus, the larger eating the smaller or both fighting until one flees. To avoid such a confrontation, potential mates have means of recognising each other and appeasing aggressive tendencies long enough for copulation to take place.

A male carries particularly large suckers on his arms, which he may display as a prelude to mating, and which seem to serve as a means for the female to recognise his sex. Once this has been established, the male inserts spermatophores into the body cavity of the female using his hectocotylus, an arm modified with a channel.

Female sacrifice To prepare for egg-laying, the female retires to a cave or other safe crevice, the roof of which she carefully cleans with repeated sweeps of her arms, other debris being removed using her suckers.

For a week or more the common octopus lays thousands of eggs which, after passing through her funnel, are manipulated by the small suckers near her mouth and attached to the cave roof, embedded in a gelatinous mass. The female guards and cares for the eggs for the rest of her life, and she may never feed again. The eggs take from one to one and a half months to hatch, and throughout this period the female octopus maintains vigilance, delicately scanning the eggs with the tips of her arms and playing jets of water across their surface. Any intruding animal is pushed away with no attempt to capture it as food. Soon after her eggs hatch the female dies.

The young The eggs of the common octopus are very small, and the tiny, newly hatched animals float as part of the plankton before settling into an adult lifestyle. Patches of minute bristles usually cover the body of a

larval octopus when it hatches; these may have assisted escape from the egg-casing but will now help the octopus to float. Eventually the bristles develop into numerous warts that cover the adult body. In the warmer parts of its range the juvenile octopus remains planktonic for a few weeks, but at the northern limits of its distribution in the English Channel this may last for three months.

From a size of about 3mm when newly hatched, common octopuses reach a length of 10mm (½in) by the time they settle on the sea-bed. Growth is very rapid; by the time they are mature after some eighteen months to two years, females may weigh over 1kg (2.2lbs). The males mature much earlier than females, when their weight is under 120gm (just over 4oz), but they seem to live longer and there are recorded weights of up to 25kg (55lb).

In most years the common octopus is fairly scarce in England even along the southern coast, and it is hardly ever found further north. Some planktonic juveniles are occasionally carried to more northern areas, but they are unlikely to survive. There have been occasions in the past, however, when numbers of the common octopus have reached plague proportions on the south coast. These plagues normally follow one or more years of warm weather.

The lesser octopus The second British species, the lesser octopus, is much more widely distributed around our coast, but it lives in deeper water than the common octopus and little is known about its life history. It starts life larger than the larval common octopus but never attains such a large adult size.

A number of features distinguish the two species. The lesser octopus has a single row of suckers down each arm, as opposed to two rows in the common octopus; a fin ridge extends around the body; the skin is smooth; and it has a distinctive musky odour. Far fewer eggs are laid, and these are not guarded

Mating behaviour

The male displays the large suckers on his second and third tentacles as a prelude to mating. Copulation consists of the male depositing sperm packets into the female's mantle cavity near the opening of the oviduct, using a specially grooved tentacle.

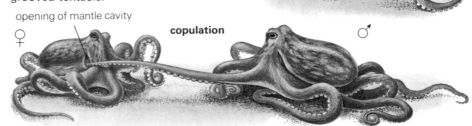

Above: It is rare to see a lesser octopus washed up on the beach. This specimen has probably been discarded from a trawl catch.

Below: A lesser octopus probing about on the sea bottom for food.

by the female. Any predator large enough to catch an octopus in open water makes short work of it.

Survival Octopuses are preyed on by a wide range of animals–they present an attractive meal in the form of a highly nutritious package of protein minus bones.

Young octopuses are particularly vulnerable, especially when still planktonic. A number of fishes specialise in probing crevices in search of food, and no doubt include a large number of octopuses in their diet. To protect itself, an octopus is able to squeeze into the tiniest gap or shoot rapidly away from danger by jet propulsion, and it can also exhibit a most effective camouflage, with changes in colour and surface sculpture to match its background.

The octopus's most familiar response to attack, however, is to discharge a quantity of cloudy ink, which acts as a visual decoy. The way in which octopus ink acts as a chemical attractant has been well illustrated using moray eels kept in aquaria. If just a tiny drop of octopus ink is added to the aquarium, the eels at once become alert and search excitedly for an octopus meal. In natural situations the eel would frenziedly follow the dispersing ink while the octopus made good its escape.

STREAMLINED CUTTLEFISH

The cuttlefish is a master of speed and concealment. With its horny jaws and eyes that can see both ahead and behind, it is one of the most perfectly adapted marine predators.

Cuttlefish are invertebrates, relatives of squid and octopuses, which are together known as cephalopods. The head (Greek: *Kephalus*) and foot (Greek: *Pous*) are virtually fused, whereas in the related bivalve molluscs they are widely separated.

The cuttlefish is divided into three sections: the tentacles, which have evolved from the flat sole-like foot of its primitive ancestor; the head with its large brain and eyes; and the body area, which houses the gut, respiratory, excretory and reproductive systems.

Tenacious tentacles There are eight short, suckered tentacles which the cuttlefish holds out in front of it as it swims. These are sometimes grouped together to form a shield in front of the head. The tentacles are equipped with touch receptors which pass information to the nervous system about the objects with which they come into contact. The suckers are used for holding on to prey, which is captured with two additional, much longer, suckered tentacles. The cuttlefish can project these from among the shorter tentacles with great accuracy to seize prey.

The head The large and highly developed brain is housed in a cartilaginous brain case. The size of the brain means that cuttlefish are relatively intelligent and capable of learning by experience. On either side of the head there are two large eyes, mounted in eye sockets, which can see ahead and behind

Above: The courtship ritual of a pair of common cuttlefish (*Sepia officinalis*). This involves the male changing colour, and precedes reproduction, where the male uses a modified tentacle to transfer a capsule of sperm from his own mantle cavity to that of his mate. The eggs are fertilised there, then released in groups and attached to weeds, where they develop into juveniles, which swim actively and feed on plankton.

Jet-propelled movement

A cuttlefish swims slowly by a rippling movement of the paired fins which run back from the head to the tip of the body. If disturbed, it can close the aperture and force water through the siphon, to jet-propel itself rapidly backwards to safety.

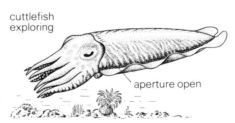

cuttlefish exploring

aperture open

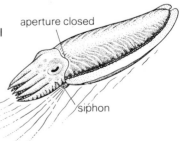

aperture closed

siphon

cuttlefish moving rapidly backwards by expelling water through siphon

Cuttlefish anatomy

The common cuttlefish reaches a length of 30cm (12in). Its skin undergoes many colour changes to mimic its surroundings. The two long tentacles, used to seize prey such as crabs and prawns, can measure up to 50cm (20in) in length.

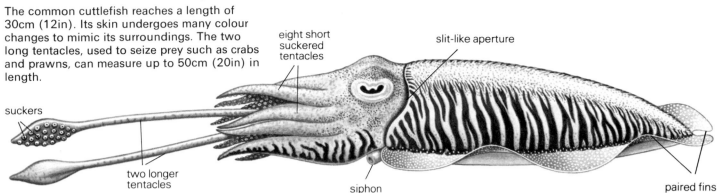

eight short suckered tentacles

slit-like aperture

suckers

two longer tentacles

siphon

paired fins

very efficiently. They are used to spot prey and predators, as well as to gauge the background colour of the sea-bed. This is important in the cuttlefish's complex protective camouflage system, which is controlled by the nervous system. Cuttlefish skin carries many hundreds of adjustable pigment cells, called chromatophores, that can rapidly expand or contract the pigment they contain, thus making the skin darker or lighter. These dramatic pigment changes can take place in seconds and allow the cuttlefish to blend in well with its background, hiding it from potential predators.

The head has a pair of horny jaws, used for breaking up the prey. These resemble the beak of a parrot in shape and size, and are similar to the jaws of squids and octopuses. Lying inside them is another structure typical of molluscs. This is the radula, a long, toothed tongue which is used for rasping at the prey. Cuttlefish also have salivary glands to assist in swallowing the food.

The body This contains the large and fairly bulky internal organs, surrounded by the mantle which, as in other molluscs, secretes the shell. In the case of cuttlefish, the shell is internal. It is the familiar white shield-shaped object commonly used as a source of calcium carbonate for cage birds. The cuttlefish shell, or 'bone' as it is incorrectly called, is porous, and comprises thousands of microscopically small cells. By filling these with gas, the cuttlefish can make itself more buoyant, and by replacing the gas with liquid, it can decrease its buoyancy. This is a great advantage for it means that the animal can adjust its depth in the water without having to swim actively. In this way, it is similar to fish, which use a gas bladder to control their buoyancy.

On the underside of the body lies the mantle cavity; this houses the two large gills, the heart, the openings of the excretory system and sex organs, and the ink sac. The cavity opens to the exterior by a large slit-like aperture which runs round from one side to the other below the animal. Situated inside this large opening is the funnel, the outer end of which looks like a tube or siphon. The gills are ventilated by movements of the muscular lower wall of the mantle, which draws water in through the large opening, passes it over the gills and then expels it through the funnel and siphon. The exhalant stream carries away any waste material at the same time.

Jet-propulsion The exhalant water stream, while essential for respiration and dispersal of waste substances, is also used in jet swimming. When the cuttlefish is alarmed, it can make a rapid escape by suddenly contracting the mantle and forcibly expelling the water contained in the mantle cavity via the funnel and siphon. This has the effect of rapidly jet-propelling the animal backwards. It is also sometimes associated with the discharge of ink from the ink sac, which distracts the oncoming predator and makes a 'smoke-screen' behind which the cuttlefish can retire.

Two factors help the effectiveness of this escape mechanism. First, the cuttlefish has an advanced nervous system, with a number of extremely large nerve cells, that rapidly transmit messages to the brain, so alerting it to the presence of danger. Secondly, this escape system would not work without a means of closing off the mantle cavity to prevent water from 'backfiring'. This is done by muscles with special stud-like cartilaginous outgrowths on the outer mantle wall which clip, like garment press-studs, into sockets on the funnel surface, closing the apertures.

Common cuttlefish distribution

The common cuttlefish is most often found in fairly shallow waters, especially over sand. It frequents bays and estuaries and is distributed throughout the Mediterranean, Atlantic, English Channel and the North Sea. By day the cuttlefish tends to stay buried in the sand on the sea-bed, but at night it emerges to become active in the search for prey. The internal cuttlebone is often found washed up on to beaches – it floats up from the sea-bed when the cuttlefish dies.

Below: The little cuttle (*Sepiola atlantica*), is a miniature cuttlefish, growing to about 5cm (2in) in length. It is rather more rounded than the common cuttlefish, and has flap-like fins and shorter tentacles. The colour varies from almost black to very pale cream, and it is sometimes found burrowing into the sand.

THE UNDERWATER WORLD OF LUNDY

Much of our current knowledge of the animals and plants living in rocky underwater areas around Britain has been gathered from Lundy – a small island off the North Devon coast which is regarded as one of our finest marine nature reserves.

Above: A view of the south end of Lundy. Lundy is only 5km (3 miles) long and 1km ($\frac{5}{8}$ mile) wide, but its precipitous granite cliffs rising to 120m (395ft) above sea level provide some of the most spectacular coastal scenery.

The island of Lundy, at the entrance to the Bristol Channel, has always attracted people interested in wildlife and wild places. It is owned by the National Trust and is leased to the Landmark Trust; both bodies are concerned to ensure that Lundy retains its unique blend of history, wildlife and wilderness. The history of Lundy is a colourful one of ancient

settlements, pirates and shipwreck. The island currently has fewer than 20 inhabitants, who are employed by the Landmark Trust to farm the island and maintain the attractive cottages and hostels let as holiday accommodation throughout the year.

Discovering an underwater world The natural history of Lundy has been widely studied on land – there is plenty of information on the grey seal population, and the kittiwakes, razorbills and guillemots that frequent the cliffs and rocks – but beneath the waters surrounding the island is a hidden world which only a few naturalists have been able to explore. Lundy provides some of the most interesting underwater scenery and colourful wildlife to be seen in the British Isles – wildlife which, until about 40 years ago, could only be sampled by the professional hard-hat diver or by dredge.

Now, with the development and widespread use of self-contained diving gear, anyone who is reasonably fit and willing to undergo training can explore the underwater areas for recreation and study. The marine bio-

120

logists who began diving from Lundy in the late 1960s soon found that the island's marine life was outstandingly rich in species.

Habitats and communities The first thing a diver with an interest in biology will see on swimming from the surface to deep water is that the rocks at shallow depths are dominated by a forest of large brown seaweeds – the kelps or oarweeds.

The seaweeds are attached to the sea-bed but do not have roots; they absorb the nutrients they require from the surrounding water. As with terrestrial plants, they need light for photosynthesis, but light intensity rapidly decreases with increasing depth below the sea surface. The kelp forest continues downwards to a depth where about 1% of surface illumination remains – about 8m (26ft) below low water level off Lundy. Red and some brown seaweeds, however, can survive in much lower light intensity, thriving under a canopy of kelp fronds to depths of about 13m (43ft). The deepest foliose algae, for example *Hypoglossum woodwardii* and *Myriogramme bonnemaisonii*, are found at 21m (69ft).

Above: A brilliantly coloured sea slug grazing a bryozoan. As many as 46 species of these amazing animals have been recorded around Lundy – many of them rarely found anywhere else in the British Isles.

The richest communities of seaweeds are found on the wave-sheltered east coast where life is less severe than it is on the wave-exposed coasts. Many of them, such as *Phycodrys rubens* and species of *Polysiphonia*, have preferred habitats like kelp stipes (stalks) or the pebbles found in the shallow tide-swept areas of sea-bed. It is the wide range of such habitats that, at least partly, accounts for the great diversity of species found around Lundy.

Animal life At depths of 13m (43ft) and more below low water level, animal species – hydroids, sea mats, sponges, starfishes and sea anemones – dominate the rocky sea-bed. Rocks around Lundy extend to depths in excess of 40m (130ft) and to distances of over a kilometre (⅗mile) from the shore in places, finally terminating in a level sea-bed of anything from thick mud, through coarser sediments, to plains of pebbles.

Tidal stream velocity and the severity of wave action are very important in determining the distribution of animal species. Around

Above: *Aglaophenia tubulifera*, with its delicate plumes, is one of the commonest hydroids (sea firs) present around Lundy. The branches are covered in minute anemone-like polyps which gather suspended food from the water.

Left: The common sea urchin is by far the most ecologically significant underwater animal around Lundy. It grazes over the rocky sea-bed, feeding on algae, bryozoa, barnacles and probably anything else it can get its teeth around. Off parts of the coast of Ireland, Scotland and south-west England, sea urchins are so abundant that the rocky sea-bed is kept bare of the majority of erect-growing species.

Lundy tidal stream velocity can be almost negligible or up to 5 knots, while wave action varies from the severe exposure of the west coast to the shelter of the east coast. Strong currents bring a large supply of food to animals such as sea firs, sea fans and brittle stars, which rely on catching organic material suspended in the water. On the other hand, vigorous tidal streams and storm-induced wave oscillation on the sea-bed dislodge or damage such erect species as the snakelocks anemone and the branching sponges. In sheltered areas, silt is deposited on the rocks and can lead to smothering or clogging of animals' feeding organs.

Animals most suited to the widely differing regimes of water movement and siltation thrive at different sites around Lundy, leading to the presence of a very wide range of communities. Many of the species on sub-tidal rocks, the cup corals for instance, are extremely long-lived and will only survive on stable rock where physical stress is low, yet tidal streams strong enough to keep them and the rocks reasonably clear of silt and supply adequate food.

Sea-bed topography is also important and different species often favour different habitats such as cliffs, caves, boulders and gullies. The northern part of the east coast of Lundy in particular appears to have the right mix of physical conditions to encourage the growth of many species, including some that are near the northern limits of their distribution.

The animals found attached to or crawling over the sea-bed around Lundy are almost all invertebrate species. Rocks around most of the island are dominated by a 'turf' of erect, branching bryozoa (sea mats); they are no more than a few centimetres high but they nevertheless contain a vast array of minute worms, molluscs and crustaceans.

Scattered among this rich turf are large and often highly colourful animals, including sponges, hydroids (sea firs), anemones, cup corals, starfishes, sea urchins and sea squirts. Close inspection of the sea-bed also reveals members of the most spectacularly colourful and diverse group of animals around Lundy—the sea slugs or nudibranchs. Each species is

Above: The beautiful yellow cup coral *Leptopsammia pruvoti* is a Mediterranean species that created great excitement when it was found to be living in abundance on some parts of the Lundy coast. The skeleton of this animal is about the size of a thimble.

Below: This map of Lundy shows the extent of the nature reserve and the water depths. Grey seals, lobsters, razorbills and sea fans are just some of the wildlife found on and around Lundy.

usually highly specific in the selection of prey. For example, *Tritonia odhneri* feeds only on the sea fan *Eunicella verrucosa*.

Desirable 'aliens' The most interesting members of Lundy's underwater community are the animal species that have their centres of distribution well to the south of the British Isles, or which appear to be restricted to coasts near oceanic water. For some reason, these Mediterranean-Atlantic species are outstandingly colourful, with shades of yellow, orange and pink making the sea-bed a veritable garden in full bloom.

One of the most exciting discoveries, made early on in the days of underwater exploration around the island, was the cup coral *Leptopsammia pruvoti*, a yellow solitary coral which lives densely crowded on many vertical faces off the east coast. The sea fan *Eunicella verrucosa* is another species rarely encountered further north but common on many parts of the sea-bed around the island. Branches of these flattened fans are covered in minute anemone-like polyps and the colonies face into prevailing water currents so that the maximum surface area is exposed to the suspended food on which the colony feeds. Sea fans are, like many of the species living on the sea-bed, extremely slow growers. The 30cm (12in) high colonies, which in the past have been considered attractive souvenirs, have taken about 30 years to reach that size.

Fishes and shellfishes The most unusual and

Lundy Island Marine Reserve

N

Stanley Bank

Hens and Chickens

Puffin Gulley
Seals Rock

Long Roost

Gannets Bay

Devil's Slide

Knoll Pins

Gull Rock

North-west Bank

Jenny's Cove

Halfway Wall Bay

Needle Rock

Dead Cow Point

East Bank

White Beach
Ladies Beach

Half Tide Rock

Mouse Island
Rat Island
The Gates

Black Rock

boundary of marine nature reserve

| | up to 20m deep | | up to 40m deep | | up to 10m deep |
| | up to 30m deep | | up to 50m deep | | |

Above: The jewel anemone *Corynactis viridis*. Dense colonies of this lovely anemone cover vertical cliffs and overhangs around Lundy. This colony is only one of many bright colour combinations that the anemone exhibits.

Left: Often known as the feather-duster anemone because of its appearance, *Metridium senile* is a rock-dwelling anemone. It has very fine tentacles with which it filters sea-water for particles of food. It can be seen round Lundy Island and is also often found on piers and oil-rigs.

Right: The habitats around Lundy's coasts are outstandingly suitable for many kinds of nearshore fishes. The kelp forests, the boulder slopes and the broken sea-bed provide the shelter needed by wrasse in particular. The ballan wrasse, the goldsinny wrasse and the beautifully coloured cuckoo wrasse (shown here) are all commonly encountered around Lundy, together with pollack, anglerfish and gobies.

fascinating of the many fishes found off Lundy is the red band fish. This spectacular red, eel-like fish with iridescent blue markings grows to a length of about 60cm (2ft) and digs vertical burrows in the muddy gravel off the east coast. Until 1974, when the first one was discovered in shallow water off Lundy, the red band fish was known only from trawls taken in depths below 60m (200ft). Following the studies around Lundy, it is now clear that the fish lives curled up in a chamber at the base of its vertical burrow, making excursions out of the hole at dawn and dusk to feed. Three species of wrasse, the ballan, goldsinny and cuckoo, inhabit the kelp forests, and pollack, anglerfish and gobies can also be found around Lundy, as well as many more common fishes.

Other fish visit Lundy on passage and both basking shark and ocean sunfish are usually seen during the summer. Scallops are found in small quantities off the east coast, but fortunately not in commercial numbers. Mussels are small and not harvestable but lobsters and crawfish are regularly caught by fishermen using traditional methods.

Conservation The essential feature of most of the coastline and its associated marine life around Britain is that it is in a largely pristine state. Although fisheries, development, pollution, land reclamation and many other activities have taken their toll of habitats and wildlife, we can still look upon most marine ecosystems as a last true wilderness in Britain. Lundy is without doubt one of those incredibly rich areas that require protection and management to ensure their continued value in the future. The island was a voluntary reserve from 1973 until November 1986 when the Department of the Environment, on the Nature Conservancy Council's prompting, designated Lundy a statutory reserve.

Birds of the open sea and islands

No less than 24 species of seabirds breed regularly in Britain and Ireland, making the British Isles the most important area for this group in north-west Europe. Seabirds often spend all of their lives at sea, except for the period when they return to land to breed and rear their young. To see the most spectacular seabird colonies you must travel to the most rugged of Britain's coasts, often having to face the rigours of a rough sea-crossing to reach the remote islands favoured by the birds. Such places are usually close to the birds' oceanic sources of food and are also isolated from predators. Many seabirds – the guillemot, razorbill, kittiwake and gannet for instance – live conspicuously in noisy colonies protected by the sheer cliffs on or near which they nest. Others live deep underground in burrows where their eggs and chicks are protected from the predatory gulls. The puffin is our best known seabird with a burrow-nesting habit, and another is the Manx shearwater.

Although relying on the bountiful sea, the feeding habit of each of these birds is different, greatly affecting the form and behaviour of each species. Feeding on fish near the surface of the sea has led to the development of two main types. There are such graceful birds as the terns – masters of the aerial pick-up, hardly touching the water to catch their fish and often travelling great distances to find food. On the other hand, there are the aquatic birds, superbly adapted for swimming underwater, with strong legs set well back for efficient propulsion and short flipper-like wings which make them effective underwater 'fliers' in the pursuit of fast-moving prey such as sand eels. The puffins, guillemots and razorbills are marvellous swimmers, and guillemots are known to dive as deep as 140m (460ft).

Below: The gannet is an important species for the British Isles, since over 70% of the entire world population is found round our coasts. The bird on the left is a young individual in its third year; the one on the right is an adult.

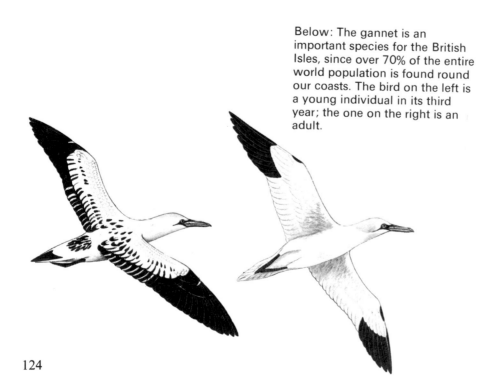

124

CHECKLIST

This checklist is a guide to some of the seabirds you can find around the coasts of Britain. Although you will not see them all in the same place, you should be able to spot many of them around the different coastal habitats of the British Isles. The species listed in **bold** *type are described in detail.*

Arctic skua
Arctic tern
Black guillemot
Common gull
Common tern
Cormorant
Eider duck
Fulmar
Gannet
Great black-backed gull
Great skua
Guillemot
Herring gull
Kittiwake
Leach's petrel
Lesser black-backed gull
Little tern
Manx shearwater
Puffin
Razorbill
Sandwich tern
Shag
Storm petrel
White-tailed eagle

Left: A colony of guillemots on the Shetland island of Unst. The guillemot is Britain's most numerous seabird. Their colonies are easy to locate because of the smell of rotting fish remains and guano, and because of the constant noise — a mixture of harsh growls and rumblings.

125

SPEEDY FULMARS AND FRAGILE PETRELS

Petrels are ocean-going birds that include the gull-like fulmar and its smaller, less robust, sooty relatives, the storm petrel and Leach's petrel. These 'tube-noses', as they are nicknamed, spend their lives gliding over the oceans in search of food, only visiting land for a few short weeks in the summer to mate, lay their eggs and rear their chicks.

Below: At their nesting site on an open cliff, fulmars will 'spit' a foul-smelling fluid (regurgitated from the stomach) to deter intruders. The large horny tubes on top of the beaks are clearly visible here. The exact purpose of these tubes is not known, but they may function as genuine nostrils.

The fulmar, together with the storm petrel and the Leach's petrel, are all related to that giant among oceanic birds, the albatross, as well as to the shearwaters, aptly named after their habit of skimming low over the waves.

The fulmar looks completely different compared to the other two petrels. It is about double the size of its relatives, mainly white and much like a gull. It nests on open cliffs and in summer can be seen all day long near the coast. The storm petrel and the Leach's petrel, on the other hand, are quite small for seabirds (lighter in weight than a song thrush) and are sooty black all over save for a white patch on the rump. They come ashore to their nests, in deep burrows or natural crevices in the rocks, only after dark.

Tubular beaks All petrels are distinguished from other seabirds by their complex beak structure. Viewed close up, the beak is made up of a series of plates of horny material, with clearly visible joints or sutures in between. In addition, the ridge of the beak is topped with a horny tube that gives the group another colloquial name – the 'tube-noses'.

The precise function of this narrow tube is not properly understood. One theory is that it serves these seabirds – most of them extremely efficient high-speed gliders – as an air-speed indicator, in much the same way as does a 'Pitot tube' on a modern aircraft. Another theory suggests that it functions as a genuine nostril. The sense of smell is poorly developed in most birds, but many petrels emit a powerful, musty odour, and returning birds may possibly 'scent out' their mates not only after dark but also deep in nesting burrows.

Success story The fulmar is at the centre of one of the most amazing bird success stories of the last 100 years. For over 900 years, the only known British breeding station was on the remote island of St Kilda, 50 miles west of the Outer Hebrides. Then, in the middle of the 19th century, the Icelandic fulmar population began to expand, and in 1878 other colonies began to be reported on Scottish islands, the first on Foula.

Since then, there has been no stopping the bird's rapid spread. First the northern islands were colonized, followed by the cliffs of both the east and west coasts of Britain and Ireland, until by 1970 fulmars were nesting on all suitable stretches of rocky coast. Even in some apparently quite unsuitable areas they find a way to succeed. In the Hebrides, there are now nests on the ground in remote and undisturbed sand dunes, and on the cliff-less coasts of southern and eastern England. The birds have even commandeered nuclear power station window sills as the nearest alternative to a cliff ledge.

Fulmars have also moved inland. Nesting was first reported on ruined buildings in the Shetlands, but now quarries several miles

Gliders and flutterers

Fulmar (*Fulmarus glacialis*), 47cm (18½in) from beak to tail. Long stiff wings, grey upper parts, white underparts.

Storm petrel (*Hydrobates pelagicus*), 15cm (6in) from beak to tail. Pale wing bar, white rump, squarish tail.

Leach's petrel (*Oceanodroma leucorrhoa*), 20cm (8in) from beak to tail. Diagonal paler wing band, white rump with dark stripe, forked tail.

from the sea in northern England have breeding pairs.

There is no certain reason for this success. It may be that there was a sudden genetic change in the birds themselves, or that the North Atlantic warmed slightly and produced more fish. A more likely explanation is related to the fulmars' diet, which consists mainly of offal. The rise in numbers coincided with the time when whaling reached a peak in the Atlantic – with abundant supplies of offal both at sea and near the shore. Although whaling has now been curtailed, modern fishing (with a great deal of the catch gutted at sea) has taken over this food-providing role.

Above: The fulmar slices through the air like a guided missile, while the much smaller storm petrel, resembling a large black moth, flutters feebly on an erratic flight path. The Leach's petrel is more positive in flight, but retains the erratic flight of its smaller cousin.

Slow breeders The fulmars' success is particularly surprising in the light of their low reproductive capacity. Once they have fledged from their simple cliff ledge nests, fulmars remain 'adolescent', roaming around the North Atlantic, for at least five years. After this period they visit the cliffs in spring and summer – prospecting for a nest site and seeking a mate – for another two or three years before they breed for the first time at about eight years old.

Only a single large chalky-white egg is laid, and this often cannot be replaced if it, or the chick, is lost to a predator. And these losses do occur, despite the fulmar's vigorous defence of its nest (see the box on aggression).

Long life The dangers inherent in such a lengthy breeding cycle seem to be offset by the lifespan of this bird. Research workers have found it difficult to make a ring that is strong enough to resist the abrasion caused by the fulmar shuffling about awkwardly on the rocks. But the results obtained from detailed studies by Aberdeen University suggest that many fulmars live for as long as 30 years, and a proportion may be a good deal older. At that rate, even laying only one egg a year, the fulmar pair have ample time to produce offspring several times over and ensure the population explosion that we have witnessed.

Fulmars in flight Out at sea or twisting and turning in the eddies and updraughts near

Aggression in birds

Birds normally resort to aggression only to protect their breeding territory from competitors, or defend their feeding areas from predators. Competition between birds is almost always confined to birds of the same species, other birds being tolerated or ignored. The response to predators varies. Starlings, for instance, just gather and swoop around – or 'mob' – a hunting kestrel, while the meadow pipit may press home an attack against a marauding cuckoo to the point of causing feathers to fly.

The fulmar is unusually well equipped to repel intruders. Once in its digestive system, the fulmar's plankton food is converted into an oily and smelly fluid. The fulmar can 'spit' this with great accuracy at predators venturing near its nest – even at several metres range. Sometimes it will pursue an intruder and 'shoot it down' in mid-air, the predator landing immediately and preening vigorously to remove the foul-smelling oil that is clogging its plumage.

Most birds, however, rely on plumage and posture to convey their aggression. The fluffed-up cock blackbirds patrolling each side of the invisible boundary between their territories are a good example. Robins use their red breasts to warn rivals off their territory. They have even been known to go to the extent of attacking with great ferocity stuffed 'model' robins placed in their territory by researchers.

Above: These fulmars are nesting among the rocks and flowering sea campion on the island of Inner Farne, off Northumberland.

Right: The fulmar lays only one large, dull-white egg in its clutch, usually in some sort of surface hollow. Incubation – at around 50 days – is long and potentially hazardous.

Below: A young Leach's petrel – a ball of sooty down. The tube 'nose' shows very clearly on this chick.

their nesting cliffs, fulmars provide the birdwatcher with a flying spectacular. They are expert gliders, rarely flapping their wings except on a still day. Gull-sized and grey and white in colour, they may look rather dumpy with short, slender and stiff wings held slightly down-curved. But they are very well streamlined. Their large eyes are set deep in grooves in the feathers and, except when the birds are on the nest, the feet are normally concealed, tucked up out of the way in the body feathers.

Near the cliffs, fulmars use their webbed feet to assist in steering or to make fine adjustments to their flying techniques. They seem able to take advantage of any wind, cutting at speed diagonally across the wind and also downwind in a shallow dive before turning sharply into the wind to gain height again. They then repeat the process. Even the slight up-currents raised by the face of oncoming waves are exploited to give that extra bit of 'free' aerodynamic lift.

Storm petrels are sooty black, save for a white patch along the rump which divides off the square, black tail. They nest on many islands to the west and north of Britain—and often apparently enormous numbers can be heard purring in their burrows. However, any census of these small black birds, which nest in holes and come ashore only after dark, is difficult to carry out with much accuracy.

The Leach's petrel is slightly larger than the storm petrel, with a grey patch on the wing, a forked tail and a dark line down the centre of its rump. One of our scarcest birds, it nests only on a handful of remote islands like St Kilda, where its wild whooping and whistling song can sound quite chilling to the birdwatcher.

Nocturnal activities Towards dusk petrels journey back home to land, either loaded with plankton food for their single dark, fluffy offspring, or anxious to relieve their mate incubating the small, almost spherical white egg. Before they enter their nest these birds gather offshore to await the dark and the safety that darkness brings from predators such as the great black-backed gull.

In winter, these small petrels truly become birds of the open sea (pelagic). They cover the oceans in their search for minute food items from the surface plankton, which they gather while swimming or by dipping down to the waves in flight. Often storm petrels follow in the wake of ships, sometimes pattering their feet on the surface, for mile after mile in the hope of collecting a meal from the scraps tossed overboard. In the days of the sailing ships this habit endeared them to sailors on long voyages and earned them the name 'Mother Carey's chickens'–the reason for which remains obscure, but probably refers to *Mater Cara*, the sailors' name for the Virgin Mary.

Above: The storm, or stormy, petrel is among the smallest and most fragile of seabirds. It touches land only during the breeding season, and then only from dusk to dawn. At other times it is a truly oceanic bird, often following ships in pursuit of scraps, and skimming low over the water.

Below: From fairly small beginnings nearly 1000 years ago on the island of St Kilda (circled in red), the fulmar population has now spread dramatically round the British coast.

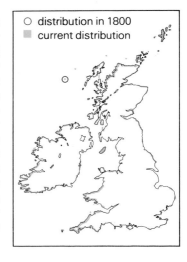

○ distribution in 1800
■ current distribution

THE MANX SHEARWATER

Manx shearwaters nest in burrows, and the sound of their wailing calls, coming from underground at dead of night, has inspired legends of trolls.

Manx shearwaters are slender-winged seabirds about the size of a small gull. As their name suggests, shearwaters at sea skim low over the water, occasionally touching and 'shearing' through a wave-top as they bank and turn.

The plumages of adults and young are similar; dark, oily black above, and white below. The boundary between dark and light comes roughly at water level when the birds are swimming on the sea; although apparently very conspicuous, this distribution of colour hides the somewhat vulnerable shearwaters well from predators such as gulls that approach from above, or large fishes approaching from below.

In flight, however, their plumage is conspicuous; together with the characteristic flight pattern, it makes them easy to recognise at all but the longest ranges. They fly fast and low, often vanishing from view in the wave troughs, which may cause some difficulty in spotting them; but then they bank and turn, first presenting a white undersurface, then black upperparts, to the birdwatcher.

Long-distance gliders At sea, shearwaters cover prodigious distances, and are masters of the art of energy-conserving flight. Most often, they fly in a long, shallow glide down and along the ocean wind, then suddenly turn into the wind, using it to gain a violent uplift at the expense of flight speed, before heading off downwind again in another long glide. Shearwaters are seen performing this spectacular type of flight as they pass along the coast, either on migration or, in the breeding season, on fishing excursions. They often fly in groups, usually in a straggling line.

They are most frequently seen off our south and west coasts. In summer they can be watched in the vicinity of any shearwater

Above: A Manx shearwater: the name 'Manx' refers to a historic colony on the Calf of Man. After centuries of breeding there, shearwaters were absent for 150 years, returning in the 1960s.

Manx shearwater (*Puffinus puffinus*). Summer visitor. Sexes alike. 36cm (14in).

Manx shearwater distribution

colony. These are located on the Isles of Scilly, Lundy, Skokholm, Skomer, Anglesey, some of the islands off the eastern Irish coasts, and many of the islands off the rocky western Scottish and Irish coasts.

Island colonies Most shearwater breeding areas are on remote islands, often uninhabited or at most with just a few human occupants. Shearwaters are clumsy on land; they have powerful webbed feet, and their legs are situated close to the rear of their bodies–which makes them effective swimmers. However, this makes walking on land rather difficult for them. They can only drag themselves along at a painfully slow rate. As a result, they easily fall victim to marauding gulls.

Greater black-backed gulls, in particular, specialise in catching shearwaters. It takes these large gulls only a couple of powerful bites to open the carcase and snip the wings off the shoulders. Then, with a few flicks of the gull's strong neck muscles, the shearwater is skinned and ready for eating. Around the nests of these predatory gulls, the discarded shearwater skins accumulate in a gruesome midden. Despite this vulnerability, shearwaters seem to be maintaining steady populations in most of the areas they inhabit.

As dusk falls, shearwaters gather offshore, floating on the sea in huge 'rafts'. They remain there for some hours, deriving a measure of safety in numbers, and venture ashore only when it is completely dark. Most colonies are on the cliff top, or close to the shore of low-lying islands. One striking exception to this norm is more than a mile from the sea and about 600m (2000ft) up on the rocky screes in the heart of the island of Rùm in the Inner Hebrides.

By day, anyone walking along the cliff top could be excused for not suspecting that there was a shearwater colony nearby. There is little outward sign of their presence in daylight except for the occasional carcase of a shearwater that fell victim to a gull the previous night.

At night, especially on a dark and stormy night, the scene changes dramatically. Homecoming birds fly past overhead with a rush of air, and call to their partners in the nesting burrows with extraordinary cackling, cooing and caterwauling calls. Those in the burrows make similar calls, and the sound of these, coming from the ground and after dark, has inspired legends. The troll legends of Norway, in particular, are said to have originated from these weird sounds.

Shearwater numbers Shearwaters are always colonial, but while some new colonies may only hold a few dozen pairs, others are huge. The one on Rùm was estimated to contain over 100,000 pairs in 1976, while the one on Skomer was estimated at 95,000 pairs in 1973. Counting birds such as shearwaters–which have black upperparts, come ashore only after dark, and nest in numbers as

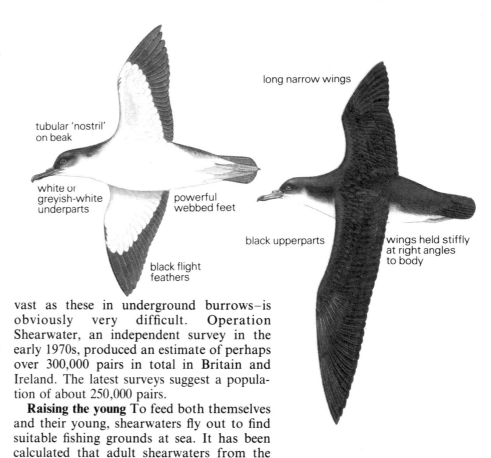

tubular 'nostril' on beak

white or greyish-white underparts

powerful webbed feet

black flight feathers

long narrow wings

black upperparts

wings held stiffly at right angles to body

vast as these in underground burrows–is obviously very difficult. Operation Shearwater, an independent survey in the early 1970s, produced an estimate of perhaps over 300,000 pairs in total in Britain and Ireland. The latest surveys suggest a population of about 250,000 pairs.

Raising the young To feed both themselves and their young, shearwaters fly out to find suitable fishing grounds at sea. It has been calculated that adult shearwaters from the

The shearwater's underground nest

Often nests are made in rabbit burrows. The shearwaters evict the hapless rabbits, using their sharp claws and hooked beaks to secure vacant possession of a suitable-sized burrow.

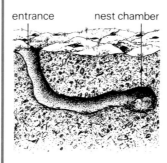

entrance   nest chamber

Above: Shearwater pairs that do not take over rabbit burrows dig new ones for themselves in the soft, peaty soil of the cliff top. A typical burrow consists of an entrance tunnel and a slightly larger nest chamber, which is lined with fronds of bracken and pieces of grass.

Right: A shearwater nesting site, as it appears after many years of burrowing.

Welsh colonies travel as far afield as the Bay of Biscay to find food, returning within one to two days. Most of their food is small in size and taken from the zooplankton, and includes many species of fishes and the young stages of crustaceans and molluscs. The shearwaters fish by diving from the surface and swimming powerfully under water.

The young shearwater, on emerging from the egg, soon develops large quantities of fluffy grey down, and resembles a ball of fluff from which eyes, beak and feet appear incongruously. The parents feed it with a smelly, oily mixture of fish and plankton which is regurgitated from the crop, where it is stored on the long fishing journeys. This mixture is highly nutritious, and the chick grows quickly, becoming very fat. The layer of fat it acquires provides a useful reserve food store for the chick. This is vitally needed, for the parental feeding visits are made after dark, and may not occur every night.

Expert navigators A shearwater has remarkable powers of navigation. Around its 70th or 80th night, the chick fledges: it spends a short time performing vigorous wing-flapping exercises before taking off on its maiden flight. On this journey, without the guidance of an accompanying parent, the young shearwater heads for the wintering grounds at sea off the coast of Brazil. Some birds, however, certainly do go astray. They are liable to be diverted by the violent winds of the south Atlantic. There is one record of a ringed shearwater washed up dead on the coast of southern Australia.

Manx shearwaters have good homing powers, too. Some years ago, an adult female was removed from the egg she was incubating in a burrow on Skokholm, Pembrokeshire, and flown (by aircraft) to Boston in the United States. There, she was released from a tall building. She had returned to her burrow before the letter announcing her release had reached the island!

Above: A Manx shearwater chick in the burrow. Its parents feed it on fishes and marine plankton.

Right: The single egg is usually laid in late May or June. It is oval in shape and a non-reflective white, although its colour soon changes, for it becomes stained by the peaty soil. The parents share the task of incubating, sitting in spells of three to five days and changing over at night. Change-overs may be delayed if bright moonlight illuminates the area and makes the returning bird easily visible to predators such as gulls. Bad weather may also delay the return of the partner bird. Incubation lasts just over 50 days.

Left: A young shearwater, about to reach the age when it will depart on its migratory flight. Fledging usually takes between 70 and 80 days; for about the last 10 days the chick is not visited or fed by its parents. By the time they cease feeding the chick, it has grown far too heavy to fly, and its excess weight is used to complete feather and muscle development as well as for day-to-day sustenance. Eventually, it will struggle out of its burrow and indulge in vigorous wing-flapping exercises to bring its muscles into tone for its maiden flight.

Above: Gannets, which usually pair for life, greet each other with raised bills.

GANNETS: PLUNGING DIVERS OF THE SEA

A gannetry in spring or summer is a breathtaking spectacle: the cliffs and rocks are white with many thousands of these large seabirds. The air, too, is filled with gannets in soaring flight, each ready to plunge into the sea for fish, perhaps from a height of 30m (100ft) or more.

The gannet is our biggest and most spectacular seabird, with a body length of about 1m (3ft) and a wingspan approaching 2m (over 6ft). It is essentially a maritime bird, breeding in cliff colonies called gannetries, although very occasionally storm-driven gannets are seen on lakes and reservoirs inland.

Goose-like bird The adult gannet is a large, almost goose-like white bird with a yellow ochre tinge to the head and nape and conspicuous black wingtips. The yellow colour is mostly lost in winter. In flight, its appearance is less goose-like, mainly because the stout neck and beak in front are counterbalanced by a long, pointed white tail, whereas geese have very short tails and a characteristically unbalanced appearance in flight. The wings, long and noticeably slender, are white for much of their length but with mostly black primaries, or flight feathers. Gannets are often seen flying along the shore, maintaining a height of about 10m (30ft) above the water. The steady flight pattern consists of a series of slow wingbeats, followed by a glide. In small flocks, often all or most birds will pause to glide with precisely timed synchrony.

Gannetry sites

1 Herma Ness; **2** Noss; **3** Foula; **4** Fair Isle; **5** Sula Sgeir; **6** Sule Stack; **7** Flannans; **8** St Kilda; **9** Bass Rock; **10** Ailsa Craig; **11** Scar Rocks; **12** Bempton; **13** Gt Saltee; **14** Little Skellig; **15** Bull Rock; **16** Grassholm; **17, 18** Alderney.

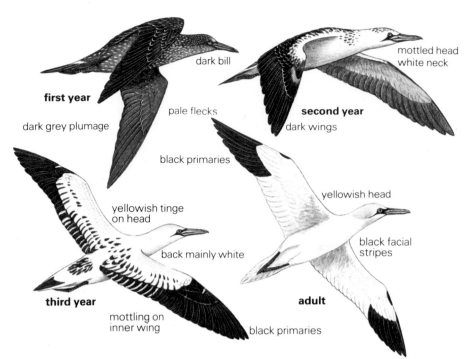

first year

dark bill

dark grey plumage

pale flecks

mottled head
white neck

second year

dark wings

black primaries

yellowish tinge
on head

yellowish head

back mainly white

black facial
stripes

third year

mottling on
inner wing

adult

black primaries

Gannet (*Sula bassana*).
Resident seabird; 70% of
world population found in
British Isles. Sexes are
alike. Length 90cm (36in),
wingspan 1.8m (6ft).

Left: A juvenile gannet. In its
first autumn and winter it has
dark grey plumage,
flecked with pale grey or
white. The plumage develops
to the adult stage over four
or five years.

Below: Herma Ness
gannetry, at the extreme
northern tip of Shetland.

In close-up view when perched, the gannet's webbed feet can be seen to be lead grey, with a neat blue-grey line running along each toe and down the front of the 'shin' or tarsus. The beak, stout and dagger-like, is almost 15cm (6in) long, and is silver coloured, with black lines. On the face a patch of grey or bluish naked skin surrounds a glaring eye with a strikingly pale iris.

Remote gannetries Gannets are colonial breeders, and their expansion in numbers over the last hundred years is one of the more striking bird success stories. There are now 18 gannetries off our coasts, no less than 11 of them founded this century.

The current increase in gannet numbers may partly be a restoration to an earlier situation following an intervening decline. Certainly during the 18th and 19th centuries gannets were persecuted by man, the fat and nutritious nestlings being slaughtered for food in tens of thousands by the inhabitants of some of our remote islands. This pressure has ended with the modernisation of our food industry, and with bird protection laws.

At the same time, it seems most unlikely that the current rate of increase, some 3% per annum, can be solely due to the relaxation of hunting pressure. Probably a major additional factor is climatic change, influencing the numbers and location of such surface-shoaling fish as mackerel, on which the gannets feed. Certainly the rate of increase is high for such a large bird which lays only one egg per season.

During the present century, the world population of the gannet has quadrupled, and with some 185,000 breeding pairs, Britain and Ireland hold around 70% of the world total. Perhaps as much as 20% of the world total now

Diving for a fish

sighting
the fish

dive may
be over
30m (100ft)

wings are
swept back
on entering
water

nests on Boreray and its associated giant rock pinnacles, Stac Lee and Stac-an-Armin, which form part of the St Kilda group of islands. This gannetry may hold over 50,000 pairs. Calculations of the daily catch of fish when the Boreray colony is fully occupied in spring and summer indicate that a prodigious 200 tons or more of fish a day are needed to supply it.

Adapted to fishing In the vicinity of a gannetry, the birds are seen performing their fishing plunge, often from a height of 30m (100ft) or more. When fish are present in huge numbers close to the surface, or when the weather is particularly rough, making visibility poor, the gannets sometimes dive at a slant into the water from a height of only a few feet.

Anatomically, the gannet is admirably well adapted to this way of life. Its eyes, for example, can swivel freely in the sockets, enabling the gannet to look vertically down into the water while maintaining its head in a horizontal position for good aerodynamic 'trim'. Feathers and tough skin assist a robust skeleton in resisting the impact of high dives, and the eyes are set in sockets lined with special 'padding' tissue which acts as a shock absorber.

Gannets differ from sea eagles, ospreys and other dive-plunging birds in the position of their wings during the dive. Instead of entering the water with their wings bent, the 'elbow' pointing forward, gannets allow their wings to trail, stretched out alongside and behind the tail as they penetrate the surface.

The food of the gannet consists almost entirely of fish, the choice depending more on easy availability than on any particular preference. Mackerel, herring, cod, capelin, saithe and pollack all feature regularly in the diet. Most food items are swallowed with a convulsive gulp just as the gannet surfaces from its dive, and can often be seen as a large bulge, steadily descending the gullet.

Colonial breeding Adult gannets begin to return to their nesting ledges in late winter, and by the spring noisy honking displays are commonplace; pairs alternately raise and lower their bills to one another in a complex and ritualised pattern. Gannets are monogamous, and usually pair for life (which is on average about 16 years), although the two sexes go their separate ways during the winter.

Over the years, most nests have become substantial mounds of seaweed and flotsam, held together with guano. As part of the courtship ritual, the male brings frequent 'gifts' of seaweed to the female on the nest, which helps it to become even bigger. The single egg is relatively small for the size of the adult bird, being 7.5cm (3in) long and 5cm (2in) broad. It is chalky blue when laid, but rapidly becomes stained brown. Some eggs are lost to predators such as gulls, or by rolling off the nest (usually during a squabble with the neighbours), but in a study of the gannets on

Bass Rock it was found that over 80% hatched. Eggs lost in the first three weeks of incubation are usually replaced.

Gannets in winter Once they leave the breeding colonies at the end of summer, adult and young gannets separate to go their own way during the winter. The adults, with their superior skills at fishing in poor conditions gained over several seasons, disperse from the colonies but tend to remain in coastal waters round Britain and Ireland or slightly to the south, rarely travelling further than Portugal or Spain. The young birds of the year, on the other hand, migrate purposefully south, first to the Bay of Biscay and later to the waters off North and West Africa.

Above: Over 20,000 pairs of gannets now breed each year on the Bass rock, off the coast of Lothian.

Below: A gannet incubating its egg. The bird has no brood patch of bare skin on the belly to warm the eggs, but instead laps the webs of its feet over the egg to warm it. Incubation takes about 45 days—the longest time for any bird of Britain and Ireland. Fledging takes about 90 days, so there is time for only a single brood each summer.

KITTIWAKES: GULLS OF CLIFF AND SEA

The kittiwake is an ocean-going seabird that nests on rocky coastlines, or even on vertical walls of buildings near the sea. To us, its spartan life seems to have few comforts, for it divides its time between the ocean, the wind and the sheer rock face.

The kittiwake, like the cuckoo, is an excellent example of a bird that clearly calls its own name. A raucous chorus of 'kitti-wa-a-a-ke' cries, with some variations on the theme, tells the birdwatcher that he is nearing a kittiwake colony. The sound is easy to hear despite the sound of waves breaking at the foot of the nesting cliffs.

The sound of the sea must be with kittiwakes all their lives, for in winter they fly far away from land, out over the Atlantic, and some even cross the ocean to the Newfoundland Banks fishing grounds. In spring and summer they can be seen almost anywhere round the coasts of Britain and Ireland, particularly where there are cliffs.

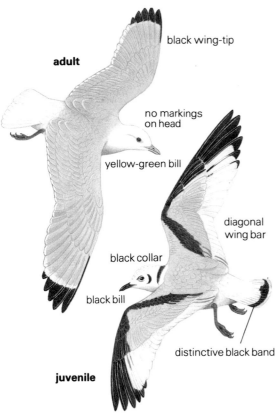

adult

black wing-tip

no markings on head

yellow-green bill

diagonal wing bar

black collar

black bill

distinctive black band

juvenile

The kittiwake is by far the most maritime of our gulls, coming to land only to breed, and then restricted almost entirely to the coast. Only very occasionally are storm-driven or sick birds seen inland, seeking a last refuge on a large lake or reservoir.

A well-mannered gull Most gulls, though elegant, seem to humans to have an unpleasant side to their character: many are nest robbers, a few are even cannibals and feed on the chicks of their own kind, and most, given the chance, scavenge greedily on refuse tips. The kittiwake is a gull, but it has none of these unpleasant habits. It is classified separately from the majority of gulls, too, and belongs to the genus *Rissa*, while most other gulls are grouped in the genus *Larus*.

The kittiwake is small and slender in comparison with most other gulls; it is all white except for the wings, which are silver grey with black tips. The wingtips differ from those of the common gull, which are also black but have clear white blobs that serve to tell the common gull apart from the kittiwake. The head of the kittiwake is small and rounded, and the beak is yellow, with a bright vermilion inside lining during the breeding season. The legs are black, further distinguishing the kittiwake from most other gulls.

Clamouring colonies On warm days during late winter, occasional single birds or groups fly in from the ocean to visit the nesting site, and visits become more frequent and prolonged during the spring. The more experienced pairs return to take up the territories they held the previous year.

Kittiwakes are primarily birds of the precipitous rocky coastline of western and northern Britain and Ireland. They nest in colonies, sometimes hundreds strong. The cliff they choose may be any size between a small outcrop to a towering precipice, and the kittiwakes are undeterred if the rock has the most intimidating overhang. Nests are sometimes built in the arch of a sea cave. The slightest projection or narrow ledge serves the bird as a foundation on which it can secure its nest.

Each nest is about 25cm (10in) in diameter, and is made of mud, pieces of seaweed and a colourful variety of flotsam and jetsam, including fragments of fishermen's nets. All this is cemented together, more and more firmly as the years go by, with liberal quantities of the kittiwake's tacky droppings.

The eggs vary in colour from blue-grey to sandy-fawn, and are covered with darker brown speckles. Egg-laying usually begins late in May. Younger birds, breeding for the first time, have the least secure and most vulnerable nests, situated on the fringes of the colony, while more established pairs occupy the centre. Young pairs often lay only a single egg, while older birds have clutches of two or, somewhat rarely, three. Each pair breeds only once each season.

As they shared the task of refurbishing the nest before laying, so both sexes share the tedious period of incubation, which lasts 21-24 days. Often it is very hot on the cliff face, and the incubating adult can be seen panting, revealing the vermilion interior of its mouth.

Fledging takes between four and five weeks, depending on how stormy the weather is and thus how easy or difficult the kittiwakes' fishing flights are, for this determines the amount of food they are able to provide for the growing young. Because of the precarious situation of the nest, kittiwake youngsters have to be specially well-behaved. Until they are able to fly, they never walk more than a few inches from the spot where they hatched—if they did, they would risk

Kittiwake (*Rissa tridactyla*); small to medium gull that spends winter mainly at sea. Nests on cliffs, rarely seen inland. British population over ½ million, increasing by 50% every 10 years. Length 41cm (16in).

Opposite page: Kittiwakes perching on a precipitous cliff. Nests are built on the narrowest of ledges and cemented with guano.

Below: Each time an adult kittiwake returns to the nest, its partner welcomes it with an effusive display, flapping its wings and bowing its head in an enthusiastic manner. Kittiwake colonies are always conspicuous because of the noise made by the birds after their return from the sea. First comes the raucous calling of the males during display, and soon after this the pairs make a great deal of noise defending their nesting ledges, and the nests themselves, from the depredations of their neighbours. Neighbourly relations may not be of the best, but as real fighting could easily dislodge eggs or young and send them tumbling into the sea, kittiwakes merely shriek at their neighbours if they come too close, adding to the bedlam of the cliffside colony.

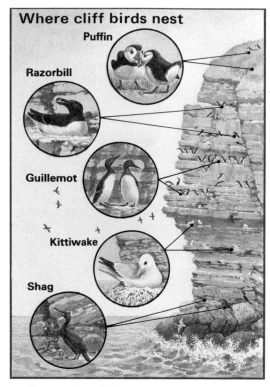

Where cliff birds nest

Puffin

Razorbill

Guillemot

Kittiwake

Shag

a plummeting fall to certain death in the sea or on the rocks below.

Changing fortunes In the last century the fashion for ornamental feathers, and indeed whole wings of birds, as decorations on ladies' hats was at its height. The millinery trade demanded huge quantities of kittiwake wings – particularly the finely marked juvenile wings. Kittiwake shooting was regarded as a fine sport, and lucrative into the bargain. Thus by the turn of the century, the kittiwake was a scarce bird except in the most remote areas. The fortunes of the bird did not improve until it was given the protection of the law; once kittiwake shooting was banned, numbers began to increase once again.

Above: Young kittiwakes are not pure white like their parents, but have grey mottling. They also have a black half-collar on the nape of the neck and a black W-shaped mark across the outstretched wings. This is a useful identification feature of the juveniles in flight, as is the black band across the tip of the tail.

Below: Kittiwakes feed close inshore during the breeding season, and their diet is mainly small fish such as sprats. When out on the ocean in winter they feed on a wide range of small invertebrates, including jellyfish, crustaceans, molluscs and worms, that all float close to the surface in the marine plankton. Occasionally kittiwakes feed on plant matter.

Indeed, the kittiwake population has continued to grow for many years after the shooting was banned. One reason for their success must be that they have few natural enemies, and they are able to defend themselves well enough from those that they have, such as the larger gulls. If a gull appears at the colony, perhaps to raid a kittiwake nest, the whole community of kittiwakes mobs the intruder furiously. The siting of the kittiwake nests on the cliff wall ensures their safety from mammal predators such as rats, stoats or foxes. Another reason for the success of the kittiwake is that the small fish and plankton on which they feed are always plentiful throughout the year.

A census of the breeding population in 1959 gave the estimated population as 180,000 pairs, although this was considered an underestimate because of the difficulties of reaching and counting remote colonies in Scotland. A decade later the RSPB conducted a more thorough survey known as *Operation Seafarer*, which estimated the population to be just under half a million pairs. Even allowing for inaccuracies caused by the difficulty of obtaining data, it was clear that a phenomenal increase had taken place. Kittiwakes had recolonized all those coasts from which they had been hunted to extinction, and spread further afield as well. In eastern England, where much of the coastline is low-lying, kittiwakes had established breeding colonies on piers, warehouses and power stations, using vertical walls and windowsills as 'replacement cliffs'. Current estimates put the population at about 543,000 pairs; the highest for at least a century.

Birdwatchers beware A kittiwake colony is well worth hours of watching, but be careful of two things: sit far enough away, so as not to disrupt the life of the seabirds, and, perhaps even more important, be careful for your own safety on the cliffs. Cliffs are always hazardous but seabird cliffs, with their coating of slime and thriving vegetation, are particularly dangerous. Beware of the temptation to crawl too near the edge to get a better view of a colony below an overhanging cliff. The ground could well be crumbly.

GUILLEMOTS: BIRDS OF ROCKY COASTS

With its comical stance and its huge breeding colonies, the guillemot bears a close resemblance to the penguin in both appearance and life-style. Yet the penguin belongs to the Southern Hemisphere, whereas the guillemot is a common British seabird.

Above: A group of guillemots with a pair of razorbills hiding behind. The two species are closely related to each other and occupy the same rocky coastal habitat, though guillemots are much more common.

All members of the auk family (of which the guillemot is one) resemble penguins to some degree, even though the two families are quite unrelated; for auks are exclusive to the Northern Hemisphere, just as penguins are to the Southern. The similarity between these two bird families is due to a well known phenomenon in which groups of animals that

are separated by vast distances but occupy similar ecological niches tend to develop along similar lines. This is known as parallel evolution.

Among auks, it is the guillemot that most closely resembles the penguin; the two species even have a similar anatomy. But the most obvious way in which they resemble each other is in their plumage.

Penguin-like plumage During the breeding season the guillemot's head and upperparts are black or a warm chocolate-brown and the underparts are white. In winter it moults and acquires white cheeks and throat and a grey-brown body.

Occasionally, guillemots show a white eye-ring and a white bar running behind each eye. These 'bridled' birds were once thought to be a separate species, but the phenomenon is now believed to be a plumage phase through which every guillemot passes.

Guillemots in the north of Britain differ somewhat from those found in the south. Their plumage is noticeably darker (almost black) and they are larger–44cm (18in) long–

Above: The guillemot's wings have become adapted for underwater swimming. Nevertheless, it is still able to fly – unlike the penguin, whose wings have become so stiffened and reduced that it is no longer capable of even the shortest flight.

Above: A typical breeding ground for guillemots is an inaccessible narrow ledge high up a steep cliff face. Guillemots happily breed on the narrowest of ledges, but the rock must have the right pattern of faults and fractures to give a reasonably horizontal surface, otherwise the eggs could roll off the ledge. Notice the quantity of white guano on the ledges.

Below: The staple diet of the guillemot is fish, crustaceans and a variety of worms. To catch them, the guillemot dives beneath the water and uses its short powerful wings to propel itself along.

than southern guillemots, which are about 4cm (2in) shorter. Northern guillemots are also more commonly bridled.

Built for swimming The guillemot has a slender, streamlined body, well adapted for swimming under water. Its wings are short and stiff-feathered. Under water, the guillemot uses them as oars to propel itself, but on the surface it swims by means of its webbed feet, which are set well back in its body for the purpose. Inevitably, this makes the guillemot a clumsy, almost comical creature on land and accounts for its penguin-like upright stance.

The guillemot's mainly aquatic life is reflected in its skeletal structure. The backbone is fused into one stiff rod, while the ribs and breastbone are both extremely robust. The ribs also overlap each other to provide extra strength. In this way, the guillemot's vital organs are protected from the tremendous pressures that occur when it dives for food – fish, worms, crustaceans and the occasional

mollusc.

Breeding colonies The best time to see guillemots is during the late spring and summer when they are at their breeding colonies on rocky cliffs and stacks of western and northern Britain and Ireland. A typical breeding site is a narrow ledge on a steep cliff-face high above the sea.

The two features of a guillemot colony that strike the visiting birdwatcher most forcibly are the noise and the smell. The noise is hard to describe but resembles something like a continuous rumbling mooing – murres, the American name for guillemots, comes from the noise they make. The smell of a guillemot colony is caused by a mixture of droppings (or guano) and the rotting fishy remains of their meals. The surrounding rocks become whitewashed with guano during the breeding season and make the colony easily visible from a distance.

The breeding season During the winter, guillemots spend most of their time in offshore waters, apart from occasional visits to the colony when the weather is fine. But, as spring and the breeding season approaches, these visits become more frequent and longer-lasting.

By the middle or the end of May, the females have begun to lay their eggs. No nest is built – the egg is simply laid on bare rock. Each female lays just a single very large egg, about 8cm (3in) long. Its colour is highly variable, ranging from cream, or pale blue or green, to a reddish-brown, with an enormous variety of dark squiggly patterns on it. Perhaps this variability helps each bird to identify its own egg in the crowded conditions of a guillemot colony. A guillemot's egg is superbly well-designed for survival on a narrow ledge, since it is long and sharply pointed, with straight sides. If knocked it rolls in a tight circle and stays on the ledge, whereas any other bird's egg would roll off the ledge.

The egg is incubated on the open ledge by both parents and takes about a month to hatch. Guillemots are poor parents and often leave their egg unprotected and at the mercy of marauding gulls.

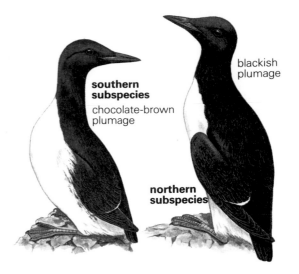

Left: A pair of guillemots shielding their young, possibly from predatory gulls. In crowded breeding colonies the parents perform the same action when feeding their young. They use their wings to protect both the chick and the food, otherwise another young guillemot nearby is likely to jump in and try to steal the food.

Above right: Guillemots in northern Britain and those in the south form two distinct subspecies. Southern birds have a warm chocolate-brown plumage, whereas northern birds are much darker and bigger.

southern subspecies
chocolate-brown plumage

blackish plumage

northern subspecies

Guillemot (*Uria aalge*). Seabird breeding around rocky coasts of the northern and western British Isles. In winter it extends its range to the east and south coasts. Length: southern subspecies 40cm (16in), northern subspecies 44cm (18in).

A mouthful of fish The young guillemot is born downy and grows rapidly. Both parents help to feed it, giving it one large fish at a time, unlike puffins and razorbills, who feed their young with small fry. When the chick is still young, the fish may be too large for it to take in at one go, in which case an inch or so of the fish's tail is left hanging out of the chick's mouth and gradually vanishes as the the fish is digested.

In a crowded colony the parents have to be careful when handing the fish over to their young or other young guillemots are likely to jump in and steal the food. To prevent this they use their wings as a screen to protect the fish while they pass it to the chick.

A more serious threat to young guillemots is predation from large gulls. To avoid this, they often make for the sea well before they are fully fledged, sometimes when they are only two or three weeks old and half-grown. To reach the sea they have to tumble down the face of the cliff. To us, this seems extremely hazardous, since they are still flightless. The vast majority reach the sea unharmed, however, protected by a thick layer of fat as they bounce off the rocks and, to some degree, supported by the strong up-currents of air that are always present near a cliff face.

Off for the winter Once at sea the young complete their development in the company of adult guillemots. In the autumn, both they and the adults disperse to spend the winter in the coastal waters of north and west Europe, the Mediterranean and North Africa.

During winter guillemots (not necessarily the same birds as breed here) can be seen at many places along the coast of Britain, not just in the north and west where they breed

but also along the coasts of southern and eastern counties. Well-known promontories such as Portland Bill, Beachy Head and Dungeness are excellent places from which to observe them.

The threat from man The guillemot is Britain's most numerous seabird. Its current population has risen to over one million birds. Over three-quarters of these are to be found in Scotland, with the largest single colonies, on the islands of Noss and Foula in the Shetlands, having over 60,000 birds. Yet the guillemot has long been threatened, both directly and indirectly, by man's activities.

In Victorian times guillemot numbers were seriously affected by egg collectors, especially at sites with large colonies, such as Bempton Cliffs in Yorkshire (now an RSPB reserve).

This century, the major threat to the guillemot has come from oil pollution. At first, this was a threat mainly during the winter when the birds were well out to sea, since that was where most of the pollution occurred. However, with the growth of the North Sea oil industry so close to the guillemot's breeding grounds, the threat has become much greater. If an oil spillage occurred close to its breeding grounds the effect on the guillemot population would be catastrophic; certainly it will be far worse than a spillage far out to sea. So far, however, the guillemot population seems to be stable enough to resist the often thoughtless pressures created by man.

Above: So-called 'bridled' guillemots show a white eye-ring with a white bar running behind each eye. This is believed to be a plumage phase and is more common in northern birds; notice the typically dark plumage of this subspecies.

Egg variations
Guillemot eggs are among the most variable of any bird's. The background colour may vary from white, through buff or brown, to red; or it may be blue or green. The markings may be brown or black dots, blotches or squiggly lines.
Guillemot eggs are long and pointed with straight sides to stop them rolling off into the sea.

COURTLY PUFFINS

The puffin is a notoriously difficult bird to study: comings and goings at the puffinry are erratic and nests are made in burrows too deep and dark to permit eggs or young to be seen.

The puffin, in its 'dinner-jacket' of black and white feathers and colourful banded beak, is one of our most charming birds. It belongs to a family of seabirds–auks–which includes guillemots and razorbills.

Distribution and dispersal For most of the year puffins live on our remote, almost inaccessible, northern coasts–particularly around uninhabited islands in the Orkneys and Shetlands. They once flourished along the Channel coast, but have now virtually disappeared from this region. In the east only suitable cliffs from Flamborough Head northwards support colonies. There are more puffinries on the western, generally rocky shoreline of Britain and Ireland. Here, the population increases towards the north.

In winter, puffins disperse widely from their breeding colonics, remaining at sea in ones or twos, not in the large groups (rafts) favoured by other auks. Some puffins stay in the North Sea or in the Bay of Biscay, while a few move south into the Mediterranean .

Puffins remain further out to sea than guillemots or razorbills, and most spend the winter scattered over the north Atlantic, feeding mainly on plankton. Even juvenile birds range far and wide: two nestlings ringed one year on St Kilda, off the Outer Hebrides, were recovered the following winter over the Newfoundland Banks.

Breeding sites The puffins return to their puffinries at varying times in spring. Many of these sites are large, and some, with tens or even hundreds of thousands of pairs, are enormous. The Farne Islands are a good place to see puffins, on the National Trust reserve, but there are also large colonies on the Scilly Isles, Bempton Cliffs in Yorkshire and Skomer off the Pembrokeshire coast. Puffins are sensitive to the presence of humans, so all the best places to see them are inaccessible.

Some puffins live in holes in sea cliffs, while others choose the extensive screes and tumbled boulders at the head and foot of the cliffs. Most puffins, however, nest in grassland burrows, usually close to the cliff top. Here they either dig burrows themselves, making use of the long sharp claws on their strong feet, or they take over a disused rabbit hole or Manx shearwater burrow.

The grassy slopes favoured by puffins are usually covered in pink thrift, white sea-campion, and often harebells–all flourishing on the guano deposited by the seabirds. This forms an attractive back-drop to the puffins' social gatherings at burrow entrances,

Above: Although puffins do not have an elaborate courtship display, the male and female bow to each other in a 'courtly' manner, and nibble one another round the back of the neck.

Far left: As their young grows, the adults visit the burrow regularly with sand eels or similar small fish held cross-wise in the beak.

Puffin *(Fratercula arctica)*; about 25cm (10in) high. Distribution on coastal, rocky shores, particularly western Britain, Ireland and northern offshore islands.

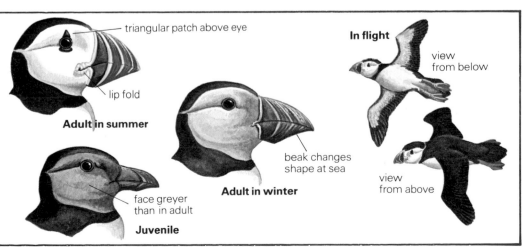

Beak-full of colour
The huge, comical-looking, parrot-like beak of the puffin, is only coloured with red, blue and yellow bands for display in the summer breeding season. The adult sheds the horny outer sheath at the end of summer. It then grows a much smaller, slimmer and strictly functional grey winter beak— much the same size as that of the youngsters. This beak change is accompanied by plumage colour changes.

triangular patch above eye
lip fold
Adult in summer
face greyer than in adult
Juvenile
beak changes shape at sea
Adult in winter
In flight
view from below
view from above

and to the communal fly-pasts that are so much a part of the puffin's life.

These fly-pasts are a spectacular sight. The Kearton brothers, (pioneer Victorian natural history photographers) who visited St Kilda late in the 19th century, complained that the vast numbers of wheeling birds overhead seriously interfered with the light for photography. They also described a pattering 'like rain' which forced them to put up umbrellas for shelter; this was not, as you might imagine, from droppings, but from thousands of small feather parasites falling from the puffins above.

Beakfuls of fish The puffin catches fish by diving straight into the water. Its beak has enormous carrying capacity. Usually the bird catches only a dozen or so small fish and fry crosswise in its beak, in each expedition. But up to 60 small fry in one beakful have been recorded.

Ornithologists still do not fully understand how the puffin manages to catch more fish without dropping those it already holds in its beak. The hinge of the jaw contains an extra small bone, so the two halves of the beak open with the edges parallel. The edges are very sharp, allowing a good grip, but too tight a grip would just chop the fish into three. The roof of the mouth has many backward-pointing sharp projections. This must help the puffin as it sweeps through a shoal of fish, snapping first to one side, then the other, to secure its meal. In rough weather, when the sea is murky, the puffin concentrates on larger prey, up to 15cm (6in) long, but on calm days with clear water much of the catch is smaller.

Danger from the air On land the puffin waddles on its bright orange webbed feet. This may appear comical to us, but its clumsiness

makes the bird vulnerable to predators, such as great black-backed gulls. These may pounce on puffins standing at their burrow entrance, or on a hungry well-grown chick peering out of the nest hole to see whether the next meal is on the way. The gulls sometimes chase and fly down an unfortunate puffin in mid-air, occasionally eating it while it is still alive. More often, they land and kill the puffin with heavy stabbing blows from the beak, before turning it inside-out to get at the flesh. Great skuas also attack puffins, especially on the water.

Crash-landings Puffins are not skilful fliers, and cannot easily escape the predators which attack them in mid-air. But they also have difficulty in landing in strong crosswinds. Their hesitant approach is exploited by some herring gulls. The gulls harass the puffins on their return runs to the burrow, and cause them to crash-land and drop their beakload of fish, which the gulls then gobble up. Although puffins are better adapted to marine life, landing on sea seems as precarious as landing on the ground. They appear to stop flying a few inches above the surface and land with a splash – rather like a thrown brick.

Once on or under the water the puffin is in its element. Short, stiff wings (similar to those of the penguin, but not so highly developed) and powerful legs provide propulsion, steering and levelling. The puffin's vertebrae are fused together, and the breastbone is very strong; the two are joined by sturdy ribs, each with an overlapping flange, so that the whole skeleton provides a rigid box girder structure, capable of protecting the vital organs from the pressure of deep dives.

Pressure on puffinries Sudden declines seem to be a feature of the puffin's history: some

Nest and young
The parent puffins inspect a likely burrow (right) to prepare for egg-laying. In the depths of this hole the female will lay her single, dirty white egg. By June the egg has hatched into a plump ball of sooty black, fluffy down (below) with a small triangular beak and dark eyes. Inside the dingy, dark hole the chick makes strange grumbling and groaning moans which may serve to guide the parents to the right hole. The chick is tended by both parents for about 40 days, after which it fends for itself.

are due perhaps to chemical or oil pollution, or to the accidental introduction of the predatory brown rat, as on Lundy – which was formerly known as the 'Isle of Puffins'.

There was also a huge puffinry on Grassholm, off the Pembrokeshire coast, until over-intensive burrowing by the puffins made the thin soil layer friable, so that erosion by wind and water left only bedrock. The puffins declined but an enormous gannetry then developed on the island. The problem is increased by the puffins' liking for grassy slopes on which sheep feed through the summer months. The sheep may easily trample in the burrow roof.

Local declines and increases are to be expected in any bird population, but the enormous decline in puffin numbers on islands like St Kilda in recent years is alarming. With the evacuation of the last islanders from St Kilda 60 years ago, the puffins were expected to expand in this remote stronghold. But *Operation Seafarer*, a seabird census taken in 1969-70, suggested that the population had fallen below 300,000 pairs–a fraction of the original. Numbers are now stable at around 155,000 pairs on the island group.

Harvested for food Against the background of this decline, it is difficult to understand the past stability of puffinries on remote islands including St Kilda, where for centuries the puffin was hunted and eaten. Each year many thousands, sometimes as many as 100,000, were slaughtered for food. Some were eaten immediately while others were split open and salted or dried for consumption during the winter.

There were no long-term drops in puffin numbers. It seems that the good husbandry of the islanders, who took a strictly rationed 'crop' that they knew the population could sustain, ensured this. Even today, in the Faroe Islands and elsewhere, puffins are snared or netted for food. Their natural inquisitiveness leads them to venture too near the fowler and his traps.

The most pressing conservation concern today is the decline in populations of sand eels, which form an important part of the puffin's diet, and is the subject of much research.

Above: Puffins breed in colonies, and communal gatherings around the burrow entrances are a common sight during the breeding season. Puffins, however, are sensitive to human disturbance. This is unfortunate for them, as more leisure time and modern transport now allow many more people to look for puffins than in the past. The moral is simple: always keep your distance and preferably look for puffins on established bird reserves, where disturbance is minimal and the birds are used to visitors. You can see puffins on the National Trust reserve on the Farne Islands, or at the RSPB reserve on Bempton Cliffs, Yorkshire, or from organised boat trips around the Scilly Isles.

CLIFF-FACE RAZORBILLS

Razorbills breed in their thousands on Britain's western and northern cliffs. They are superb divers and underwater swimmers. While they are moulting, they cannot fly.

The razorbill is notable for its distinctive stance, elongated silhouette and striking black and white summer plumage. The stance of this bird on its breeding cliffs is usually upright, whereas on the water it appears low-lying and short-necked and about the size of a teal, but with the rather long, pointed tail usually held up at an angle.

Summer and winter appearance In summer the razorbill's underparts are pure white, while the tail, back, wings, neck and head are jet black, relieved only by a white vertical mark near the tip of the black beak, by a white line of 'furry' feathers stretching from the 'bridge of the nose' to the eye, and by a bold white wing bar. In flight this wing bar forms a conspicuous trailing edge on the inner half of the wing, visible both from above and below, and more striking than the wing bar of the otherwise confusingly similar guillemot.

In winter, when some of our razorbills remain well offshore in British waters, confusion with guillemots is even more likely.

Above: A razorbill in the typical upright stance. The white wing bar and beak stripe are particularly conspicuous. The beak is smaller in winter, the summer beak having been shed at the autumn moult.

Below: A group of razorbills —the wings are noticeably flipper-like in appearance.

razorbills nest on open ledges, but many prefer cavities in the cliff face or seek similar shelter from such predators as the great black-backed gull deep beneath the rocks in the screes at the top or foot of the cliffs.

Most razorbill colonies are relatively small and interspersed with those of other auks; few colonies reach 10,000 pairs and only one, on Horn Head in County Donegal, is of any great size, perhaps exceeding 12,000 pairs. *Operation Seafarer*, a survey of British Isles seabirds conducted in 1969-70, suggested an estimated 144,000 pairs as our grand total, and the latest estimates of observers indicate a combined total for Britain and Ireland of 182,000 pairs.

Courtship and breeding Razorbills may visit their breeding cliffs in fine weather almost any time after the New Year, but attendance becomes much more regular from March onwards. On the cliffs, pairs indulge in mutual neck-nibbling, but the sky is full of pairs involved in the 'butterfly' display. In this, the wing-beats are slowed right down and are exaggeratedly deep – hence the name.

The single massive egg is laid in mid-May and incubated in turn by both parents. As might be expected from the protected nature of the nest site, the razorbill egg is of normal chicken-like shape, not pointed and top-shaped like that of the exposed ledge-nesting guillemot. However, the spots and squiggles of dark markings, and the background colour

Both birds moult to a nondescript grey above, with smudgy margins, while the dark head is replaced by a pale greyish neck and face. As many are seen at long range, identification is often uncertain and only birds close enough to see the longer tail of the razorbill, or its square-ended beak, can be positively named.

Coastal distribution The results of ringing studies of British and Irish razorbills show that, in general, they travel further than guillemots, many reaching Mediterranean waters by mid-winter. In common with some other birds (gannets and gulls for example) razorbills, as they become older, tend to travel shorter distances during the winter, rarely moving further than the North Sea or the Bay of Biscay. Ringing recoveries also show that man plays a large part in causing the death of these birds: about half of those found dead are reported killed either by oiling, by being shot by Continental sportsmen, or by being drowned in fishing nets.

About 20% of the world razorbill population breed in Britain and Ireland. What makes our islands so special in this respect? Compared with much of Europe, our western and northern coasts, and the off-shore islands, are girt with precipitous cliffs. They form natural reserves, protected by treacherous and often rough seas. The rock of these cliffs, too, is often of just the type needed by the razorbills, cracking and fracturing to provide appropriate ledges and crevices. Some

Above: About 20% of the world population of razorbills breed in Britain and Ireland, finding security on the inaccessible cliffs of our coasts.

Right: Only one large egg is laid each year by the razorbill; it is incubated by both parents.

Below: At the age of two or three weeks the razorbill chick must make its way down the cliffs to the sea, where it is safer from the predations of gulls.

of the shell, are just as varied as those on the guillemot egg, and presumably help the returning bird to identify its own egg among many others. During the nesting season the pair communicate with each other and with their neighbours using a variety of sepulchral, grumbling, low-pitched groans, but at other times they are totally silent.

The egg hatches about a month later, in mid-June, and is then fed by both parents. Like puffins, razorbills return to the nest carrying a beakful of several small fishes held crosswise. The approach to the nest is often difficult in the winds blowing about the cliff face. Razorbills, being heavy-bodied, with short, stiff wings, are not very manoeuvrable and may have to make several approaches before achieving a good landing.

Taking to the sea The razorbill chick remains on the nesting cliffs for only two or three weeks. Then, usually under cover of darkness to protect it from gull predation, it jumps from the cliff down into the sea. At this stage it is only half-grown, its wings little more than stubs and certainly incapable of sustaining flight for any length of time. Nonetheless, most chicks seem to survive perfectly well, protected by their down and fat from injury on the rocks on the way down. The chick then sets off for the open sea, accompanied by at least one of its parents. Whatever the apparent hazards, it would seem that this is less risky than staying on the cliffs to be persecuted by the gulls. While they are still at sea caring for the flightless chick, the adults moult all their flight feathers at once, thus themselves becoming flightless.

Diving and swimming The chicks can swim and dive well by the time they take to the sea, and beneath the water the birds are fast and expert swimmers, using both feet and wings for propulsion and steering.

Razorbill recognition features

The juvenile razorbill (below) looks much like the adult in shape, but has a shorter, blunter bill with no white stripe. In colour it resembles the adult in winter plumage, having greyish-white cheeks and throat patches. Male and female razorbills have similar plumage, both in summer and in winter.

juvenile
white throat and cheek patches

black upperparts
white eye stripe
white bar on beak
adult in breeding plumage
white wing bar

The body skeleton is better suited to life beneath the water than to flight, being a robust 'box girder' structure. A stout, inflexible backbone is joined to a strong breastbone by thick ribs, each with a backward-pointing projection overlapping the rib behind for additional strength. Within this rigid box the body organs are protected from the pressure of water during dives often many metres below the surface. The razorbill's prey includes sand eels, small sprats and the fry of a wide range of fishes and also some shellfishes and shrimps.

Above: Razorbills, like the other auks, have a whirring style of flight. The wings are used as much to propel the bird through the water as the air, while the large webbed feet (which act rather like the flaps on aircraft wings) are often used to steady and control the bird while landing—they are held in a 'straddled' position away from the body. The narrow, stiff wings and heavy body combine to make the razorbill somewhat clumsy in the air.

black guillemot   **puffin**   **razorbill**   **guillemot**

Above: Four members of the auk family occur in Britain and Ireland: the puffin, razorbill, guillemot and black guillemot. They are all black and white birds characterised by an upright stance and the fact that they are expert divers and underwater swimmers. (Another member of the family, the great auk, became extinct in 1844 because of the depredations of egg collectors.) The puffin is the smallest of the four at 30cm (12in) long; the next smallest is the black guillemot (34cm/13½in), while the razorbill and guillemot are much the same size (41cm/16in long).

Razorbill distribution

Razorbill (*Alca torda*). Resident seabird in British and Irish waters, breeding on precipitous cliffs on western and northern coasts and offshore islands; seagoing for rest of year. Length 41cm (16in).

Left: On the water razorbills appear low-lying and rather short-necked.

PIRATICAL SKUAS

Great and Arctic skuas harry and bully other seabirds until they disgorge or drop the food they are carrying. Skuas are so agile that they can often catch the food in mid-air.

Arctic and great skuas – large, aggressive, gull-like birds – are migrants that visit the northernmost shores of the British Isles from April to November. They put their exceptionally agile flying skills to good use in robbing other birds of their food.

Arctic skua In size and shape the Arctic skua resembles a middle-sized but rather slim, long-winged gull. The two central tail feathers of the adult birds are greatly elongated into slightly flexible streamers, perhaps half as long again as the body. Although the tail feathers sometimes become broken, this plumage feature is most useful in field identification of adults; it is lacking in young birds.

Colour phases Arctic skuas sometimes cause birdwatchers problems because they can appear in quite different plumages, called colour phases: in one phase the bird is dark brown all over (the dark phase), in the other the body is predominantly creamy white with a dark cap, back, wings and tail (the pale phase). There are numerous intermediate phases with different amounts of pale coloration. The juveniles are always dark all over – a very distinct rich chocolate brown, with grey feather fringes giving the plumage a scaly appearance.

Aerial piracy In view of the difficulties presented by such a variety of plumage colours, it is fortunate that the flight of the Arctic skua is distinctive enough to provide a valuable aid to field identification. The slender build, long whippy wings and long tail make them fast and nimble in flight, capable of astonishing agility in the air. In addition, there is a large white patch in the centre of each wing, visible only in flight, formed by the pale bases of the primary feathers.

Bully-birds Arctic skuas seem to rely mostly on their sheer bullying capability and expert flight to extract their food; rarely is there much physical contact or actual damage to the homecoming bird, which soon shakes its feathers back into position and returns to its feeding grounds to try again. The attacks are random, too, so that no single pair is remorselessly parasitised and overall their young lose no more than the odd meal.

Above: The great skua is known as the bonxie in Shetland, a word derived from the Norse language and implying aggression and strength, two characteristics this bird has in abundance.

Below: The April-November British range of the great skua. The Arctic skua's range is very similar, except that it can sometimes be found in some of the remoter parts of mainland Scotland.

Great skua distribution

Great skua (*Stercorarius skua*), 58cm (23in) from beak to tip of tail. Only one colour phase. Relatively late migrant, in Britain from April to November.

Arctic skua (*Stercorarius parasiticus*), 45cm (18in) long from beak to tip of tail. Two main colour phases with numerous intermediate phases. Migrant, in Britain from April to November.

Below: Arctic skua with a young fledgling. Note the adult's exceptionally long tail—a helpful feature if you want to identify the adult. Like great skuas, Arctic skuas do not hesitate to defend their territory from other birds and even humans, flying straight at them and attacking them with their strong beaks and webbed feet.

For some of the year at least, and perhaps especially during the winter months, Arctic skuas can, and do, forage largely for themselves. Much of their diet is fish caught on the sea surface or by shallow plunge-diving; on the breeding grounds in years when vole or lemming numbers are especially high, these rodents feature in the birds' diet, as do the eggs or chicks of other birds that have been left unprotected. However, the Arctic skua's dependence on rodents for food is never so great as in the closely related pomarine skua, which has a breeding season diet largely composed of lemmings–to such an extent that, in years when lemmings are low, the pomarine skuas may not breed at all.

Breeding colonies Arctic skuas breed in a relatively narrow circumpolar belt that fringes the northern coasts of North America, Eurasia and the various island land masses in the Atlantic, Pacific, and Arctic oceans. Most breed in colonies, with the colour phases indiscriminately mixed. These colonies are often large, sometimes of hundreds, or even thousands, of pairs. In Britain, the Arctic skua's strongholds are on the offshore islands to the north of Scotland, but occasionally you may see solitary pairs in remoter parts of the Scottish mainland. Elsewhere, the habitat is damp tundra, but British birds nest on open damp grassland or moorland near the coast or, in the south of their range, on open areas of hill country.

Great skua

adult

Arctic skua

pale phase adult

juvenile

The nest is simple, consisting of a depression in grass or moss, often rounded-off and lined with dried grasses. The clutch size normally varies between one and four olive-brown or olive-green eggs, and incubation and fledging each take about one month. The eggs (and the young that hatch from them) are fiercely defended against intruders, be they buzzards, gulls, foxes or man. All the nearby pairs will take to the wing in defence of the nesting area, but the brunt of the aggression comes from the pair whose territory has been invaded. These birds swoop ferociously at the intruder, coming within inches and often making physical contact.

Summer visitor The Arctic skua is a summer visitor to Britain, leaving during the autumn, and flying south, usually over inshore waters, to winter in equatorial or southern hemisphere waters. If you cannot enjoy the thrilling experience of visiting the remote breeding islands, the best opportunity of seeing all the skuas is at their times of passage. The cross-Channel and Irish Sea ferries provide an ideal grandstand, but a less

expensive view can be had from many headlands around the coast, such as Dungeness, Spurn Head or Portland Bill, all well known as good sea-watching locations.

Skuas are relatively late migrants (like most terns), passing northwards from late April through May. Often they travel in small purposeful parties. In the autumn, their passage is more leisurely, and skuas may be seen offshore at any time between August and November.

The great skua is also best seen in autumn when it migrates south. It, too, winters in equatorial seas. Great skuas are usually seen only in ones or twos, rarely in groups like other skuas. They are easily distinguished from their relatives by their large size (which is very similar to the great black-backed gull), their short blunt tail with only tiny projections of central tail feathers, and their dark brown plumage. There is only one colour phase—brown with buff speckles, relieved by large and conspicuous white flashes in the centre of the wings.

In habits, great skuas can be even more brutal than great black-backed gulls; they may seem ponderous in flight, but this is misleading as they are fast enough to fly down and kill puffins and petrels in mid-air, sometimes using their feet and powerful claws like a hawk. They, too, earn much of their living as pirates (see box feature).

The great skua has a fascinating breeding distribution since it is the only bird in the world that lives near *both* Poles. Indeed, it is rather commoner in the Antarctic than the Arctic, and was recorded very far south indeed by Captain Scott. In Britain, at the southern limit of its northern range, most colonies are sited on islands to the north of Scotland, on coastal cliff tops and moorland.

Above: Great skuas are the largest of all the skuas. The adults make such an easy living off piracy in summer near the massive sea bird colonies that they can afford to 'loaf', or stand about, for the greater part of each day.

Right: A clutch of Arctic skua eggs. Incubation may take up to 28 days and the chicks hatch in late May or early June.

The ferocious attack of the great skua

Great skuas, like Arctic skuas, earn much of their living as pirates, attacking other birds and forcing them to disgorge their food. Although they persecute gulls and occasionally terns, as you would expect from their size, they specialise in larger victims carrying a more worthwhile size of meal. They make piratical attacks even on gannets, coming alongside and seizing a wingtip in an attempt to overturn the gannet. They may attack them in flight, or (right) after the victim has fallen into the water. Faced with this treatment, most gannets disgorge their meal and escape. Such ferocity is not just limited to feeding either. In defence of their nests and young, great skuas will fly directly at human intruders, sometimes operating together from different angles of attack, some swooping at the head, others approaching at ground level before suddenly climbing towards the face. Physical contact with humans is commonplace and painful. Perhaps in the circumstances it is not surprising that the all-over milky coffee coloured down of the youngsters lacks any form of camouflage marking—with such aggressive and effective parental care none is needed.

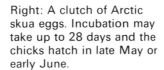

Left: The white-tailed eagle is a huge brown bird with a massive yellow bill and yellow feet. Adults have short, somewhat wedge-shaped white tails and noticeably pale heads. Juvenile and immature birds are darker, with brown tails, the latter showing progressively more white until complete adult plumage is attained at about seven or eight years of age. By 1982 some of the eagles released on Rùm were approaching this age, as is the one shown here.

Cartwheels in the sky

Below: A pair of birds soar together, calling. The male dives towards the female; she rolls over and they touch talons. Sometimes they grapple talons and even 'cartwheel' downwards.

the pair lock talons together and whirl downwards

Below: The area in which white-tailed eagles have been reported and may occasionally be seen.

THE WHITE TAILED EAGLE

The white-tailed eagle, once common in Scotland, had been exterminated there by 1916. Now a bold attempt has been made to reintroduce it.

The 'sea eagles' of the genus *Haliaeetus*, all large birds of prey, are more closely related to kites and Old World vultures than to other eagles. Most of them are adept fishers, taking prey from the surface in their talons and sometimes even wading after it. They are also efficient hunters of birds and small mammals. Scavenging, carrion feeding and piracy – stealing the prey of other predatory birds, gulls and even otters – are important aspects of their way of life.

Britain's other eagle One of these sea eagles – the white-tailed eagle – occurs in Britain today. It is a rare but thrilling sight in the Hebrides and on the north-west Scottish mainland and, though it is comparable in a broad sense to the golden eagle, the two species are not difficult to tell apart. Of the two, the white-tailed eagle is slightly bulkier, although a big female golden eagle may be larger than a male white-tailed eagle. There is a pronounced size difference between the sexes in both species, and female white-tailed eagles may be 15-25% larger and heavier than males.

In shape and movement, the two species are rather different from one another. The white-tailed eagle has a more vulturine outline, with long, broad wings, much shorter tail and much more prominent head and bill. The golden eagle has more balanced proportions with its longer tail and slimmer wings, and its flight is more elegant. It soars with its wings slightly raised and pressed forward, while the generally more ponderous-looking white-tailed eagle soars on flat wings held straight out from the body.

Giant nests Pairs of white-tailed eagles form breeding territories, with a home range averaging 50-65sq km (20-25sq miles) in most cases. Water is an essential element for these birds – river valleys, large lakes (or chains of smaller ones), extensive marshes and rocky sea-coasts being their preferred habitats on the Continent. Nests may be on crags (especially those of coastal birds) or in tall trees inland. The biggest may be up to 2m (6ft) in diameter and some tree nests may be as much as 3m (10ft) deep. One four-year-old nest

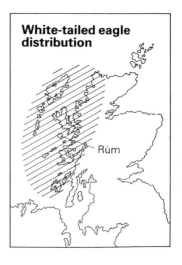

White-tailed eagle distribution

Rùm

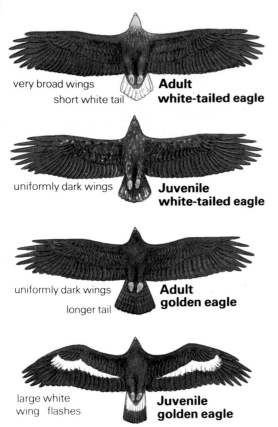

Adult white-tailed eagle
very broad wings
short white tail

Juvenile white-tailed eagle
uniformly dark wings

Adult golden eagle
uniformly dark wings
longer tail

Juvenile golden eagle
large white wing flashes

examined in detail weighed over 230kg (500lb) and contained no fewer than 2900 branches over 2m (6ft) in length!

Persecuted species The birds' prey includes small mammals, up to the size of hares and rabbits, but there is little evidence of lamb killing or indeed of much damage to any livestock. It would not be impossible for a white-tailed eagle to kill a lamb, but so far all lambs that the birds have been observed to eat were taken as carrion. The persecution that the birds have suffered on the basis of preventing damage to livestock is therefore unjustified.

Even so, deliberate and relentless human persecution has been at the root of the white-tailed eagle's great decline–and local extinction–over most of its former wide European range. Two hundred years ago, the white-tailed eagle must have been a familiar sight around the western coasts and islands of Scotland where, judging by all the contemporary accounts, it was quite common. By the middle of the 19th century, however, it was in rapid

The eagle's financial ally

The Eagle Star Insurance Group has publicised endangered eagles on a world scale through its well-known posters. The first one of these to appear featured the white-tailed eagle, using the magnificent painting which is reproduced here (right). Since then posters have shown nine other species of eagle from all over the world, but the insurance group has made itself a special ally of the white-tailed eagle. It provided the funds for the RSPB reintroduction programme and, for the following couple of years, maintained a scheme designed to monitor and protect the eagles' nests.

White-tailed eagle
(*Haliaeetus albicilla*). One of the world's eight sea eagles; large predator breeding in Europe and northern Asia east to the Bering Sea. Length of females 84-91cm (33-36in), males 70-77cm (27-30in).

Below: Swimming birds such as ducks and auks form a distinct and important category of prey. Often two white-tailed eagles hunt together for this type of quarry. The hunting pair take turns to harry the victim, plunging at it from a height. The attacks are too fast for it to escape by flying, and its only option is to dive underwater for safety until, finally exhausted, it becomes an easy victim for the eagles.

decline in the face of persecution; and the final pair last bred on Skye in 1916.

A fresh start In recent decades man's persecution of eagles–though still continuing –is somewhat less intense, and so the conditions were judged suitable for a reintroduction. The first real attempt was made in 1968 when the RSPB brought four eaglets from Norway, reared them and released them on Fair Isle, halfway between Shetland and Orkney and a former breeding area. For various reasons the experiment failed, but it has been repeated since then on a large scale and over a longer time-span by Scottish Natural Heritage and RSPB, based on the Rùm National Nature Reserve in the Inner Hebrides. The RSPB also monitors eagles that leave Rùm, and sets up protection schemes for those that abandon the island.

Between 1975 and 1985, 82 young birds were brought in from Norway under licence; three died in captivity but the remaining 79 were reared and released. Of five birds found dead so far, two have died of unknown causes, one was killed through striking an overhead power cable, one was poisoned through eating an illegally laid poison bait and the other was suspected of having been poisoned. By spring 1985, birds had been reported from many areas in western Scotland and the survival of these young white-tailed eagles remains encouragingly high.

In 1983 and 1984 eggs were laid in two nests but all four clutches failed to hatch. In 1985 there was a tremendous breakthrough in the return of the white-tailed eagle to Scotland: one pair successfully hatched and reared a chick, the first in 70 years to be raised in the wild in Britain. They have bred successfully every year since and the recolonisation of this magnificent bird is slowly gathering pace.

Hunting in pairs

distant eagle waits its turn

attacking eagle

prey surfaces exhausted after repeated dives to escape attacks

ELEGANT ARCTIC AND COMMON TERNS

The Arctic tern is one of the world's greatest travellers, and the common tern is not far behind it; these two maritime birds, both notable for their graceful flight and endurance, well deserve their popular name of 'sea swallows'.

Below: Common terns calling. Despite their propensity for long-distance travel, common terns can be seen from spring until mid-autumn, feeding close inshore near many coastal resorts.

Terns have aptly been given the popular name 'sea-swallows', for they are perhaps the most graceful and elegant of our seabirds. Silver-grey and white, with darker wing-tips and black cap, and long tail streamers, they are smaller and much slimmer than any of the gulls. All are migrants, travelling to fish in the oceans of the southern hemisphere during our winter, and returning to our coasts to breed in the summer.

The two species most often seen off British coasts during the summer months are the common tern and the Arctic tern. Both fit the general description above, and are so similar in size, shape and plumage that they may often be very difficult to identify with certainty. Because of this, birdwatchers have coined the jargon term 'comic terns' for those whose identity has not positively been confirmed.

Telling them apart If a really close view can be obtained in good light, then you can see some plumage differences which distinguish the two. In a mixed group (and on passage mixtures of the two are often seen) standing on a beach, Arctic terns are noticeably shorter in the leg than common terns: they are so short-legged in fact, as to seem to be sitting rather than standing. Especially during the height of the breeding season, Arctic terns have a totally blood-red beak, while common terns have black tips to their orange-red beaks, extending to half the beak's length.

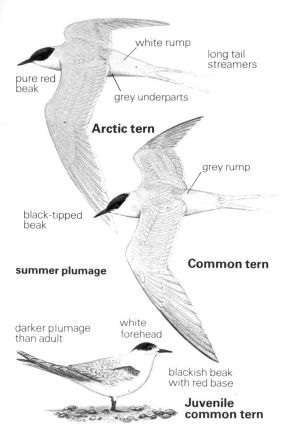

white rump

long tail streamers

pure red beak

grey underparts

Arctic tern

grey rump

black-tipped beak

summer plumage

Common tern

darker plumage than adult

white forehead

blackish beak with red base

Juvenile common tern

Terns in spring During the breeding season, terns fish close inshore, 'flickering' along lazily in the air a few feet above the waves before suddenly turning and plunging head-long into the sea. Often these dives result in an audible 'plop' and a considerable splash, but the bird penetrates only a few inches rather than submerges deeply.

Arctic terns are colonial breeders, and the colonies may be thousands strong. They are birds of the Arctic, as their name suggests, nesting on barren beaches and tundra. The nest is a shallow scrape, lined with fragments of shell and sometimes vegetation, and containing one, two or three eggs which are incubated for about a month. The young wander about soon after hatching, and fly four or five weeks later. In Britain and Ireland, not surprisingly, they are birds of remote islands and beaches in the north and west.

Generally, Arctic terns shun areas disturbed by man, but at one of their more southerly breeding colonies, on the Farne Islands, they have become accustomed to the regular but well-managed parties of visitors that are allowed to pay brief visits to their

Above: An Arctic tern brings food to the nest after a fishing flight close inshore. The prey is usually small fish or shrimps, and the fish are caught one at a time, not in a beakful as with puffins. Early in the season the male feeds his mate, an activity known as courtship feeding.

Arctic tern (*Sterna paradisaea*); summer visiting seabird, almost entirely coastal. Breeding range more northerly than that of common tern, wintering grounds more southerly. Length 36cm (14in).

Common tern (*Sterna hirundo*); summer visiting seabird, mainly coastal but sometimes nesting inland· length 36cm (14in).

Below: A common tern alights at its simple nest.

Towards the end of the summer, as the adults moult into winter plumage, beak colours become drabber and this feature is less reliable. Both species acquire white foreheads in the autumn. Young birds have blackish beaks and so cannot be separated by this feature. Again, with the birds seen at rest, the tail streamers of the Arctic tern (part of the origin of the term 'sea swallow') extend for a couple of inches or more beyond the folded wing tips, while the common tern's streamers and wings are about the same length.

Perhaps the best separation feature of all is the wing pattern, seen when the birds are in flight. The primaries, or flight feathers, of the Arctic tern appear slightly translucent in the light, giving the impression of an almost luminous white patch in the outer section of the wing. This noticeably bright area has only a very narrow grey-black border along the leading edge of the outermost feather and along the trailing edge of the outer part of the wing. In contrast, the common tern has a pale smoky-grey outer half to its wing, above and below, and its grey-black feather margins are more extensive, especially on the upper wing surface.

Listen to the call There are also slight differences in the calls of the two species, but these require a great deal of experience before they can be successfully used as an identification feature. Both have a long-drawn-out 'keeee-yaaaah' call. In the common tern, the emphasis is strongly placed on the first syllable, which forms the longer part of the call, while in the Arctic tern the two syllables have roughly the same length and emphasis. On migration, the common tern uses a 'kik-kik-kik' call which can sometimes be distinguished from the higher pitched, whistling 'kee, kee' of the Arctic tern.

Above: Arctic terns breed on islands and beaches in the north and west; common terns breed further south and inland.

Above: A pair of common terns feed their young.

Left: Arctic tern eggs and young alike are perfectly camouflaged: a mixture of greys, fawns, blacks and whites that makes them almost invisible against a background of sand flecked with fragments of seaweed, vegetation and shells. Because of this, it is imperative that a birdwatcher coming across a tern colony should exercise extreme care in moving around: it is far better to sit and watch the goings-on from a distance.

Below: Arctic terns roosting on a reef.

colonies. Indeed, they can be extremely aggressive to intruders, be they predatory birds or mammals such as foxes, weasels or stoats, and will often press home their vociferous dive-bombing attacks to the point of physical contact.

Although many common terns nest in the north of Britain and Ireland, others nest all around our coasts on isolated sandy beaches and shingle peninsulas, or on grassy islands among the mudflats of sheltered estuaries. Additionally, an increasing number are nesting inland, sometimes on natural islands in rivers but, more often, on man-made islands in flooded gravel pits and similar waters. Conservationists now even make large gravel-covered floating rafts, and moor them out in extensive areas of water, finding it relatively easy to tempt a few pairs of common terns to breed on them.

Global travellers Arctic terns probably see more hours of daylight each year than any other bird. Breeding in northern Britain and north into the Arctic Circle, they experience a virtually nightless summer. Having raised their young, they migrate southwards, crossing the equator and passing down the African coast and then on south to spend the winter in the Antarctic Ocean, often as far south as the edge of the ice shelf. Here, of course, it is again summer, and the Arctic terns have the benefit of an immense supply of small fish and plankton. One ringed bird, that lived for 26 years and travelled almost from pole to pole twice a year, must have had an unthinkably high lifetime mileage: certainly several million miles!

Apart from their differences in distribution and nesting habitat, common and Arctic terns are as alike in habits as they are in plumage. As most common terns migrate south to winter off West Africa, it would be easy to suggest that they had a much less extensive range than their Arctic cousins. That is not always true, for ringed common terns have been recovered in Australia, on the opposite side of the world from their British breeding grounds.

A VISIT TO THE FARNE ISLANDS

Birds have been protected on the remote, rocky Farne Islands ever since the 7th century. Today the islands are breeding grounds for an impressive 20 species of seabirds, and a large colony of seals also thrives on the abundant marine life.

The Farne Islands lie off the north-east coast of England, just to the north of the village of Seahouses, which is the embarkation point for visitors to the two islands open to the public. The islands form the eastern end of the Great Whin Sill, a formation of a type of igneous rock known as whinstone which runs for some 110km (70 miles) across the north of England. Whinstone is extremely hard, with vertical faulting which provides numerous ledges suitable for cliff-nesting seabirds; consequently these are

the most prominent attractions of the islands.

Bird protection started here when St Cuthbert lived in a retreat on Inner Farne during the 7th century. He introduced rules for the care of nesting eider ducks, with the result that even today this species is known locally as 'Cuddy's duck'. Today the islands are in the care of the National Trust, which provides wardens to protect the breeding birds.

Twenty species of birds nest each spring, totalling over 60,000 pairs, and more than 1000 grey seal cows pup each winter, making the Farnes one of the most important nature reserves in Europe. Wildlife survives here because food is readily available, because the isolation of the islands by sea and weather ensures that there is little disturbance, and because of the protection given by man. The adjacent waters are a good breeding ground for sand eels and small fish. Tidal currents swirling around the islands produce upwellings which bring large quantities of these and other marine creatures from the seabed to the surface, making them easily available to the seabirds and seals.

Clifftops and ledges The cliff nesting birds all compete for nest sites, the different species adapting themselves to the various habitats on the cliffs and utilising all the space available. Shags nest earlier than other species and tend to fill the larger ledges with their untidy, sprawling nests. The shag is an aggressive bird which readily fends off any predatory gulls, and therefore acts as a general 'policeman' for the area. Kittiwakes take advantage of this protection by building their nests on the smaller ledges between the

Above: Arctic terns arrive on the Farne Islands to breed in May, when there is a good supply of fish to feed their nestlings.

shags, so filling up all the nest sites on the remaining ledges and on the tops of the stacks (the rock pillars that rise from the sea); they keep close together to present a common defence against predators. Young shags start nest building earlier than the older shags, to try to obtain good sites, but they are often dislodged by the older birds taking over the partially built nest, forcing the young birds to colonize new areas. Here they are quickly followed by the other species taking advantage of their protection.

The clifftops and the highest ledges are the property of the fulmars, which appear to like a respectful distance between their nests, so that they can launch into the air or land without the risk of coming into conflict with neighbours. These birds are masters at using air currents and seem to prefer the extra windy conditions and up-draughts prevailing on the clifftops. Razorbills appear to be less particular, nesting among other species or completely on their own.

Nesting in the grass The thin cover of soil and vegetation on the islands is used by eiders, terns, puffins and gulls. Eider numbers vary each year between 1000 and 1500 breeding ducks. The numbers probably depend upon the amount of food available during the previous winter; it is essential for the ducks to build up a good body weight for the four week incubation period, when the birds

Map

Berwick-upon-Tweed
Holy Island (Lindisfarne)
A1
Farne Islands
Seahouses

Longstone
North Wamses
South Wamses
Big Harcar
Brownsman
Staple Island
Knocks Reef
Farne Island

■ islands   ▪ rock exposed at low tide only

There are 28 islands at low water and 15 at high water; the furthest are 8.4km (5¼ miles) from the mainland. All have their highest point to the south-west, sloping towards sea level at the north-east. Five have a covering of soil which supports a varied plant community.

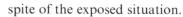

spite of the exposed situation.

Grey seals haul themselves out on to the rocky outer islands in spring and summer, usually at low water. They breed from late October to December, with a peak of births in mid-November. The cow gives birth to one white-coated pup, whose colour was once an excellent camouflage when seals used to breed on ice. The pup is suckled for approximately three weeks, then it is deserted by the cow; it spends one to two weeks moulting its white coat before taking to the sea. The effect of seals breeding on any soil capped islands has, in the past, been devastating, for they make huge 'wallows' where their constant movement and rolling reduces the surface to mud. When this dries, it is open to erosion by wind and storms, so reducing the habitat for plants, birds and other wildlife.

Marine life Ruins of small stone shelters are seen on two of the islands. These are the old 'ware cutters' houses, relics of the days when seaweed, probably kelp, was harvested from the islands and used on farms as a fertiliser. At low water the zonation of the

rarely leave their nests to feed. Eider ducks blend in well among the vegetation, their colour camouflage being their main defence against predators.

Underground abodes The soil itself houses the most numerous species of bird on the islands, namely the puffin. Approximately 30,000 pairs of these birds make their underground burrows. While these are only 30cm (1ft) or so beneath the surface, they extend for some 1.5m (5ft) into the soil, and are liable to collapse if any weight is applied above them. To save the puffins' fragile habitat from destruction, visitors are restricted to set paths and are not allowed to walk over areas where there are burrows. The shallow soil above the burrows can only support small plants, but plant cover is essential to soak up excess water and prevent flooding of the burrows during heavy rainfall, and also to bind together the loose soil excavated by the birds when making or cleaning them out.

The outer islands Because of soil erosion by violent sea storms, the outer islands have virtually no vegetation cover. On these islands a colony of cormorants breed, congregating together for protection; about 350 pairs survive in this bare, hostile environment. They are not disturbed by the lesser black-backed and herring gulls which breed all around them and the cormorants are usually successful in raising their young in

Right: Thrift growing on a cliff top on Inner Farne. In the distance are two smaller islands—note the sloping top of the higher one.

Below: Seals on the Farne Islands. The pups are born in white fur, which is moulted after about three weeks.

159

Above: A typical grassland plant community on Inner Farne. Sea campion is clearly visible, as well as various grasses. Gulls and terns nest among the vegetation.

Left: Shags occupy the larger rock ledges, where they build sprawling nests of seaweed.

Opposite page: Kittiwakes are common on the Farnes. Note the yellow bill and black legs of this adult bird.

Below: Yorkshire fog, one of three species of grass that grow on the islands where there is enough soil.

various algae can be seen on the few flat sloping shores and rock pools, while in the deeper water the dominant species of plant is the long-stalked *Laminaria* seaweed. Sea urchins are plentiful and can be seen clinging to the cliff faces when exposed at low water in spring, while the intertidal zone is inhabited by limpets, barnacles and mussels.

Salt tolerant plants Sixty-six species of plants have been recorded on the Farnes. The richness of plant species decreases as you go further from the mainland. The vegetation is heavily exposed to sea spray, and consists of salt-tolerant species only; sea-campion is dominant among them. Three grasses, red fescue (*Festuca rubra*), salt-marsh grass (*Puccinellia maritima*) and Yorkshire fog (*Holcus lanatus*), flourish on certain islands. These form meadows which used to be grazed by livestock kept by the resident monks, and later by the keepers who manned the lighthouses; since lighthouse keepers are no longer required on the islands, and no farm animals are kept, the grass tends to grow longer than it used to in the past.

Long grass, when it is wet, soaks the plumage and chills the bodies of young birds; it is an insurmountable barrier to them, causing a high mortality rate among nestlings. Rabbits are now the only grazing animals on the Farne Islands, and they play an essential part in cropping the grasses. However, Yorkshire fog is less palatable to the rabbit and this grass is kept short by mechanical cutting after each breeding season.

One relatively rare plant, *Amsinckia intermedia*, was probably introduced by accident when keepers fed their poultry with grain imported from America. This modest plant with its tiny orange-yellow flower is to be seen on a few of the islands.

Mammals of the open sea and islands

Many biologists believe that man himself had an aquatic period during his evolution. Such a period would account for the largely hairless body we now possess and for various other features of our appearance. But there are many mammals which today live wholly or partly in the sea, depending upon its plentiful food supply and protected from its cold by thick blubber.

These mammals – the whales, dolphins and seals – have developed many specialised features to cope with the peculiar difficulties as well as the advantages of living in the sea. The whales are particularly well adapted to life in the sea. Many have become accomplished divers, able to descend to much greater depths than man can go. At over 1000m (3300ft) deep, the enormous pressures the whales experience are absorbed not only by a superb adaptation of the lungs and airways but also by a highly flexible chest wall. The periods of up to an hour spent underwater are made possible by a restriction of blood circulation, slowing of the heart rate, storage of oxygen in the muscles and a rich supply of haemoglobin (the red oxygen-carrying pigment in the red blood corpuscles) in the enlarged blood supply.

Among these marine mammals, the dolphins are exceptionally fast swimmers; they use their speed to pursue fish and seem to enjoy their agility as they leap above the waves and play in the wash of ships. Whales and dolphins cannot exist on land at all, but seals are tied to the coast because they give birth to their pups out of the water. Seals also spend much time hauled-out, apparently resting and basking in the sun.

Seals (Britain has two species, the grey and the common) are among the few mammals which colonize islands naturally. Most of the larger mammals inhabiting islands have been brought there by man for food – they include the Soay sheep, the feral goat and the rabbit. Or the animals have arrived by accident through shipwreck or through the transport of goods from the mainland.

Left: The Hebridean sheep, distinguished by its magnificent horns (it can have up to six), is a primitive breed of sheep originating from the islands from which it takes its name. Island sheep such as the Hebridean are characterised by their ability to survive in bleak climates and on poor quality food.

Left: A bottle-nosed dolphin leaps clear of the waves off the coast of Cornwall. Once common in British waters, this species is now in decline, perhaps because it is particularly susceptible to pollutants in the water.

163

AN INTRODUCTION TO WHALES

Whales and dolphins spend all their lives in the sea – feeding, playing, mating, giving birth to their young and migrating in the great oceans of the world. Many species, including the huge blue whale, have been seen in British waters.

Above: This southern right whale (*Eubalaena australis*) has its mouth open, displaying the hornlike baleen plates which hang down from each side of the upper jaw. The inside edge of each plate is covered with bristles. The whale sucks in water and plankton (small plant and animal organisms) then strains the water out through the baleen plates, using its massive tongue to push the water out. The plankton gets caught on the baleen and is swallowed.

Superficially whales resemble some of the large sharks, but certain features clearly identify them as mammals – they are warm-blooded, breathe air with lungs, and give birth to living young that are suckled on milk secreted by the mammary glands of the mother.

Two groups of whales There are approximately 80 species of whales and dolphins, all belonging to the order Cetacea. Of these, 86% belong to the sub-order Odontoceti, the toothed whales; the rest belong to the Mysticeti, the whalebone or baleen whales.

The most obvious difference between these two groups of whales is their feeding apparatus. The Odontoceti have teeth, although

in some they are not visible as they do not emerge through the gum. The toothed whales feed mainly on fish and squid, which they pursue and capture with their teeth. The killer whales, however, may also eat the flesh of penguins, seals and dolphins.

Another feature of toothed whales is that the arrangement of bones in their skulls is asymmetrical and consequently there is only one external opening, or blowhole. The nasal passages either unite close to the blowhole or one is suppressed, leaving the other as the sole breathing tube.

Among the Odontoceti are the small whales we call dolphins and porpoises, which usually measure only 1.5-4m (5-12ft) in length. There are also some larger toothed whales, such as the 18m (60ft) sperm whale, and the killer whales, beaked whales and pilot whales, all measuring between 4-9m (12-30ft) in length. Also included in the Odontoceti, but rather distinct, are the river dolphins, thought to be the most primitive cetaceans now living.

The other group of whales is the Mysticeti. Instead of teeth the members of this group have a system of horny 'plates' (called baleen and also known as whalebone) with which they filter or strain planktonic organisms from the sea. Plankton forms most, and in a few cases all, of their diet. The skulls of the Mysticeti are symmetrical and they have two blowholes. Most of the Mysticeti are large

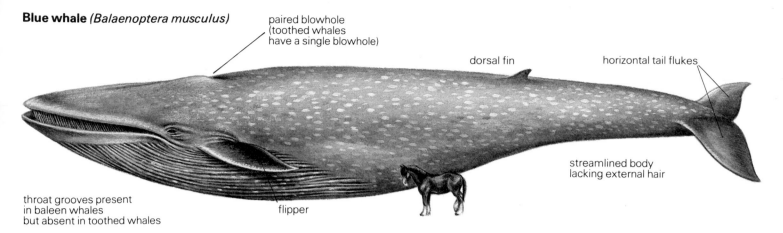

Blue whale *(Balaenoptera musculus)*

paired blowhole
(toothed whales
have a single blowhole)

dorsal fin

horizontal tail flukes

streamlined body
lacking external hair

throat grooves present
in baleen whales
but absent in toothed whales

flipper

whales. There are three main groups: the rorquals, which includes the blue whale (the world's largest animal) and the distinctive humpback whale; the right whales; and the grey whale.

The largest animal on earth How is it that animals the size of whales can have evolved? The answer lies in the fact that they live in water. Water provides support for the enormous body, which on land would require limbs so large that mobility would be very restricted, and the animal would be in danger of seriously injuring itself if it should fall.

Despite their size and weight, whales and dolphins are very mobile. This is because, in the course of evolution, they have evolved a streamlined body which is the ideal shape for moving through water. The head has become elongated compared to other mammals, and passes imperceptibly into the trunk with no obvious neck or shoulders. The body has two horizontal fins called flippers and tapers to a boneless tail fluke. In many species there is also an upright dorsal fin. There is no special nose structure, the nostrils opening by a single or double blowhole on the top of the head.

Further streamlining has been achieved by reducing protruding parts that would impede the even flow of water over the body. The hind limbs have been lost, although there are still traces of the bony skeleton within the body. There are no external ears—just two minute openings on the side of the head which lead directly to the organs of hearing. In order to maintain the body's smooth shape, the male's penis is completely hidden within muscular folds, and the teats of the female are hidden within slits on either side of the genital area.

Keeping warm Like all mammals, whales are warm-blooded animals. However, unlike most land mammals they do not have a hairy covering to keep them warm. Hair or fur would be an impediment in water: it would become waterlogged and heavy and would then chill the animal rather than keep it warm. The whale's answer to this problem is a thick insulating layer of fat, called blubber, immediately beneath the skin. This layer

of blubber is another very obvious difference between cetaceans and land animals.

How do whales move? Whales drive themselves through the water using their powerful tails, but unlike fishes which move their tails from side to side, whales move their tails up and down. The upward stroke provides the propulsion and the downward stroke is passive. Most cetaceans have a well defined dorsal fin which is assumed to have a stabilising effect.

The fore limbs have a skeletal structure similar to that of the human arm but they have been modified to form paddle-like flippers which are used for steering.

The problem of breathing Cetaceans spend most of their life under water, some of it at considerable depths. Because they are mammals they breathe air direct, instead of extracting oxygen dissolved in water as fishes do. Whales must therefore return to the surface at regular intervals to take air, and when they dive they must hold their breath. Because of their unique physiology whales can hold their breath for lengths of time

Above: One of the most striking features of the Cetacea is the enormous size of some of their species. The blue whale is the largest animal that has ever lived and can reach 30m (100ft) in length and weigh up to 150 tonnes, 150 times the weight of Britain's largest land mammal – the Shire horse.

Below: This group of southern right whales is engaged in an energetic mating chase. They are found in the southern oceans and in the northern hemisphere are replaced by the closely related *E. glacialis* which some people consider to be a different race of the same species.

Food for big mouths

The huge concentrations of plankton that occur in the polar seas during the summer months provide the food for many animals—fishes, squid, seals and seabirds as well as cetaceans. Baleen whales such as the right whale, humpback whale and the blue whale eat krill—a shrimp-like plankton that lives in huge shoals in the sea. Some toothed whales, such as the sperm whale, eat squid, while others, including most dolphins and porpoises, feed mainly on fish. The killer whale may also feed on penguins and other warm-blooded animals— even the blue whale.

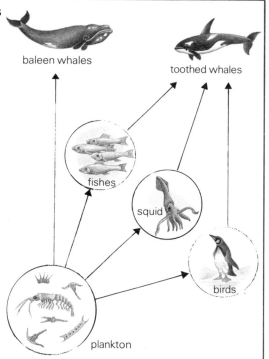

baleen whales

toothed whales

fishes

squid

birds

plankton

that seem improbable; for instance, the sperm whale can remain under water for more than an hour at a time. When the whale returns to the surface its blowhole opens wide and the foul air is expelled explosively. A cloud of steam, known as the spout, is produced as the moisture in the warm breath condenses on coming into contact with the cooler air. This is known as 'blowing' and occurs in all whales, although the spout is less visible in smaller species. As soon as the animal has exhaled it takes in more air and dives again.

How do whales see? There is little light deep under water so cetaceans rely mainly on senses other than sight to inform them about their surroundings and help them to locate food. They have a very highly developed sense of hearing, and communicate with each other by making a variety of sounds.

The toothed whales, which pursue fast-moving fish and squid, locate their prey by using sonar. The whale emits intense, short pulses of sound in the ultrasonic range. These clicks, and other sounds, bounce off objects in their path producing echoes from which the whale is able to build up a sound picture of its surroundings. The whalebone whales have not yet been shown to use echolocation and may instead rely on sight to locate the dense swarms of plankton on which they feed.

Family life The gestation period in whales varies from species to species, but is usually about 12 months. The single young is born head first and is immediately nosed to the surface by its mother so that it can breathe. The young whale is able to swim at birth. Its mother's milk is rich in protein so the calf grows quickly. Maternal care is well developed in all cetaceans and the calf is dependent on its mother for many months, in some cases for a year or more. Maturity is reached after a relatively long period.

Above: The killer whale (*Orcinus orca*) is one of the larger toothed whales, adult males reaching 9m (30ft) in length. It is a handsome animal with three large splashes of cream on the body. It has a tall dorsal fin which may be up to 1.8m (6ft) high in the male. The two rows of sharp teeth are clearly visible.

Right: Common dolphins (*Delphinus delphis*) are found throughout the world in waters that are not colder than 15°C (59°F). They seem to enjoy playing around ships and are often seen riding in the wave at the bow.

OCEAN GIANTS: BALEEN WHALES

The huge baleen whales of the northern hemisphere migrate from the equator during spring, arriving in northern waters in mid-summer when plankton and fish are most plentiful. They feed by filtering food-laden seawater through their baleen fringes.

Above: The humpback whale tends to swim near the surface of the water. It gets its name from the way it arches its body as it submerges its head after taking a breath of air. Its very long flippers—the longest of any whale—are also helpful in identification.

The great whales of our oceans are, with one exception—the sperm whale—members of the sub-order Mysticeti. These are the baleen whales, so named because they have huge jaws lined with horny plates called baleen, which sift out organisms from small planktonic crustaceans to fishes as large as herrings. The Mysticeti are divided into three families: the Balaenopteridae, the Balaenidae and the Eschrichtiidae.

Baleen sieves Baleen is an extraordinary substance, unlike anything else found in the animal kingdom, and bearing no relationship to teeth. It is a fibrous yet flexible material that grows as a series of thin plates, each the shape of an elongated triangle, hanging down from the margins of the upper jaw by its shortest side.

The outer edge of the baleen is smooth, but the inner edge is frayed into a fringe of coarse filaments which form a dense fibrous filter system. This is used for straining plankton from the sea water (see overleaf). This type of feeding, called 'gulping', is used by all the balaenopterid whales—blue, fin, sei, Bryde's and minke, and by the humpback. The baleen of the humpback is comparatively short, although there may be as many as 400 plates in each jaw, and its throat is covered with a system of grooves, rather like tramlines, which enable it to expand.

However, some baleen whales, notably the North Atlantic and Greenland right whales, and the grey whale, capture prey by 'skimming', as does the sei whale on occasion. These swim slowly forward with mouth slightly open, allowing water to flow into the mouth cavity and out again through the baleen plates at the sides.

In the right whales the head is large, often up to a third of the total length of the body, so as to accommodate the highly developed baleen apparatus. The rostrum (the 'bonnet' on top of the head) is long, narrow, and arched upwards. The lower jaw-bones are not arched in the same way, so that the space between the upper and lower jaws is closed by the huge lower lips that rise from the jaw-bones and enclose the long narrow plates of

Above: The minke whale (*Balaenoptera acutorostrata*) is the smallest of the baleen whales. It weighs 10 tons and is up to 9m (30ft) long. It is sometimes seen from ships, jumping out of the water, and is relatively common around British coasts.

baleen that hang from the edges of the rostrum.

The grey whale has a shorter baleen and fewer throat grooves (usually 2 or 3) than the balaenopterids. These differences in the size and arrangement of the baleen plates reflect not only differences in the mode of feeding, but also the types of food taken. Those with the finest baleen plates, such as the right and minke whales, take the smallest plankton. Species with coarser baleen, such as the fin whale, eat such food as prawns and shrimps.

Food and feeding It is the differences in diet of the different species that prevent too much competition where these species occur together, although clearly the impact of one

whale species on its main food has repercussions on its relatives. For example, around the beginning of this century the largest of all whales, the blue whale, was hunted to near extinction. The reduction in numbers of this species must have provided a great abundance of food, not only for the remaining blue whales but for other species as well, since blue, fin and sei whales all started to grow faster, reproduce at an earlier stage, and a higher proportion of females in the population became pregnant.

The principal food of all these species, at least in the Southern Ocean, is krill. It is shaped like a shrimp, though quite unrelated to one, and is very rich in protein. For this reason man has concentrated efforts where the species is abundant round Antarctica, to harvest it for food, and this may bring us once more into conflict with the great whales. The baleen whales are not the only species to feed on krill, for it forms the base of the food pyramid of many other predators, particularly certain species of seals, penguins, albatrosses and other petrels, many fish, and probably also squid.

It has been calculated that the large rorqual whales feed at a rate of about 4% of their body weight a day during the 120-day feeding period they spend in the Southern Ocean. Since a large whale, such as a fin or blue whale, can take a meal of 800-1000kg of krill, it is possible to calculate, given the

Black right whale
Balaena glacialis
18.5m (60ft), 40–50 tons

Humpback whale
Megaptera novaeangliae
14m (46ft), 31 tons

Gulping: how whales feed

As the whale moves forward, swimming through the water with its mouth wide open, the floor of the jaw is lowered, the skin of the throat expanded as the grooves open out, and water loaded with plankton is forced into the mouth, which then closes. The muscles of the throat grooves contract, causing the floor of the mouth to tighten and driving the tongue forward, and the

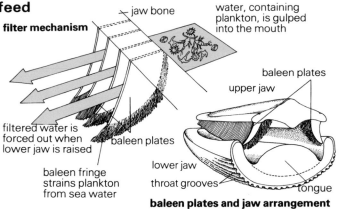

filter mechanism

jaw bone

water, containing plankton, is gulped into the mouth

filtered water is forced out when lower jaw is raised

baleen plates

baleen plates

upper jaw

baleen fringe strains plankton from sea water

lower jaw

throat grooves

tongue

baleen plates and jaw arrangement

water is then forced out through the baleen fringes. The spacing of the parallel baleen plates allows a rapid flow of water without loss of rigidity to the filaments, so that the food contained in the water is left stranded on the mat from where it is swallowed, possibly aided by the tongue driving the food backwards to the gullet. This method of feeding is called 'gulping', and it is used by all the baleen whales.

known average densities of krill, the number of gulps it needs to make each day. For both species this is estimated to be between 70 and 80 gulps. Smaller species require proportionately more gulps. Clearly, very great quantities of krill are consumed, and the whales accordingly become very fat, increasing their body weight by 50-70% over this short period. This is necessary to last them the rest of the year, which they spend in the warmer, yet relatively unproductive, regions nearer the equator.

Not all the great whale populations migrate to the Southern Ocean. Some move north from the equator to Arctic and sub-Arctic waters where krill is not the principal food.

Instead, there is a range of food organisms at lower concentrations than the krill of the Antarctic. The blue whale has a restricted diet in all oceans, taking only euphausiids such as krill. Minke whales have perhaps the most catholic diet, and together with humpbacks, also take large quantities of shoaling fish. The northern right whale, like the blue whale, has rather a restricted diet, principally calanoid copepods.

Migration The great migrations of the large whales take place annually. In the northern hemisphere, whales move north from the equator during spring, arriving in high latitudes by mid-summer when plankton and fish concentrations are at their greatest. As

Below: Some of the baleen whales which may spend part of the year around the coasts of Britain. Here they have no natural predators and, although many are protected species, their greatest enemy is man. They feed on a variety of food organisms, from small floating plankton to medium-sized fishes.
The weights and sizes given here are for average male specimens.

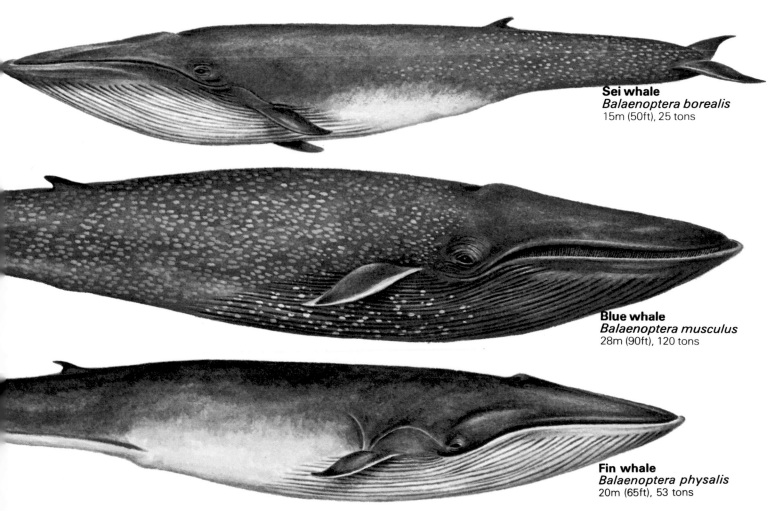

Sei whale
Balaenoptera borealis
15m (50ft), 25 tons

Blue whale
Balaenoptera musculus
28m (90ft), 120 tons

Fin whale
Balaenoptera physalis
20m (65ft), 53 tons

Left: The tail of a right whale, showing its two horizontal tail flukes. If you manage to get a good view of the tail fin of a whale, the chances are that it will be a humpback, right or sperm (toothed) whale. They tend to raise their tail flukes right out of the water before diving.

Whale songs

Whales can produce a great variety of moans, screams, grunts and whistles. In baleen species these are generally of low frequency, transmittable over great distances. Detailed studies have been carried out on right and humpback whales and these have shown the existence of dialects with song phrases which may differ both geographically and from year to year.

The song of humpback whales is made up of a constant number of themes repeated in the same order and lasting a considerable time. The themes are composed of phrases whose number may vary between successive songs of a particular whale. No theme is left out completely, although a whale may repeat a phrase many times. Phrases may change gradually so that one at the end of a theme may be quite different from what it was at the beginning. Such songs are apparently only uttered in warm waters by migrating animals, and each year the population has a characteristic pattern of themes.

Tape recordings of right and grey whale calls have been played to a group of right whales: right whales reacted to their own calls by approaching the tape recording, but avoided those of the grey whale, a possible competitor.

the autumn gales start to disperse the plankton swarms, the whales return southward, arriving in equatorial waters by November or December, where they mate, or, twelve months later, give birth to their single calves. The same procedure is followed in the southern hemisphere but since the southern winter is at the opposite end of the year to the northern winter, these whales are never in equatorial waters at the same time as the northern group, and so there is little contact between populations.

The most extensive migrants are the blue, fin, minke, grey and humpback whales. They annually cover distances of 5-6000 nautical miles, and observations of migrating grey whales in the north-east Pacific suggest that they do not stop at all during migration, averaging about two knots when travelling north and four knots when swimming south. The rorquals tend to travel faster at speeds up to 16 knots, so it is feasible that they could travel between summer and winter grounds in a week or two. There is some suggestion that whales travel faster when moving to their wintering grounds, but this may not be related to the actual speeds at which they swim but to the number of stops they make on the way.

It is possible that on a journey to their summer feeding grounds the whales are exploiting spring blooms of plankton which they encounter en route. At the end of the summer, however, the food supply declines rapidly, the water temperature drops in the polar regions, and the whales, which already have a huge fat store to last them through the winter, need to migrate quickly to warmer waters.

Navigation and the senses How do whales in such a wide expanse of seemingly uniform ocean manage to find their way five thousand miles from one end of our globe to the equator? It is extraordinary to think that these animals can return year after year to the same tropical lagoon to calve, and then be found six months later in the same areas as the ice floes they frequented the previous year.

Yet individual recognition, either by natural markings, such as the arrangement of callosities on the 'bonnet' on a right whale, or by tags attached by research zoologists, has confirmed the regular use of particular regions by individual whales, just as migrating birds may breed or winter in the same area from year to year.

One method of navigation is almost certainly visual clues—prominent features of the sea-bed topography such as coastal escarpments and sea mounts. In the north-east Atlantic whales probably migrate along the edge of the Continental shelf, and this is supported by early 20th century whaling records which show concentrations of animals caught along the shelf edge.

It is likely, however, that a combination of senses is used by migrating groups of whales. In whales smell and taste are apparently unimportant, while vision, and obviously touch, are only useful over short distances. Information about the distant environment must therefore come principally from sound. Unlike toothed whales, there is no evidence that baleen whales use echo-location for navigation or communication between individuals.

Instead they emit low-frequency sounds which may be audible over tens to hundreds of miles across the deep ocean channels (the denser the medium, the longer the distances at which sounds can be propagated). This is how individuals keep in constant contact.

Where to see whales, dolphins and porpoises in British and Irish waters

Many species of whales and dolphins occur around our coasts. The large whales are generally here only during summer, having migrated northwards in spring from warmer water near the equator, where they go to mate or calve. The smaller whales and dolphins do not undergo such extensive migrations, although they tend to move away from the coasts, and sometimes southwards, in autumn. British waters become so rich in these species in summer because of the high productivity in the seas at this time which provides food for swarms of plankton, which in turn are eaten by many fishes and cephalopods (squid). All these fall prey to seabirds, and to whales and dolphins.

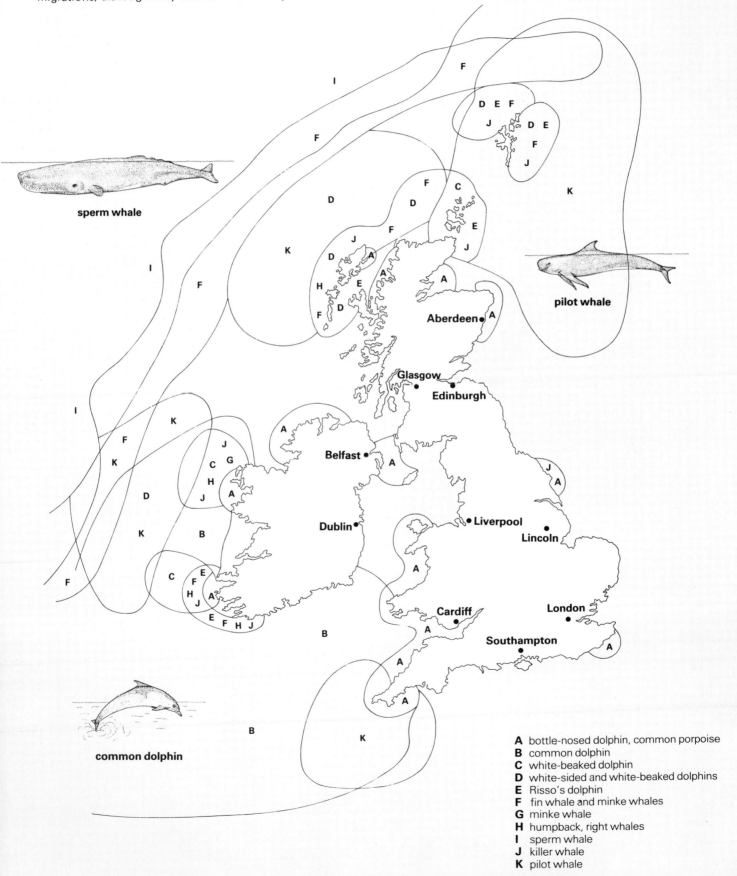

sperm whale

pilot whale

common dolphin

A bottle-nosed dolphin, common porpoise
B common dolphin
C white-beaked dolphin
D white-sided and white-beaked dolphins
E Risso's dolphin
F fin whale and minke whales
G minke whale
H humpback, right whales
I sperm whale
J killer whale
K pilot whale

TOOTHED WHALES OF THE OCEANS

Toothed whales are mostly social animals, living together in various combinations of males, females and young, a few, such as the sperm and killer whale, being polygamous. They live mainly in deep waters, although some become stranded around our coast.

Below: Bottlenose whales, the largest and most sociable of the beaked whales, are fairly common around the British coast and are usually seen in schools of a dozen or so, and occasionally up to 50 animals.

Of the 80 species of whales and dolphins, the great majority belong to the sub-order Odontoceti, the toothed whales. Five of the six families of toothed whales occur occasionally in British waters. It is often difficult to tell whales apart, but all toothed whales have a single blow-hole, and all but the sperm whale, white whale and narwhal have a dorsal fin of distinctive shape and location.

In general the large toothed whales are known as whales, and the small ones as dolphins although, rather confusingly, three members of the dolphin family–pilot, killer and false killer whales–are usually called whales. Other species of toothed whale include the sperm and pygmy sperm whale, several beaked whales–bottlenose, Cuvier's, Sowerby's, True's and Gray's–and a number of dolphins and porpoises. Only one species of porpoise visits British waters but five species of dolphin are commonly seen.

Most toothed whales have conical teeth. Some species, such as most dolphins, have rows of continuous pointed teeth in both jaws; others, such as the beaked whales, have a single tusk-like tooth in the lower jaw and very often the females just have gums. In the male narwhal the left upper incisor tooth undergoes extraordinary modification, forming a single long spiralled tusk.

Feeding The sperm whale eats mainly squid and other cephalopods, often catching them at great depths. It is not unknown for squid

almost the size of the sperm whale itself to be eaten by males, although they mostly take squid of 30-100cm (1-3ft) long. Because squid are difficult to catch with man-made equipment the analysis of sperm whale stomachs has provided scientists with useful information about these elusive creatures. Furthermore, as some squid only occur in certain parts of the world, the stomach contents can give clues to the areas the whale has visited.

The capture of fast-moving prey requires different skills from those needed by the baleen whales, which simply sift plankton out of the oceans. Some people think this is why toothed whales tend to mature slowly and have relatively well-developed nervous systems.

Most toothed whales do not show great north-south movements, although local migrations do occur. However, the sperm whale (particularly a lone male) undergoes extensive migrations, often of several thousand kilometres, from the tropics to feeding areas in high latitudes.

Other toothed whales eat both fishes and

Deep-sea diving

The male sperm whale is the deepest diver of all the cetaceans, and this ability may well be associated with the enormous spermaceti organ contained in the whale's vast head. In a 30,000kg (30ton) whale this organ may contain 2,500kg (2½tons) of waxy spermaceti oil. This oil is liquid at 33°C (91°F), its temperature in the whale at the water surface, but it begins to solidify at 31°C (88°F), becoming denser, and therefore less buoyant, as it does so. Scientists think that careful regulation by the whale of the temperature, and thus the density, of the spermaceti oil through various means may enable the animal to control its buoyancy on very deep diving expeditions, and actually allow it to be neutrally buoyant at depth.

The names 'sperm whale' and 'spermaceti' were originally given to this species by people who believed it carried its semen in its head. In the past the oil has been used in the making of cosmetics, lubricating oils and cleaning materials.

Above: The vast sperm whale, the largest of the toothed whales. Its head is a third as heavy and large as its body. This species is found in all the oceans of the world, although only single males occur in Polar waters and the records of stranded sperm whales on British coasts have all been of male animals. Sperm whales take in oxygen for about ten minutes and then dive as deep as 1000m (3300ft). and stay underwater for up to an hour.

Below: The pilot whale is all black except for a conspicuous white throat patch. It becomes stranded, often with other pilot whales, comparatively frequently around the British coast. Stranded schools may exceed 200 animals.

Above: The killer whale. The reputation of this species as an animal dangerous to man is almost certainly false, or at least greatly exaggerated. It might occasionally attack man, mistaking him for a sea mammal. But certainly a killer whale in captivity, well-fed with fishes, co-exists amicably with dolphins, upon which it preys in the wild, and allows its trainer to play with it at close quarters.

dorsal fin is usually attacked first and then the tongue, a favourite morsel.

Distribution Sperm and killer whales are distributed throughout the world's oceans, but some species are much more localised, including the distinctive narwhal and the white whale (or beluga), both of which occur in Arctic waters and only rarely come into British waters.

Sperm whales are deep-sea animals and so they tend to be seen just off the Continental shelf around the British coast, particularly south-west Ireland and north-west Scotland where the shelf edge comes closest to the mainland. Occasionally they may come right into the coastal waters: a herd of females and young was seen one recent autumn in the Pentland Firth, and there have been several sightings close to the Shetlands.

The pilot whale is relatively common, particularly in autumn when it follows mackerel shoals to inshore waters of south-west England and Shetland. It spends most of the remainder of the year ranging over the northeast Atlantic and the northern North Sea in herds of up to 100 animals, and is one of the most frequently stranded.

Killer whales occur in much smaller herds, usually fewer than 15 individuals, particularly along the west coast of Britain in coastal waters, where they feed on grey seals and seabirds, as well as fish. Some sites are traditionally visited, especially in mid to late summer: the coast of Lewis and Harris, the Outer Hebrides and the Farne Islands are good places to spot them.

cephalopods. The pilot whale, for example, feeds mainly on cephalopods but also takes shoaling fishes such as herring. During the last few centuries pilot whale populations in the Faroes have fluctuated according to herring catches. The white whale also feeds on fishes such as herring, salmon and cod, as well as squid.

The killer whale has an even more varied diet. It takes a variety of fishes and squid, and commonly eats seabirds. It is the only species known to be predatory on other marine mammals, including seals. Packs of killer whales even feed on large whales twice their size – usually old or sick individuals. The

Elusive whales Although quite a lot is known about sperm, killer and pilot whales,

Toothed whales

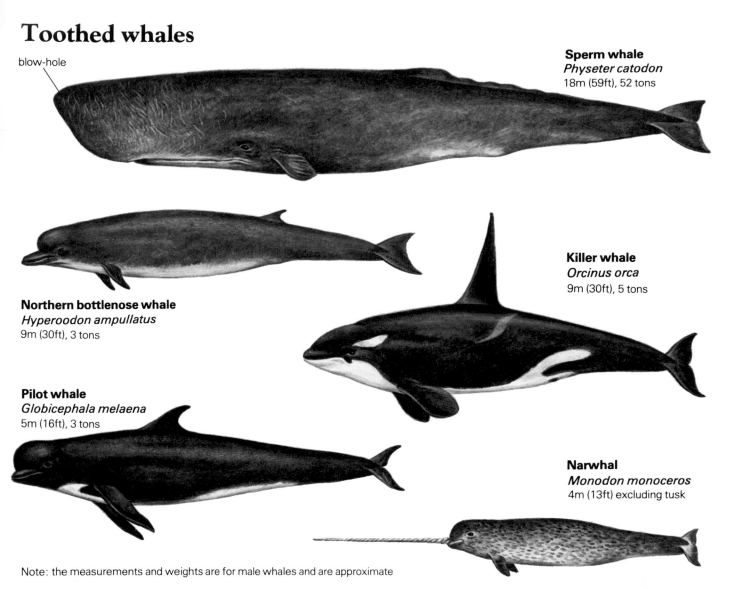

blow-hole

Sperm whale
Physeter catodon
18m (59ft), 52 tons

Killer whale
Orcinus orca
9m (30ft), 5 tons

Northern bottlenose whale
Hyperoodon ampullatus
9m (30ft), 3 tons

Pilot whale
Globicephala melaena
5m (16ft), 3 tons

Narwhal
Monodon monoceros
4m (13ft) excluding tusk

Note: the measurements and weights are for male whales and are approximate

little is known about the beaked whales. This is almost certainly because they tend to be pelagic, living in deep waters, and are rarely observed. Some, such as True's and Cuvier's whale are known almost exclusively from stranded specimens. More is known of the northern bottlenose whale. It occurs in concentrations in particular areas of the north-eastern Atlantic, right up into the Arctic near Spitsbergen and Bear Island.

The false killer whale occasionally comes inshore and becomes stranded in large numbers. The reason for these mass strandings is not clear. Despite its name, this species is not related to the killer whale and, indeed, it looks quite different; it is much smaller, with a rounded snout and underslung lower jaw, and it looks rather like a bulbous shark.

Social structure During the relatively long period of maturation, the young learn from their elders how to find and capture prey. The sperm whale has perhaps the most complicated social system of the toothed whales. Groups may comprise any of the following: all female or bachelor male herds, females with calves, or one male with a group of females and a few sub-adult males. If a male with a harem becomes old or injured he may

be replaced by a younger male from a bachelor herd and he then goes off alone, covering great distances into higher latitudes. It is probable that there is fairly intensive fighting between males in competition for a harem.

Inside the male sperm whale's head is a vast spermaceti organ which may contain up to 2500kg (2½ tons) of spermaceti oil. It is possible that the greatly enlarged head is used for sparring between males in fights for females, as deer use their antlers. Yet another theory links the temperature and density of the spermaceti oil with the amazing deep diving ability of this species.

The head of a group of sperm whales, whether a harem master or a female with a herd of calves, tends to be an older member and the most experienced. The practice among whalers of taking the largest animal has been very disruptive to the social organisation of schools of whales.

Killer whales exist in similar social groups. Killer whale herds have been studied closely in various parts of Canada where scientists have been able to recognise individuals and follow their movements. The groups appear fairly stable and faithful to the same areas.

Above: Some of the toothed whales that may visit British waters. The left tusk-like tooth of the male narwhal may grow to 2.5m (8ft) while the right tooth remains embedded in the upper jaw. In the female neither of the teeth is visible.

Opposite: A beached sperm whale. Mass strandings of toothed whales are not uncommon, although they are little understood. One theory is that they cannot echo-locate properly in shallow water. Another is that roundworm parasites in the ear may prevent effective echo-location. When people have tried to drag the whales out to sea, they have often merely turned round and become stranded again.

GREGARIOUS DOLPHINS: MAN'S FRIEND AT SEA

Dolphins have long symbolised friendliness and intelligence. Some, such as the common dolphin, take pleasure in riding the bow waves of boats, at the same time giving us an excellent opportunity to watch them at close quarters. Many routinely follow ferries, either in herds or alone.

Below: Common dolphins. Dolphins are highly gregarious, living in social groups and using their combined sensory abilities to hunt and herd fish and evade predators, notably sharks and killer whales. Such species as the bottle-nosed dolphin form groups of 3-15 individuals in coastal waters and search for shoaling fish together, as well as feeding alone. They communicate by ultra-sonic clicks, vocalisations and tail-smacking.

Dolphins and porpoises are members of the whale sub-order Odontoceti, the so-called toothed whales, such as the killer, sperm and beaked whales. They can usually be distinguished from other toothed whales by their small size, the largest dolphin being no more than 4m (13ft) long. In British waters five species are commonly seen – white-beaked, white-sided, bottle-nosed, common and Risso's dolphins. The harbour porpoise is the only porpoise found in British waters. It is distinguished from its larger dolphin relatives by its small triangular dorsal fin (the dorsal fin of dolphins curves backwards), its spade-like teeth (dolphins generally have conical teeth), and by its smaller size – it is only 1.2m (4ft) long.

Links with man Ever since the writers of classical Greece dolphins have figured highly in the culture of man. Greek legends tell of Arion, the wandering minstrel who travelled widely, playing his music and saving his earnings. The crew of a ship taking him home set upon him to steal his money. His final request was to play his lute for the last time. As he played, dolphins swam to the ship, whereupon he jumped overboard and one of the dolphins bore him on its back safely to the shore. The dolphin expert, Horace Dobbs, tells a similar modern-day story – his son was carried by a friendly dolphin called Donald. There have been tame bottle-nosed dolphins at Amble in Northumberland and elsewhere.

This type of activity may be connected with the care-giving behaviour between dolphins. Herd members help a mother to raise a new-born calf to the surface for its first breath, and an injured dolphin is often helped in a similar way. It is partly this kind of response that has led man to consider dolphins to be highly intelligent, altruistic behaviour tending to be regarded as primarily a human feature.

Clearly, dolphins learn tricks fast in dolphinaria, and they appear inventive and quick to imitate. However, it is difficult to assess how intelligent they are. The problem in comparing them with man is that dolphins live in a medium where different senses have different relative importance from those used by man. For example, dolphins can hear noises of a wider frequency range than man.

Dolphins live in social groups and co-operate to find food and other dolphins. When in the open ocean, groups are generally larger and move over greater distances than those closer inshore. The larger aggregations may be due in part to the need to provide better protection against rare predator species, notably the killer whale, out in mid-ocean. Larger groups are probably more effective in navigation and food-finding, using their collective experience.

Communication With such a gregarious existence good communication between individuals and groups is important. Dolphins have a rich repertoire of vocalisations and actions, ranging from echolocatory clicks to squeaks and squeals. Different sounds are produced at different levels of excitement, and dolphins in a group constantly seem to be emitting calls which may keep the group together in the same way as contact calls made by birds in flocks.

Although the food source of dolphins tends to be patchily distributed, it is often abundant. It has been estimated that dolphins require between four and ten per cent of their body weight in fish daily – about five to ten fish of mackerel or herring size. Thus it is likely that there is much time for social interactions.

In most species group membership seems to be fairly fluid, comprising both males and females. There is usually one annual calving peak, although in some species, such as the bottle-nosed, courtship occurs throughout the year, possibly because it enables individuals to determine their status in relation to each other, and hence the dominance hierarchies in the group. The bond between mother and calf is strong, and the calf may remain with her for many months. However,

Above: A beached harbour porpoise. In the past it was common to see small herds of porpoises around such resorts as Brighton and Blackpool, but recently these have become much less frequent. Porpoises are quite difficult to observe: they rarely do more than skim the surface, their small fins or arched backs being all that you tend to see.

Below: Common dolphins in rough seas. This is the dolphin most often seen in the Channel approaches, off southern Ireland and western France, and it often occurs in large herds.

Above: The white-sided dolphin, like its close relative the white-beaked dolphin, may commonly be seen in the Minches of west Scotland, and in Orkney and Shetland waters. It generally moves in large schools.

Below: The common dolphin is slender and graceful. Only the harbour porpoise is more frequently stranded around the British coast.

the bond between adult male and female is apparently weak, and mating seems to be fairly promiscuous. Unlike other dolphin species, Risso's dolphin is probably polygamous, with one male having a harem of females.

British dolphins Much of our information about dolphins is based on information from stranded dolphins around our coasts. It is supplemented by data from live sightings by numerous observers, but there is still much to learn. The bottle-nosed dolphin, once the commonest dolphin in the stranding records, has clearly undergone a decline in recent years in British and European waters. It is an inshore species of sheltered bays and estu-

aries. Here it is particularly susceptible to pollutants such as heavy metals and pesticides and these, together with the pressure of over-fishing of its food prey (such species as cod, herring and halibut) in such areas as the southern North Sea and the Channel, may be responsible for its decline. The greater disturbance from vessels in these inshore waters may also have played a part.

The same influences may have contributed to the apparent decline in the harbour porpoise, although it is still probably the commonest of these species around our coast. White-beaked dolphins, on the other hand, seem to be benefiting from the large numbers of mackerel off north-west Britain in areas once frequented by great shoals of herring.

The white-sided and the white-beaked dolphins both have a more northerly distribution, and further south they tend to be replaced by the common dolphin. This species often occurs in large herds, usually away from the coast where it catches fast-moving shoaling small fishes such as sardine and anchovy.

Although the white-sided and white-beaked dolphins tend to be restricted to the cooler waters of the north Atlantic, the common dolphin is distributed world-wide, from warm temperate regions to the tropics. It is one of the commonest species in the Mediterranean, sharing these comparatively sheltered and warm seas with the euphrosyne dolphin, which it closely resembles. The euphrosyne

Dolphins of British waters

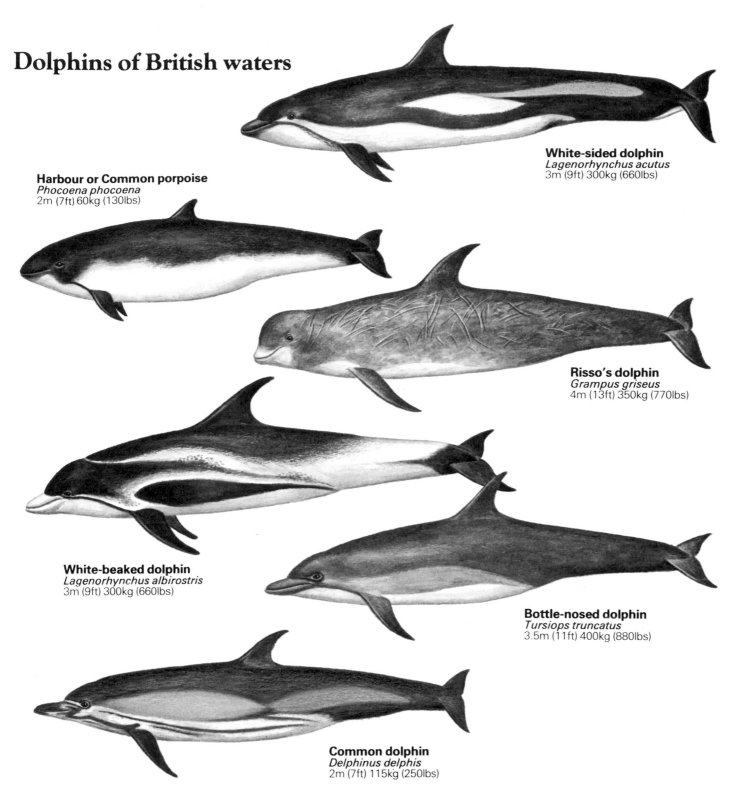

White-sided dolphin
Lagenorhynchus acutus
3m (9ft) 300kg (660lbs)

Harbour or Common porpoise
Phocoena phocoena
2m (7ft) 60kg (130lbs)

Risso's dolphin
Grampus griseus
4m (13ft) 350kg (770lbs)

White-beaked dolphin
Lagenorhynchus albirostris
3m (9ft) 300kg (660lbs)

Bottle-nosed dolphin
Tursiops truncatus
3.5m (11ft) 400kg (880lbs)

Common dolphin
Delphinus delphis
2m (7ft) 115kg (250lbs)

dolphin occurs off the French coast, and rarely off south-west Britain where there have been strandings and two sightings in recent years.

Risso's dolphin also tends to occur in warmer waters, although it is not uncommon along the west coast of Britain and Ireland. Here it is much more of an inshore species and may even be seen from headlands, such as Tiumpan Head near Stornoway in the Isle of Lewis.

Some dolphins, such as the common and euphrosyne dolphins, often come to the head of a boat and ride the bow wave. They use the push provided by the wave by angling their tails against it and riding under water, rather as humans do when surfing on waves above water. Besides the advantage of moving forward and saving their energy, dolphins seem to engage in this behaviour simply for pleasure. 'Pelorus Jack,' a famous Risso's dolphin in New Zealand, regularly accompanied ships through the narrows of the Marlborough Sound in the early part of this century.

There are no freshwater dolphins in the British Isles, although a few species live in such rivers as the Amazon and Plate of South America, and the Ganges of India and Pakistan. However, habitat changes and pollution may all have contributed to the decline of some of these species, some of which are now threatened with extinction.

Above: The dolphins and harbour porpoise of the British Isles. When searching for dolphins, look out for distant splashing as the animals break the surface of the water. This behaviour is probably for panicking and then driving fish. It may also alert other dolphins, organise the herd for more effective food capture and help in navigation, as well as provide sheer enjoyment.

VAGRANT SEALS

Occasionally, vagrant seals from the far north appear off Britain's coasts. Ringed, harp, hooded and bearded seals have all been seen in British waters.

The order Pinnipedia (seals, sea-lions and walrus) contains some 31 species which are distributed throughout the world. Around the coasts of Europe two families are represented: the true seals or Phocidae, and the walrus or Odobenidae. Grey or common seals are familiar residents in the British Isles, but ringed, harp, hooded and bearded seals and the unmistakable walrus have also been seen occasionally in British waters.

The four seals which occasionally visit British shores are perhaps less distinctive and therefore harder to identify than the walrus; but they have all travelled southwards from their Arctic habitats to reach our coasts. Ringed, harp, hooded and bearded seals breed on ice and must therefore live in the cold north

where ice will be certain to form, advancing and retreating with the change of season. It is likely that as recently as 10,000 years ago, at the end of the last Ice Age, these species may have lived much nearer to the coasts of the British Isles. For example, a harp seal jawbone was found in the Dordogne in France, associated with an upper Paleolithic cave settlement dating back to the end of the last glacial period.

Why do they come? If the natural homes of these northern species are now so far away, why do they turn up as vagrants, albeit irregularly? Many of the vagrant seals are young individuals. Dispersal of newly weaned pups away from the breeding areas occurs in many species of seals. It seems likely that a particularly adventurous individual travels further than usual, then gets caught by the current and wind to be swept southwards out of its normal range. As far as adult vagrant seals are concerned, if there is no competition for food it may be a positive advantage for an individual to forage further afield than usual. However, so far we have no information on whether or not vagrant seals which have visited our shores have been able to find their way back to their normal range.

Ringed seal This species is about half the size of other seals. Its name comes from its distinctive coat pattern of scattered dark spots surrounded by a white ring. Individuals weigh about 60kg (130lb), although they may go up

RINGED SEAL (*Phoca hispida***)**
Weight of male 60kg (130lb).
Length of male 135cm (53in).
Colour light grey background with black spots surrounded by white ring.
Breeding season 1 pup born March to April.
Gestation 270 days.
Lifespan 15-20 years.
Food crustaceans and fish.
Predators polar bears, arctic foxes, walruses, killer whales, man.
Distribution Arctic Ocean, Bering Sea, N Pacific, Baltic, Lakes Ladoga and Saimaa.

HARP SEAL (*Phoca groenlandica***)**
Weight of male 135kg (300lb).
Length of male 183cm (72in).
Colour silver-grey with black head and harp-shaped band along flanks, across back.
Breeding season 1 pup born Feb to March.
Gestation 7 months.
Lifespan 30 years.
Food mainly capelin, cod.
Predators man, killer whales.
Distribution off Newfoundland, Gulf St Lawrence, Jan Mayen, White Sea.

Above: A hooded seal pup and (below right) a male hooded seal. This species gets its name from the enlargement of the nasal cavity in the males which can be inflated to form a hood or crest. The males, like this one, can blow from one nostril a curious bright red balloon shaped structure formed from the nasal septum.

Opposite page: A harp seal and pup in their normal icy habitat in Canada.

HOODED SEAL (*Cystophora cristata*)
Weight male 400kg (880lb).
Length male 300cm (118in).
Colour blue-grey background with irregular dark patches, dark face.
Breeding season 1 pup born in March.
Gestation 7½ months after suspended development of 4 months.
Lifespan 20-25 years.
Food squid and fish.
Predators man, killer whales.
Distribution off Newfoundland, Jan Mayen, Davis Strait.

BEARDED SEAL (*Erignathus barbatus*)
Weight male 350kg (770lb), female slightly larger.
Length male 215cm (85in), female 225cm (88in).
Colour silver-grey to tawny or dark brown.
Breeding season 1 pup born March to April.
Gestation about 10½ months.
Lifespan 25-30 years, max. 31 years.
Food crustaceans and molluscs.
Predator man, polar bears, killer whales, large sharks.
Distribution circumpolar.

to 80kg (180lb) when in peak condition at the start of the breeding season; just under half the body weight of these tiny rotund torpedoes consists of blubber which insulates them on the icy waters where they normally feed and breed.

The ringed seal is the most numerous and successful of the northern seals. The world population may be as high as five million, but they are difficult to count because, unlike most other seals, they do not haul out on the ice surface or on land to mate and pup.

The ringed seal is unique in that it excavates a cave in the snow overlying land-fast ice. It keeps open an access hole from the water below by clawing at the ice with its fore-flippers. Both sexes excavate lairs which they use for resting, but females create additional lairs for pupping, perhaps up to three within 100m (330ft) of each other. This complex of birth caves probably provides alternative refuges to which a female can move her pup if a prowling polar bear or arctic fox threatens one lair.

Females give birth to a single pup bearing a white fluffy coat and weighing about 5kg (11lb). Pups are fed on fat-rich milk for six to seven weeks, which is one of the longest lactation periods of northern phocid seals. Towards the end of lactation females come into oestrus, and mating occurs in the water under the ice. Then, as the warmth of spring cracks and melts the ice, both young and adult seals claw through the snow to bask in the sunshine. The adults moult at this time, spending much of their days loafing on the surface, scratching at their loosening fur. The pups have already moulted in their snow lairs, exchanging a fluffy white coat for spotted adult fur. As the ice breaks up, the seals move off into open water to feed actively during the brief, northern summer. It is probably stragglers from the summer feeding forays which stray far south and occasionally land on our shores. Ringed seals could easily be confused with our native common seal, as the only identification points are the small size and coat pattern.

Harp seal This species is a member of the

Left: Long whiskers and square foreflippers are two of the distinctive features to look for in a bearded seal. When its abundant sensitive whiskers are wet they hang straight down on either side of the muzzle but in drying they curl up, often forming corkscrew whorls at the tips. The foreflippers look as though they have been trimmed to form a straight edge, giving rise to the Norwegian sealers' name of 'square-flipper'. Bearded seals are solitary animals, seldom found in groups. Their scattered distribution makes them difficult to census, so estimates of total numbers vary widely; the world population may be as high as half a million.

same genus (*Phoca*) as the ringed seal, but adults are easily recognised by their black head and harp-shaped black bands which run along the flanks and across the back, contrasting with the silvery fur of the rest of the body. Young harp seals might be confused with our native species because of their variable spotted coat pattern before the 'harp' forms and the animals become sexually mature. Adult harp seals are about twice the size of ringed seals and slightly bigger than common seals.

During summer harp seals are gregarious and live along the edge of the loose pack ice, migrating northwards as the edge of the ice retreats. As the ice begins to re-form and push southwards again, the seals travel ahead and eventually congregate in traditional pupping or 'whelping' areas in early spring. Newborn pups weigh about 9kg (20lb) and are covered in a coat of white silky fur. They are fed by their mothers for about ten days, growing at a rate of over 2kg (4½lb) a day–fast even by seal standards. The short suckling period is undoubtedly an adaptation to their habitat: the pack ice may break up in storms or even melt in warm springs. After lactation the females mate and then abandon their pups. The pups moult their white fur for the first adult coat, then move into the ocean to seek their own food.

Hooded seals A close neighbour of the harp seal during the breeding season is the much larger hooded seal. Hooded seals form scattered groups of solitary females with one or more males. Adults of both sexes have a strikingly marked coat of black angular patches on a silver background. The distinctive hood of the male and the red balloon are usually inflated in fighting, during sexual activity or disturbance by humans, or even when the animal is lying quietly.

Females give birth in late March to a single pup of about 15kg (33lb). Its coat is one of the most beautiful of all seal coats: silver bluegrey on the back and creamy white on the belly, and much prized by seal hunters. A white fluffy coat forms during development but is shed before birth. The suckling period is short, not more than ten days, during which time the females defend their pups fiercely against intruders.

After mating at the end of the suckling period the adults and pups disperse, apparently adopting a solitary existence. They are found further from land than harp seals, usually in deeper water in the Atlantic and Arctic Oceans. Hooded seals gather together

Above: A recently born harp seal pup stained yellow with amniotic fluid. Harp seals are probably the best known of the pinnipeds because for many years they have been the object of controversial hunts. Thousands of young seals have been taken since the late 18th century; but current estimates of 2-3 million animals mean that the harp seal is still an abundant marine mammal.

Right: Walruses are the most distinctive of the vagrant pinnipeds.

again in summer to moult, forming large groups in the Denmark Strait and off the north-east Greenland coast. After the moult they disperse to spend the winter at sea.

The coat coloration of adult hooded seals is not dissimilar to that of our native grey seal, but the larger size–up to half as much again–should make any straggler to our coasts easy to spot. The strikingly enlarged hood should certainly confirm identification of the male, as should the characteristic fur of the 'blue-black' pup.

Bearded seals These seals are solitary animals which normally live on pack ice over relatively shallow water of 30-50m (100-160ft). Apparently they cannot maintain breathing holes in thick ice, so they avoid the fast ice area which is the breeding haunt of the ringed seal. Their distribution is circumpolar, from the Arctic and north Atlantic Oceans round the coasts of northern Canada and Alaska to the northern Pacific. In summer they may haul out on beaches, but must follow the end of the pack ice as it advances and retreats with the seasons. They feed on bottom-living animals, shrimps, crabs, clams and fish.

The females give birth to a single pup from the end of March to mid-May. Pups are born on open ice floes and weigh about 35kg (77lb). They are covered in a grey-brown woolly fur, often with white patches on the head and back. This coat is moulted towards the end of the 12-18 day suckling period in exchange for the first adult coat of stiff hairs. The adults mate towards the end of lactation. During the breeding season males make a distinctive underwater sound, described as a warbling whistle, which may be a proclamation of territory. As spring turns into summer the seals migrate northwards following the re-treating ice.

Rare visitors

ringed seal *(Phoca hispida)*
world population 2–5 million

harp seal *(Phoca groenlandica)*
world population 2–3 million

hooded seal *(Cystophora cristata)*
world population 400,000

bearded seal *(Erignathus barbatus)*
world population 500,000

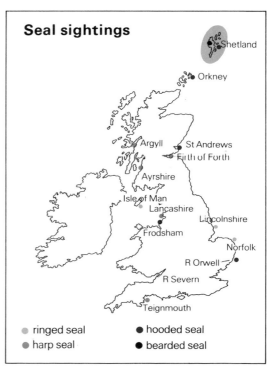

Seal sightings

Shetland
Orkney
Argyll
St Andrews
Firth of Forth
Ayrshire
Isle of Man
Lancashire
Lincolnshire
Frodsham
Norfolk
R Orwell
R Severn
Teignmouth

● ringed seal   ● hooded seal
● harp seal   ● bearded seal

ISLAND MAMMALS

Many of the islands dotted around Britain have developed distinctive mammal populations – how and why they have evolved pose some fascinating questions.

Mammals can reach an island in any of three main ways. They may swim to it. They may be carried there – by man, on drifting wood or, in the case of bats, blown there by strong winds. Or they may be present on the island because they were already there before rising seas separated the island from the mainland and left isolated populations.

As soon as isolation from the mainland occurs, there are possibilities for populations of a particular species to diverge from others of that same species. However, this only occurs if environmental conditions are different in the two localities so that the selection pressures on the two populations differ; or if the population is very small so that simply by chance the individuals may be genetically different from those of the other population.

Random genetic drift The latter process is

Above: There are no truly wild goats in Britain, but feral herds live in remote areas, including islands.

Opposite page: Shetland ponies are smaller than their mainland relatives because of the harsher conditions of island life – particularly the wind and the scarcity of nourishing food. Even so, they are remarkably sturdy.

Below: The black rat enters islands through ports.

called random genetic drift and requires some explanation. It is perhaps best understood by considering the following example. If you take a classroom of 20 children and measure the height of each child, you can arrive at an average height for the group. If two of these children at random are now separated (with no attention to their height or any other characteristics), and you now measure the height of the two groups, the first group of 18 is likely to have an average height very similar to that obtained previously for the complete class of 20. However, the chances are that the group of two will have an average height that differs more markedly from the average for the class as a whole.

Left: A rabbit grazing the turf among the clumps of thrift on Skokholm Island off Dyfed in Wales. The prolific rabbit population on this island means that the turf is grazed hard which allows numerous species of low-growing flowers to thrive.

Right: The map shows areas where there are noted island mammal populations. They vary in differing degrees from their mainland relatives. Some, such as the greater and lesser white-toothed shrews, are absent from mainland Britain and occur only on islands, in this case the Channel and Scilly Islands, and on mainland Europe. In others, island and mainland sub-species exist, distinguished on the basis of size, colour, bone and tooth structure. In the case of the mountain hare the differences are more apparent in winter.

Island mammal haunts

Westray
Rousay
Sanday
Orkney mainland
Fair Is.
S. Ronaldsay
Orkney
Shiant Is.
St Kilda
Raasay
Skye
Mull
Bull Is.
Skokholm
Skomer
Lundy Is.
Great Blasket
Isles of Scilly
Guernsey
Herm
Alderney
Sark
Jersey
Channel Is.

So it is with populations in general. If an island has a population of only a few individuals, it is likely that it will differ from the larger population from which it is derived. Height is partly determined by genes and the variation in the genes of individuals of a population. Natural selection can only act upon the genes that individuals possess, and so the genetic constitutions (the assemblage of genes) of a population will dictate to some extent how it will evolve.

If that population is isolated and the evolutionary route differs greatly from the parent population, then a new species may be formed. This has occurred for example with a number of mammals on small isolated off-shore British islands–the white-toothed shrews from the Isles of Scilly and the Channel Islands; the Orkney vole from Orkney, off the north of Scotland; and the Soay sheep from St Kilda, off north-west Scotland. These species are today quite distinct from their nearest mainland relatives.

Why are they there? It is often a problem determining why one but not another may be present on islands. The mammals of most of our small offshore islands probably arrived with the help of man. Many of the islands along the western seaboard of Britain and Ireland have their own population of wood-mice (sometimes forming distinct island races, as on St Kilda and Fair Isle), and these almost certainly arrived in grainstores with human settlers.

House mice too are likely to have arrived on islands in sacks of grain and other materials.

Below: An unusual picture of a swimming hedgehog. Although it can swim to safety from a pond or swimming pool, it is rarely found on islands far from the mainland. In south-west Ireland it occurs on a few small inshore islands, usually in sheltered bays, but it never reaches the islands well offshore.

Even islands or rocks inhabited only by lighthouse keepers have their house mouse populations, presumably established in this way. House mice occur only on islands with human habitation: St Kilda, and Great Blasket island off south-west Ireland, both had populations when they had human communities but soon after the islands became uninhabited these populations became extinct. It seems that the food and/or shelter which man inadvertently provides is a

Island mammals

Stoat
(Mustela erminea)

Mainland stoat
(Mustela erminea stabilis)

Right: The Irish stoat, a sub-species solely represented on the Irish mainland, is distinguished by its darker upperparts and an irregular, smaller area of white fur on the underparts.

Irish stoat
(Mustela erminea hibernicus)

Mountain hare
(Lepus timidus)

Mountain hare (winter)
(Lepus timidus scoticus)

Irish hare (winter)
(Lepus timidus hibernicus)

Above: The mountain hare of Scotland and northern England turns white in winter, while the slightly redder Irish race does not (even when in experiments it has been transported to Scotland).

House mouse
(Mus musculus)

Mainland house mouse
(Mus musculus)

Bull Is. house mouse
(Mus musculus jamesoni)

Above: The flavistic (yellow-coloured) house mice from North Bull Island are a different colour from mice on the Irish mainland.

Bank vole
(Clethrionomys glareolus)

Mainland bank vole
(Clethrionomys glareolus glareolus)

Bank vole (Mull)
Clethrionomys glareolus alstoni

Above and left: Five island sub-species of bank vole are recognised in the British Isles from their external appearance and bone structure. They differ from the Continental species and occur on the mainland and on the islands of Mull, Skomer, Jersey and Raasay.

Orkney/Guernsey vole
(Microtus arvalis)

Orkney vole (southern)
(Microtus arvalis orcadensis)

Orkney vole (northern)
(Microtus arvalis orcadensis)

Skomer vole
(Clethrionomys glareolus skomerensis)

Guernsey vole
(Microtus arvalis sarnius)

Above: In the British Isles this species is confined to the islands of Guernsey and Orkney, although it occurs elsewhere in Europe. Individuals from the northern Orkney islands of Sanday and Westray are paler than those from the southern islands of mainland Orkney, South Ronaldsay and Rousay.

Greater white-toothed shrew
(Crocidura russula)

Channel Islands

Above: In the British Isles this species is confined to the Channel Is. of Alderney, Herm and Guernsey where it is the only shrew species present.

Lesser white-toothed shrew
(Crocidura suaveolens)

Isles of Scilly

Above: In the British Isles this species is confined to Jersey, Sark and the Isles of Scilly. It is the only shrew species present (with the exception of Jersey).

Left: An island wood mouse. Separate sub-species of wood mouse are found today on St Kilda and on the Shetland Isles of Foula and Fair Isle; there are also slight variants of the mainland wood mouse on a number of islands such as Lewis, Rhum, Raasay, Mull and the Channel Islands, but their differences are not sufficient for them to be classified as sub-species.

crucial factor to the survival of house mice on islands in winter.

Some species of mammals have been introduced by man. The rabbit, for example, occurs on nearly all offshore islands where man has lived or frequently visits. It was probably originally introduced for meat. Other species such as the mink have been introduced by man and bred in captivity, but escapees have colonized neighbouring areas. Thus mink are found on islands in the Hebrides, where they pose a potential threat to ground-nesting birds, particularly the eider duck and black guillemot on which they prey.

There are few cases of mammals which have arrived on islands by natural means. Some islands such as Lundy in the Channel and the Shiant Isles in the Minch have brown rat populations which may have come ashore on drifting timber from shipwrecks. The brown and black rats have caused widespread damage to native populations worldwide, but most of our uninhabited islands are rat-free, probably because of the harsh winters and

Right: The mink loses no time in establishing itself on islands if it is released or manages to escape from mink farms. It has spread to a number of Hebridean islands without farms, presumably by swimming. It is a good swimmer and climber and is well suited to conditions found on many of our offshore islands. Its presence in some cases causes great concern to ornithologists because of its habit of taking young birds.

Below: The famous Soay sheep of St Kilda, the only truly wild sheep to be found in their natural state in the British Isles, although there are numerous flocks kept in mainland parks.

lack of food. There are many records of rats coming ashore on islands, occurring in abundance for a year or two and then dying out.

Island influences Islands have various characteristics which can profoundly influence the ecology of their mammal populations. Most of the islands around Britain and Ireland occur off our west and north coasts, facing the Atlantic. They therefore receive an oceanic climate with mild winters and relatively cool summers. If they are some distance from land they tend to receive less rainfall than the mainland because there is less high ground around which clouds can collect.

Unless they are sheltered from other land masses they are also windy places, and this often has consequences for the amount of vegetation cover. Trees are uncommon on small offshore islands.

Because islands are bounded by the sea mammals rarely have the opportunity to disperse, so that if conditions are unfavourable they cannot move elsewhere. This has probably strongly influenced how island populations exist–their body size, number of young and length of time they live in relation to their mainland counterparts.

Most island races of mice, for example, are larger than their mainland counterparts. It is the same with many other species. Various

Left: The European otter which is equally at home on land and water. Swimming long distances as an agency to colonize an island is a method that few species seem capable of using. Mink have spread to a number of Hebridean islands without mink farms, presumably by swimming, and otters have probably done likewise to reach Shetland, Orkney and the Outer Hebrides. However, both these species are strong swimmers, and most other mammal species are probably only able to cross very narrow straits of water.
Some species are adapted to swim–the grey and common seals for example, and offshore islands afford important and safe refuges from human disturbance for them to haul out and to pup.

Below right: The Skomer vole, a sub-species of the mainland bank vole. On the island of Skomer off west Wales it lives in tall bracken and brambles, a habitat elsewhere occupied primarily by field voles. The Skomer vole has creamy markings on its underside in the winter months.

explanations have been put forward: lack of ground predators such as stoats and weasels, enabling them to grow bigger without risk of predation (although gulls and skuas also feed upon them); greater competition between individuals within a species so that larger individuals are likely to be dominant over smaller ones; or in some cases animals may have been brought inadvertently from populations further north where the species is larger anyway. However, the fact that individuals cannot escape unfavourable conditions may be the principal reason why they tend to be larger on islands, since larger animals can carry around proportionately more fat.

Changing populations We know rather little about the detailed ecology of island mammal populations, but studies of rabbits and mice have indicated that populations may fluctuate greatly in size from year to year. A favourable summer may provide a boom in births with the population rising dramatically. Because individuals cannot disperse, there may then be intense competition and when food becomes scarce a high mortality, so that the population crashes once more. Recurring outbreaks of myxomatosis amongst rabbits on islands may be a consequence of high densities after favourable conditions followed by mass mortality and breeding failure as the disease spreads quickly.

Generally speaking, the smaller the island, the fewer habitats it possesses and the more isolated it is, the fewer the number of species that occur upon it. On small islands the chances of competition are greater should two similar species arrive there. This may explain why the bank vole and field vole occur on large islands such as Skye, but only the former on Raasay and Skomer, and only the latter on neighbouring Skokholm. When only one of the two species occurs, the lack of competition may allow it a wider range of habitats. For example, the house mouse–the only mouse on Skomer–occupies bracken habitats used by the wood mouse elsewhere, while closely related species such as the stoat and weasel, and the pygmy and common shrew, are only rarely found together.

The entries listed in **bold** type refer to main subjects. The page numbers in *italics* indicate illustrations. Medium type entries refer to the text.

ACKNOWLEDGEMENTS
Photographers' credits Penny Anderson 44 (top): Heather Angel 8, 9 (bottom), 17, 18, 21 (top), 29 (top), 31 (top, bottom left), 33, 35 (top), 43 (middle), 50, 51, 63 (top), 64 (top, middle), 81, 83 (top), 88 (top), 90 (top), 91 (middle), 95, 96 (top), 99, 101 (bottom), 104, 107, 108 (middle), 110 (top), 114 (bottom), 117 (middle), 128 (top), 136, 139, 142, 151 (top), 155 (top), 157, 166 (bottom), 176, 186 (top): Aquila Photographics/ GG & IM Bates 147 (bottom); Dr & Mrs JP Black 141 (middle); PT Castell 132 (top, middle), 147 (middle); S & BA Craig 150; M Leach 46 (bottom right); Sawford & Castle 45: Ian Beames 126, 134 (bottom), 138 (bottom): Biofotos/G Kinns 185 (bottom), 188 (top left, top right), 189 (bottom right); S Summerhays 183: FV Blackburn 154: Bob Gibbons Photography/Bob Gibbons 47, 49 (middle), 160 (top): Bruce Coleman Ltd/Ken Balcomb 167, 170, 173 (top); J & D Bartlett 164; E Breeze-Jones 130; John R Brownlie 174 (bottom); J Burton 72, 73 (top); Bruce Coleman 174 (top), 178 (top), 180, 182; LR Dawson 30; Francisco Erize 165; Inigo Everson 64 (bottom); J Foott 91 (bottom), 113 (bottom); G Langsbury 62; L Lee Rue IV 128 (bottom); NR Lightfoot 181; Hans Reinhard 152, 186 (bottom); James Simon 173 (bottom); K Taylor 103; RJ Tulloch 172-3, 184; G Williamson 168; Bill Wood 114 (top): NE Buxton 53, 54, 55: David Corke 96 (middle), 159 (middle): Dr Horace E Dobbs 162-3: Euan Dunn 177 (bottom): Eric Edwards 63 (bottom): Peter Evans 36 (top), 38, 178 (bottom): Caroline Flegg 11 (top): Jim Flegg 144: Nigel Forteath 9 (top): Colin Graham/Kenneth Allsopp Memorial Trust 40, 42 (top left): Dennis Green 56, 133, 135 (top), 140 (bottom), 145, 156 (top): Jim Greenfield 12, 13 (top), 16 (top), 22

(bottom), 23 (top), 26 (top), 27 (top), 92-3: Melvin Grey 159 (bottom): Keith Hiscock 13 (middle), 14, 15, 16 (middle, bottom), 21 (middle), 101 (top), 121 (middle), 123 (middle): CM Howson 26 (bottom): RW Ingle 10 (top): P Kelley 77: Frank W Lane 166 (middle): Michael Leach 147 (top): John Mason 27 (middle): Richard T Mills 32 (bottom), 66, 137, 141 (top): W Mojsiewicz 68: Pat Morris 25 (top), 36 (bottom), 71, 73 (middle), 74 (bottom), 83 (middle, bottom), 84 (bottom), 89, 106, 115, 116 (bottom), 118, 119, 121 (bottom), 177 (top): Natural History Photographic Agency/J & M Bain 105; L Campbell 134 (middle); S Dalton 158-9; J Good 80 (bottom); J Goodman 82, 109; Brian Hawkes 70, 160 (middle); WJC Murray 151 (middle); LH Newman 32 (top); P Wayre 189 (middle): Nature Photographers Ltd/SC Bisserot 49 (top), 102 (bottom), 116 (middle), 185 (top), 188-9; FV Blackburn 42 (top right); D Bonsall 37 (middle), 52, 149; B Burbidge 138 (top), 161; H Clark 41 (top); A Cleave 6-7, 42 (middle), 111, 121, 160 (bottom); AK Davies 110 (bottom), 155 (bottom); ME Gore 148; P Knight 35 (bottom); CK Mylne 11 (bottom); O Newman 37 (bottom), 49 (bottom), 131, 140 (top left); 143; N Picozzi 59 (top), 156 (middle); T Schilling 41 (middle); Don Smith front cover, 20 (bottom), 44 (bottom), 135 (bottom), 182 (top); P Sterry 31 (bottom right), 46 (top), 50 (bottom), 121 (top), 122, 129, 140 (top right); R Tidman 34, 46 (bottom left), 146 (top): Oxford Scientific Films/ Peter Parks 94: Bernard Picton 10 (bottom), 20 (top), 21 (bottom), 22 (top), 23 (bottom), 25 (bottom), 27 (bottom), 28, 29 (middle), 74 (top), 76, 78, 80 (top), 98, 100, 102 (top), 108 (top), 117 (bottom), 123 (middle, bottom): Premaphotos Wildlife/KG Preston-Mafham 41 (bottom), 43 (top): Imants Priede 86, 87, 88 (top): Richard Revels 37

(top): John Robinson 48: Bryan Sage 57 (bottom), 58, 59 (middle, bottom), 124-5: Peter Scoones 60-1: Seaphot/Peter David 112 (top); Daniel Gotshall 113 (top); William Howes 84 (top), 90 (bottom); Mike Laverack 112 (bottom): Roger Tidman 57 (top), 146 (bottom): BS Turner 128 (middle): Alwyne Wheeler 67: P Williams 79.

Artists' credits Graham Allen/Linden Artists 165, 168-9, 175, 179, 183, 187: Fred Anderson/The Garden Studio 82: Norman Arlott 143, 144: Craig Austin/The Garden Studio 45: Russell Barnett 62, 63, 76, 77 (line), 89, 110 (bottom), 114, 122 (insets), 158 (insets), 166, 169 (bottom): T Boyer/ courtesy of Eagle Star Insurance Group 153 (top right): Eugene Fleury 39 (map), 186: Wayne Ford 124, 127, 131 (top), 134, 137, 141, 148, 150, 151, 153 (left, bottom), 155: Will Giles 171 (insets): Hayward Art Group 88 (line), 129, 149: Elaine Keenan 162: Richard Lewington/The Garden Studio 95: Kathryn Lunn 131: Denys Ovenden title page, 19, 24, 27, 28-9, 33, 60, 66, 67, 69, 71, 73, 75, 79, 81, 85, 87, 88 (dorsal fins), 92, 97, 103, 104, 105 (line), 111, 113, 117, 138: Sandra Pond 39 (insets), 58 (insets), 65 (fish), 99, 100, 107, 108, 110 (middle), 116, 152: Andrew Riley/The Garden Studio 77 (colour), 90-91: Gordon Riley 118, 119: Colin Salmon 13, 14, 43, 47, 51, 52, 55, 58 (map), 65 (map), 70, 105 (map), 109, 122 (map), 130, 133, 148 (map), 152 (map), 156 (map), 158 (map), 171 (map), 183 (map).

Distribution map data on page 171 courtesy of Dr Peter Evans.

Index compiled by Richard Raper, Indexing Specialists, Hove, East Sussex.